IN LOVE WITH
crochet

A LEISURE ARTS PUBLICATION
PRESENTED BY OXMOOR HOUSE

EDITORIAL STAFF

Vice President and Editor-in-Chief:
Anne Van Wagner Childs
Executive Director: Sandra Graham Case
Editorial Director: Susan Frantz Wiles
Publications Director: Carla Bentley
Creative Art Director: Gloria Bearden
Senior Graphics Art Director: Melinda Stout

PRODUCTION
Managing Editor: Susan White Sullivan
Senior Technical Editor: Cathy Hardy
Instructional Editors: Sarah J. Green and
Jackie Botnik Stanfill

EDITORIAL
Managing Editor: Linda L. Trimble
Associate Editor: Tammi Williamson Bradley
Assistant Editors: Terri Leming Davidson,
Robyn Sheffield-Edwards, and Darla Burdette Kelsay
Copy Editor: Laura Lee Weland

ART
Book/Magazine Graphics Art Director: Diane M. Hugo
Senior Graphics Illustrator: M. Katherine Yancey
Photography Stylists: Sondra Daniel, Aurora Huston,
Christina Tiano Myers, Pam Choate, and Courtney Frazier Jones

BUSINESS STAFF

Publisher: Bruce Akin
Vice President, Marketing: Guy A. Crossley
Marketing Manager: Byron L. Taylor
Print Production Manager: Laura Lockhart
Vice President and General Manager: Thomas L. Carlisle
Retail Sales Director: Richard Tignor
Vice President, Retail Marketing: Pam Stebbins
Retail Marketing Director: Margaret Sweetin
Retail Customer Services Manager: Carolyn Pruss
General Merchandise Manager: Russ Barnett
Vice President, Finance: Tom Siebenmorgen
Distribution Director: Ed M. Strackbein

CROCHET COLLECTION SERIES

Library of Congress Catalog Number: 96-78952
Hardcover ISBN 0-8487-1580-2
Softcover ISBN 1-57486-021-6

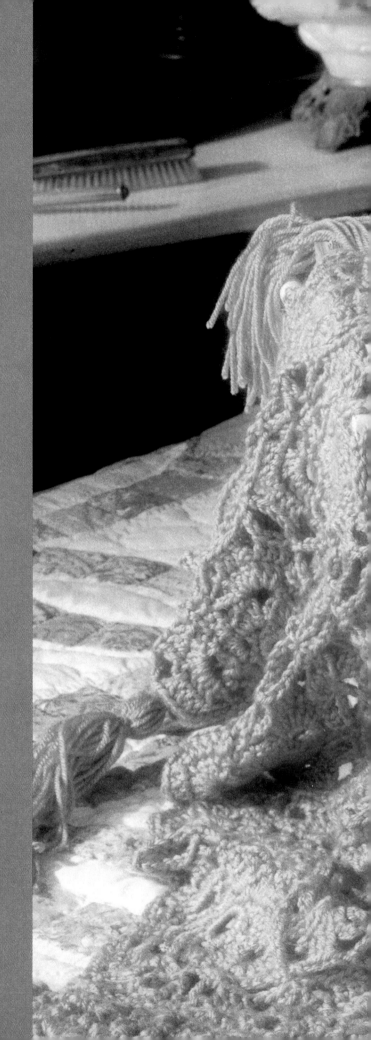

IN LOVE WITH
crochet

It's so easy to fall in love with crochet! It's simple to learn, fun to do, and inexpensive to get started! To help you get hooked on this fabulous pastime, we created In Love with Crochet, the newest volume in our Crochet Collection series. With more than 60 original designs from which to choose, this beautiful treasury will inspire you to brighten your decor, shower your loved ones with gifts, decorate for the holidays, and more!

The cozy throws in Wrapped Up in Afghans include a wonderful mix of styles that will complement any decorating theme. All Through the House offers pretty accents to wake up your living room, bedroom, bath, and kitchen. Brighten a special day with a handmade token from the Gifts for All section, or craft a watermelon rug and cute little piggy just for the fun of it! Our charming Rock-A-Bye Collection makes it easy to celebrate baby's arrival, and the trendy designs in our Fashion Corner will add personal style to your family's wardrobe. We also included one-of-a-kind holiday creations to highlight occasions all year.

Whether you're starting your first crochet project or the latest in a long line of successful endeavors, our easy-to-follow instructions, diagrams, and helpful hints will guide you to beautiful results every time. You're going to love having this delightful collection at your fingertips!

Anne Childs

LEISURE ARTS, INC.
LITTLE ROCK, ARKANSAS

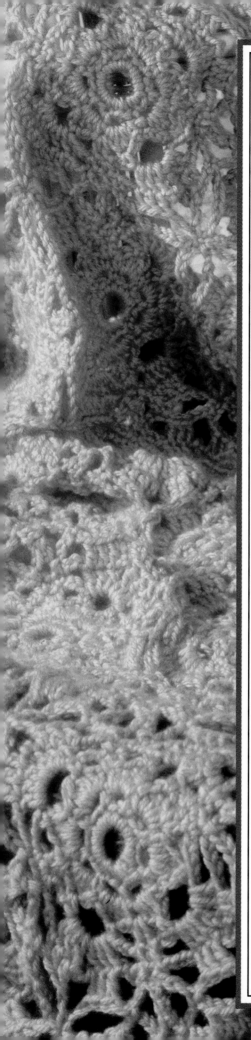

table of contents

wrapped up in afghans.....6

all through the house 24

gifts for all......................48

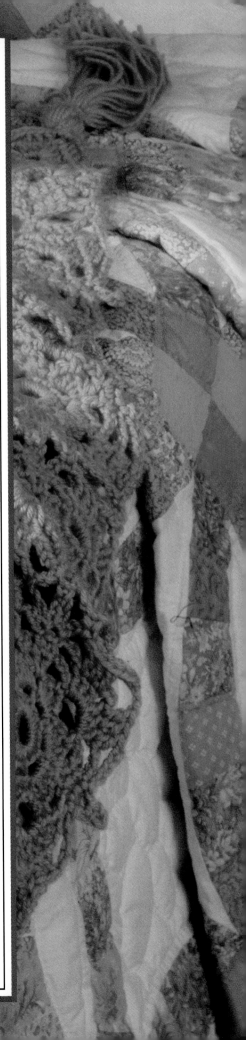

just for fun 64

rock-a-bye collection 78

fashion corner 94

hooked on holidays......112

wrapped up in afghans

Afghans have a charm that everyone loves, whether for snuggly warmth, delicate softness, or decorative appeal. With that in mind, we chose a wonderful mix of styles and stitching techniques for the cover-ups in this collection, including lacy feminine throws, a reversible striped afghan, a brilliant "stained glass" wrap, and more. There's a choice selection of projects for beginning and advanced stitchers alike, so bring out your yarn, grab a hook, and get wrapped up in afghans!

GRANNY STARS

Your flair for creativity will shine with this radiant wrap! Soft and inviting, it's made with one- and two-color granny squares that are whipstitched together to form the stars.

Finished Size: 48" x 68"

MATERIALS
Worsted Weight Brushed Acrylic Yarn:
Blue - 42 ounces, (1,190 grams, 2,660 yards)
White - 15 ounces, (430 grams, 950 yards)
Crochet hook, size I (5.50 mm) **or** size needed for gauge
Yarn needle

GAUGE SWATCH: 4" square
Work same as One-Color Square.

ONE-COLOR SQUARE
(Make 104 with Blue and 24 with White)
Ch 4; join with slip st to form a ring.
Rnd 1 (Right side)**: Ch 3 (counts as first dc, now and throughout)**, 2 dc in ring, ch 2, (3 dc in ring, ch 2) 3 times; join with slip st to first dc: 12 dc.
Note: Loop a short piece of yarn around any stitch to mark Rnd 1 as **right** side.
Rnd 2: Slip st in next 2 dc and in next ch-2 sp, ch 3, (2 dc, ch 2, 3 dc) in same sp, ch 1, ★ (3 dc, ch 2, 3 dc) in next ch-2 sp, ch 1; repeat from ★ around; join with slip st to first dc: 24 dc.

Rnd 3: Slip st in next 2 dc and in next ch-2 sp, ch 3, (2 dc, ch 2, 3 dc) in same sp, ch 1, 3 dc in next ch-1 sp, ch 1, ★ (3 dc, ch 2, 3 dc) in next corner ch-2 sp, ch 1, 3 dc in next ch-1 sp, ch 1; repeat from ★ around; join with slip st to first dc, finish off: 36 dc.

TWO-COLOR SQUARE (Make 48)
With White, ch 4; join with slip st to form a ring.
Rnd 1 (Right side)**: Ch 5 (counts as first dc plus ch 2, now and throughout)**, 3 dc in ring, cut White, with Blue, YO and draw through loop on hook, ch 1, 3 dc in ring, ch 2, 3 dc in ring, cut Blue, with White, YO and draw through loop on hook, ch 1, 2 dc in ring; join with slip st to first dc: 12 dc.
Rnd 2: Slip st in first ch-2 sp, ch 5, 3 dc in same sp, ch 1, 3 dc in next ch-2 sp, cut White, with Blue, YO and draw through loop on hook, ch 1, 3 dc in same sp, ch 1, (3 dc, ch 2, 3 dc) in next ch-2 sp, ch 1, 3 dc in next ch-2 sp, cut Blue, with White, YO and draw through loop on hook, ch 1, 3 dc in same sp, ch 1, 2 dc in same sp as first dc; join with slip st to first dc: 24 dc.
Rnd 3: Slip st in first ch-2 sp, ch 3, (2 dc, ch 2, 3 dc) in same sp, ch 1, 3 dc in next ch-1 sp, ch 1, 3 dc in next corner ch-2 sp, cut White, with Blue, YO and draw through loop on hook, ch 1, 3 dc in same sp, ch 1, 3 dc in next ch-1 sp, ch 1, (3 dc, ch 2, 3 dc) in next corner ch-2 sp, ch 1, 3 dc in next ch-1 sp, ch 1, 3 dc in next corner ch-2 sp, cut Blue, with White, YO and draw through loop on hook, ch 1, 3 dc in same sp, ch 1, 3 dc in next ch-1 sp, ch 1; join with slip st to first dc, finish off: 36 dc.

ASSEMBLY

With **wrong** sides together and using either color, and working through **inside** loops only, whipstitch Squares together, forming 11 vertical strips of 16 Squares each following Placement Diagram *(Fig. 30b, page 139)*; then whipstitch strips together, securing seam at each corner.

PLACEMENT DIAGRAM

EDGING

Rnd 1: With **right** side facing, join Blue with slip st in any corner ch-2 sp; ch 1, ★ (sc, ch 2, sc) in corner ch-2 sp, † sc in each dc and in each ch-1 sp across to next joining, hdc in joining †, repeat from † to † across to last Square, sc in each dc and in each ch-1 sp across to next corner ch-2 sp; repeat from ★ around; join with slip st to first sc, finish off.

Rnd 2: With **right** side facing, join White with slip st in any corner ch-2 sp; ch 1, (sc, ch 2, sc) in same sp, ★ ch 1, (skip next st, sc in next st, ch 1) across to within 1 sc of next corner ch-2 sp, skip next sc, (sc, ch 2, sc) in corner ch-2 sp; repeat from ★ 2 times **more**, ch 1, skip next sc, (sc in next st, ch 1, skip next st) across; join with slip st to first sc, finish off.

Rnd 3: With **right** side facing, join Blue with slip st in any corner ch-2 sp; ch 1, ★ (sc, ch 2, sc) in corner ch-2 sp, ch 1, (sc in next ch-1 sp, ch 1) across to next corner ch-2 sp; repeat from ★ around; join with slip st to first sc.

Rnd 4: Slip st in first ch-2 sp, ch 6, dc in same sp, ch 1, (dc in next ch-1 sp, ch 1) across to next corner ch-2 sp, ★ (dc, ch 3, dc) in corner ch-2 sp, ch 1, (dc in next ch-1 sp, ch 1) across to next corner ch-2 sp; repeat from ★ around; join with slip st to third ch of beginning ch-6.

Rnd 5: Slip st in first ch-3 sp, ch 1, ★ (sc, ch 2, sc) in corner ch-3 sp, ch 1, (sc in next ch-1 sp, ch 1) across to next corner ch-3 sp; repeat from ★ around; join with slip st to first sc, finish off.

Rnd 6: With **right** side facing, join White with slip st in any corner ch-2 sp; ch 1, ★ (sc, ch 2, sc) in corner ch-2 sp, ch 1, (sc in next ch-1 sp, ch 1) across to next corner ch-2 sp; repeat from ★ around; join with slip st to first sc, finish off.

Rnd 7: With **right** side facing, join Blue with slip st in any corner ch-2 sp; ch 1, ★ (sc, ch 3, sc) in corner ch-2 sp, ch 2, (sc in next ch-1 sp, ch 2) across to next corner ch-2 sp; repeat from ★ around; join with slip st to first sc, finish off.

This cozy afghan makes a quiet spot especially inviting for reading. The reversible throw works up quickly using single and double crochets in the back loops to create a textured pattern. Crocheted with a large hook and two strands of yarn, the easy-and-elegant afghan is completed with a generous fringe.

Finished Size: 50¹/₂" x 65"

MATERIALS
Worsted Weight Yarn:
    Grey - 37 ounces, (1,050 grams, 2,325 yards)
    Tan - 35 ounces, (990 grams, 2,200 yards)
Crochet hook, size P (10.00 mm) **or** size needed for gauge

Note: Entire afghan is worked holding 2 strands of yarn together.

GAUGE: In pattern, 9 sts = 4" and 10 rows = 6"

Gauge Swatch: 4"w x 6"h
With Grey, ch 10 **loosely**.
Rows 1-10: Work same as afghan: 9 sts.
Finish off.

COLOR SEQUENCE
One row Grey *(Fig. 28a, page 139)*, 2 rows Tan, (2 rows Grey, 2 rows Tan) to last row, 1 row Grey.

Note: Each row is worked across length of afghan.

With Grey, ch 148 **loosely**.
Row 1: Sc in back ridge of second ch from hook and in each ch across *(Fig. 2a, page 133)* changing to Tan in last sc: 147 sc.
Row 2: Ch 1, turn; sc in first sc, (dc in next sc, sc in next sc) across: 147 sts.
Row 3: Ch 1, turn; working in Back Loops Only *(Fig. 21, page 136)*, sc in first sc, (dc in next dc, sc in next sc) across changing colors in last sc.

Row 4: Ch 1, turn; working in both loops, sc in first sc, (dc in next dc, sc in next sc) across.
Repeat Rows 3 and 4 for pattern until afghan measures 50", ending by working Row 3 with Tan.
Last Row: Ch 1, turn; sc in both loops of each st across; finish off.

Add fringe using 6 strands of matching color, each 16" long *(Figs. 33a & b, page 139)*; spacing evenly, attach across ends of rows on each end of afghan.

EARTHY MILE-A-MINUTE

*T*ake this warm wrap along on your next hayride or campfire cookout!
Crafted in a trio of earthy colors, the intricate mile-a-minute design is
worked in strips that are whipstitched together to create the scalloped edges.

Finished Size: 47" x 63"

MATERIALS
Worsted Weight Yarn:
Tan - 20 ounces, (570 grams, 1,380 yards)
Rust - 20 ounces, (570 grams, 1,380 yards)
Turquoise - 11 ounces, (310 grams, 760 yards)
Crochet hook, size E (3.50 mm) **or** size needed for gauge

GAUGE SWATCH: 1¹/₂"w x 4"h
Work same as Center through Row 6.

STITCH GUIDE

FRONT POST TREBLE CROCHET (abbreviated FPtr)
★ YO twice, working in **front** of previous rnd, insert hook
from **front** to **back** around post of dc indicated *(Fig. 1)*,
YO and pull up a loop, (YO and draw through 2 loops on
hook) 3 times. Skip hdc behind FPtr.

Fig. 1

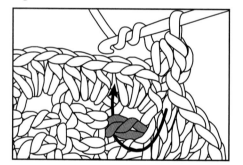

STRIP (Make 9)
CENTER
With Turquoise, ch 9 **loosely**.
Row 1 (Right side): Dc in fourth ch from hook and in each
ch across: 7 sts.
Note: Loop a short piece of yarn around any stitch to mark
Row 1 as **right** side and bottom edge.
Rows 2-89: Ch 3 **(counts as first dc, now and
throughout)**, turn; dc in next dc and in each st across.
Finish off.

EDGING
Rnd 1: With **right** side facing, join Tan with slip st in end of
first row; ch 2, 2 hdc in same row, 3 hdc in end of each row
across; skip first 3 dc, (4 dc, ch 1, 4 dc) in next dc; 3 hdc in
end of each row across; skip first 3 chs, (4 dc, ch 1, 4 dc) in
free loop of next ch *(Fig. 22b, page 136)*; join with slip st to
top of beginning ch-2.
Rnd 2: Ch 2, hdc in same st, † work FPtr around dc **below** next
hdc, working in Back Loops Only *(Fig. 21, page 136)*, (hdc in
next 2 hdc, work FPtr around dc **below** next hdc) 88 times,
2 hdc in next hdc and in each of next 4 dc, 2 hdc in next ch,
2 hdc in each of next 4 dc †, 2 hdc in next hdc, repeat from
† to † once; join with slip st to top of beginning ch-2, finish off.
Rnd 3: With **right** side facing and working in both loops, join
Rust with slip st in first FPtr; ch 3, 2 dc in same st, skip next 2 hdc,
sc in next FPtr, (skip next 2 hdc, 5 dc in next st, skip next 2 hdc,
sc in next st) 45 times, skip next hdc, 3 dc in each of next 2 hdc,
skip next hdc, sc in next hdc, (skip next 2 hdc, 5 dc in next st,
skip next 2 hdc, sc in next st) 47 times, skip next hdc, 3 dc in
each of next 2 hdc, skip next hdc, sc in next hdc, skip next
2 hdc, 5 dc in next hdc, skip next 2 hdc, sc in next hdc, skip
last 2 sts, 2 dc in same st as first dc; join with slip st to first dc,
do **not** finish off.

FIRST SIDE
Row 1: Ch 1, sc in same st, (ch 5, sc in center dc of next
5-dc group) 44 times, leave remaining sts unworked: 44 ch-5 sps.
Row 2: Ch 1, turn; sc in first sc, (4 sc in next ch-5 sp, sc in
next sc) across: 221 sc.
Row 3: Ch 1, turn; sc in each sc across; finish off.

SECOND SIDE
Row 1: With **right** side facing, skip 4 sc from First Side and
join Rust with sc in center dc of next 5-dc group *(see Joining
With Sc, page 136)*; (ch 5, sc in center dc of next 5-dc
group) 44 times, leave remaining sts unworked: 44 ch-5 sps.
Rows 2 and 3: Work same as First Side.

ASSEMBLY
With **wrong** sides together, bottom edges at the same end and
Rust, and working through **both** loops, whipstitch Strips
together *(Fig. 30a, page 139)*.

LAVISH CABLES

Featuring alternating columns of richly textured cables and delicate fans, this lavish afghan has a classic Aran look. It's crafted using clusters, front post stitches, and a unique cross stitch that creates the cables. Ideal for any decor, this wrap will delight an advanced stitcher.

Finished Size: 53" x 70"

MATERIALS

Worsted Weight Yarn:
52 ounces, (1,480 grams, 3,390 yards)
Crochet hook, size K (6.50 mm) **or** size needed for gauge

GAUGE: 6 dc and 3 rows = 2"

Gauge Swatch: 4" square
Ch 14 **loosely.**
Row 1: Dc in fourth ch from hook **(3 skipped chs count as first dc)** and in each ch across: 12 dc.
Rows 2-6: Ch 3 **(counts as first dc)**, turn; dc in next dc and in each dc across.
Finish off.

STITCH GUIDE

CROSS STITCH (uses next 3 sts)
YO, insert hook in next st, YO and pull up a loop, YO and draw through 2 loops on hook, YO twice, skip next st, insert hook from **front** to **back** around post of next st *(Fig. 1a)*, YO and pull up a loop, (YO and draw through 2 loops on hook) twice, YO and draw through all 3 loops on hook, working **behind** st just worked, dc in skipped st, YO twice, working in **front** of last 2 sts worked, insert hook around post of st **below** first st made in group *(Fig. 1b)*, YO and pull up a loop, (YO and draw through 2 loops on hook) twice, YO, insert hook in next st, YO and pull up a loop, YO and draw through 2 loops on hook, YO and draw through all 3 loops on hook.

Fig. 1a **Fig. 1b**

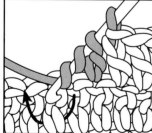 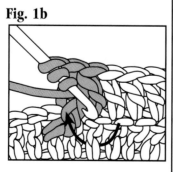

FRONT POST TREBLE CROCHET *(abbreviated FPtr)*
YO twice, insert hook from **front** to **back** around post of st indicated, YO and pull up a loop, (YO and draw through 2 loops on hook) 3 times *(Fig. 18, page 135)*.

BACK POST TREBLE CROCHET *(abbreviated BPtr)*
YO twice, insert hook from **back** to **front** around post of st indicated, YO and pull up a loop, (YO and draw through 2 loops on hook) 3 times *(Fig. 19, page 135)*.

6-DC CLUSTER
★ YO, insert hook in Front Loop Only of st indicated *(Fig. 21, page 136)*, YO and pull up a loop, YO and draw through 2 loops on hook; repeat from ★ 5 times **more**, YO and draw through all 7 loops on hook *(Figs. 10a & b, page 134)*, ch 1 to close.

5-DC CLUSTER
★ YO, insert hook in st indicated, YO and pull up a loop, YO and draw through 2 loops on hook; repeat from ★ 4 times **more**, YO and draw through all 6 loops on hook, ch 1 to close.

Ch 155 **loosely.**

Row 1: Dc in fourth ch from hook and in next 27 chs **(3 skipped chs count as first dc)**, † ch 2, skip next 4 chs, dc in next ch, (ch 1, dc) 3 times in same ch, ch 2, skip next 4 chs †, dc in next 13 chs, repeat from † to † once, dc in next 33 chs, repeat from † to † once, dc in next 13 chs, repeat from † to † once, dc in last 29 chs: 133 dc.

Row 2 (Right side): Ch 3, turn; dc in next 6 dc, work Cross St, (dc in next dc, work Cross St) twice, dc in next 7 dc, ★ † work FPtr around next dc, dc in next 3 dc, ch 2, skip next ch-2 sp, (sc, ch 3, sc) in each of next 3 ch-1 sps, ch 2, skip next ch-2 sp, dc in next 3 dc, work FPtr around next dc †, dc in next 2 dc, ch 1, skip next dc, dc in next 2 dc, repeat from † to † once, dc in next 7 dc, work Cross St, (dc in next dc, work Cross St) twice, dc in next 7 dc; repeat from ★ once **more**: 9 Cross Sts.

Row 3: Ch 3, turn; dc in next 6 dc, † (work BPtr around next FPtr, work 6-dc Cluster in Front Loop Only of next st, work BPtr around next FPtr, dc in next dc) 3 times, dc in next 6 dc †, ★ work BPtr around next FPtr, dc in next 3 dc, ch 2, skip next ch-2 sp and next ch-3 sp, dc in center ch of next ch-3, (ch 1, dc) 3 times in same st, ch 2, skip next ch-3 sp and next ch-2 sp, dc in next 3 dc, work BPtr around next FPtr, dc in next 2 dc, work 5-dc Cluster in next ch, dc in next 2 dc, work BPtr around next FPtr, dc in next 3 dc, ch 2, skip next ch-2 sp and next ch-3 sp, dc in center ch of next ch-3, (ch 1, dc) 3 times in same st, ch 2, skip next ch-3 sp and next ch-2 sp, dc in next 3 dc, work BPtr around next FPtr, dc in next 7 dc, repeat from † to † once; repeat from ★ once **more**.

12

Row 4: Ch 3, turn; dc in next 6 dc, work Cross St, (dc in next dc, work Cross St) twice, dc in next 7 dc, ★ † work FPtr around next BPtr, dc in next 3 dc, ch 2, skip next ch-2 sp, (sc, ch 3, sc) in each of next 3 ch-1 sps, ch 2, skip next ch-2 sp, dc in next 3 dc, work FPtr around next BPtr †, dc in next 2 dc, ch 1, skip next 5-dc Cluster, dc in next 2 dc, repeat from

† to † once, dc in next 7 dc, work Cross St, (dc in next dc, work Cross St) twice, dc in next 7 dc; repeat from ★ once **more**. Repeat Rows 3 and 4 until afghan measures 70", ending by working Row 4.

Add fringe using 12 strands, each 18" long *(Figs. 33a & b, page 139)*; spacing evenly, attach across each end of afghan.

STRIKING STAINED GLASS

The beauty of stained glass is reflected in this brilliant jewel-tone throw. Each motif resembles a flower with four giant petals that you create by changing colors during the rounds. Black centers and edging provide a striking backdrop for the vivid hues. What an eye-catching accent!

Finished Size: 46" x 61"

MATERIALS

Worsted Weight Yarn:
    Black - 21 ounces, (600 grams, 1,440 yards)
    Green - 6 ounces, (170 grams, 410 yards)
    Burgundy - 6 ounces, (170 grams, 410 yards)
    Purple - 6 ounces, (170 grams, 410 yards)
    Blue - 6 ounces, (170 grams, 410 yards)
Crochet hook, size I (5.50 mm) **or** size needed for gauge

GAUGE: Each Motif = 7¹/₂"

Gauge Swatch: 3" square
Work same as Motif through Rnd 2.

MOTIF (Make 48)

With Black, ch 4; join with slip st to form a ring.
Rnd 1 (Right side)**:** Ch 3, dc in ring, ch 2, (2 dc in ring, ch 2) 3 times; join with slip st to top of beginning ch-3: 4 ch-2 sps.
Note: Loop a short piece of yarn around any stitch to mark Rnd 1 as **right** side.
Rnd 2: Slip st in next dc and in next ch-2 sp, ch 3, 6 dc in same sp, ch 1, (7 dc in next ch-2 sp, ch 1) around; join with slip st to top of beginning ch-3, finish off: 28 sts and 4 ch-1 sps.
Note: Colors are joined on Rnd 3 in the following order: Burgundy, Purple, and Blue.
Rnd 3: With **right** side facing, join Green with slip st in same st as joining; ch 2, sc in same st and in next dc, ch 2, skip next dc, (2 dc, ch 2, 2 dc) in next dc, ch 2, ★ skip next dc, sc in next 2 dc changing to next color in last sc worked *(Fig. 28a, page 138)*, drop yarn, do **not** cut dropped yarn unless otherwise instructed, ch 1, sc in next 2 dc, ch 2, skip next dc, (2 dc, ch 2, 2 dc) in next dc, ch 2; repeat from ★ 2 times **more**, skip next dc, sc in last 2 dc; join with slip st in beginning ch-2 sp.
Rnd 4: Ch 1, turn; ★ † sc in next sc, skip next sc, 2 sc in next ch-2 sp, ch 2, (2 dc, ch 2, 2 dc) in next ch-2 sp, ch 2, 2 sc in next ch-2 sp, skip next sc, sc in next sc †, drop yarn, ch 1 with next color; repeat from ★ 2 times **more**, then repeat from † to † once, ch 1; join with slip st to first sc.

Rnd 5: Ch 2, turn; ★ † sc in next sc, skip next 2 sc, 2 sc in next ch-2 sp, ch 2, (2 dc, ch 2, 2 dc) in next ch-2 sp, ch 2, 2 sc in next ch-2 sp, skip next 2 sc †, sc in next sc changing to next color, ch 1; repeat from ★ 2 times **more**, then repeat from † to † once, sc in last sc; join with slip st in beginning ch-2 sp.
Rnd 6: Ch 1, turn; ★ † sc in next sc, skip next 2 sc, 6 dc in next ch-2 sp, (3 dc, ch 2, 3 dc) in next ch-2 sp, 6 dc in next ch-2 sp, skip next 2 sc, sc in next sc †, drop yarn, cut dropped yarn, ch 1 with next color; repeat from ★ 2 times **more**, then repeat from † to † once, ch 1; join with slip st to first sc, finish off: 80 sts and 8 sps.
Rnd 7: With **right** side facing, join Black with slip st in any corner ch-2 sp; ch 1, ★ sc in corner ch-2 sp, ch 1, sc in next 10 sts, working in **front** of next ch, tr in ch-1 sp on Rnd 2, sc in next 10 sts, ch 1; repeat from ★ around; join with slip st to first sc.
Rnd 8: Ch 1, turn; sc in same st, ch 2, sc in next 7 sc, skip next 3 sc, (dc, ch 3, dc) in next tr, skip next 3 sc, sc in next 7 sc, ch 2, ★ sc in next sc, ch 2, sc in next 7 sc, skip next 3 sc, (dc, ch 3, dc) in next tr, skip next 3 sc, sc in next 7 sc, ch 2; repeat from ★ around; join with slip st to first sc, finish off.

ASSEMBLY

Join Motifs into 6 vertical strips of 8 Motifs each as follows:
With **right** sides together and working through **outside** loops only, join Black with slip st in any corner sc, ch 1, sc in same st, 2 sc in next ch-2 sp, sc in next 7 sc, 3 sc in next ch-3 sp, sc in next 7 sc, 2 sc in next ch-2 sp, sc in next corner sc; finish off. Join strips in same manner.

EDGING

Rnd 1: With **right** side facing and working in Back Loops Only *(Fig. 21, page 136)*, join Black with slip st in any corner sc; ch 1, sc in each st around working 2 sc in each corner sc, and 3 sc in each ch-3 sp; join with slip st to first sc.
Rnd 2: Ch 1, turn; sc in both loops of each sc around; join with slip st to first sc, finish off.

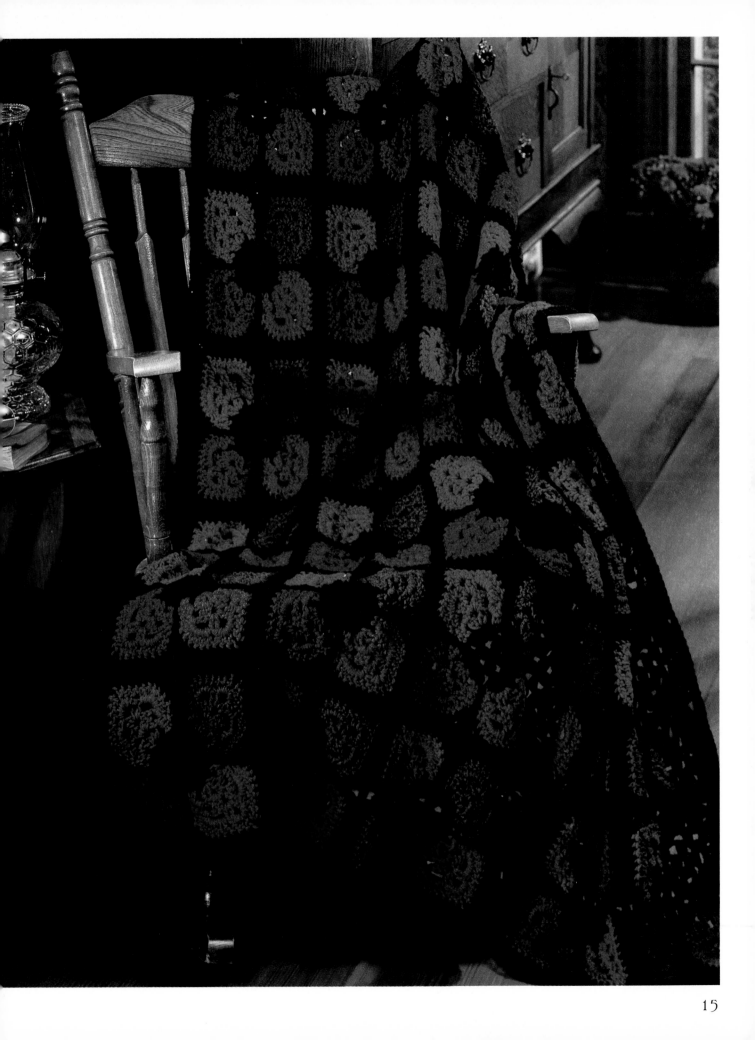

RICH DIAMONDS

Our diamond-studded afghan is sure to please girls of all ages! Worked separately and then whipstitched together, each vibrant motif is accentuated with an inner border of contrasting clusters. Tassels offer a rich finish to this priceless beauty.

Finished Size: 48" x 69"

MATERIALS

Worsted Weight Yarn:
Blue - 20 ounces, (570 grams, 1,130 yards)
Maroon - 15 ounces, (430 grams, 850 yards)
Tan - 13 ounces, (370 grams, 735 yards)
Crochet hook, size H (5.00 mm) **or** size needed for gauge
Yarn needle

GAUGE: Each Diamond = 8"w x 11½"h

Gauge Swatch: 3¾"w x 5½"h
Work same as Diamond A through Rnd 2.

STITCH GUIDE

> **BEGINNING CLUSTER**
>
> Ch 3, ★ YO, insert hook in sp indicated, YO and pull up a loop, YO and draw through 2 loops on hook; repeat from ★ once **more**, YO and draw through all 3 loops on hook *(Figs. 10a & b, page 134)*.
>
> **CLUSTER**
>
> ★ YO, insert hook in st or sp indicated, YO and pull up a loop, YO and draw through 2 loops on hook; repeat from ★ 2 times **more**, YO and draw through all 4 loops on hook.

DIAMOND A (Make 36)

With Blue, ch 4; join with slip st to form a ring.
Rnd 1 (Right side)**:** Ch 3 **(counts as first dc, now and throughout)**, in ring work (2 dc, 2 tr, ch 3, 2 tr, 3 dc, ch 2, 3 dc, 2 tr, ch 3, 2 tr, 3 dc), ch 2; join with slip st to first dc: 20 sts and 4 sps.
Note: Loop a short piece of yarn around any stitch to mark Rnd 1 as **right** side.
Rnd 2: Ch 3, dc in next 4 sts, † (dc, 2 tr, ch 2, 2 tr, dc) in next ch-3 sp, dc in next 5 sts, (dc, ch 2, dc) in next ch-2 sp †, dc in next 5 sts, repeat from † to † once; join with slip st to first dc, finish off: 36 sts and 4 sps.
Rnd 3: With **right** side facing, join Tan with slip st in last ch-2 sp worked, work (beginning Cluster, ch 2, Cluster) in same sp, † ch 1, (skip next st, work Cluster in next st, ch 1) 4 times, skip next st, work (Cluster, ch 3, Cluster) in next ch-2 sp, ch 1, (skip next st, work Cluster in next st, ch 1) 4 times, skip next st †, work (Cluster, ch 2, Cluster) in next ch-2 sp, repeat from † to † once; join with slip st to top of beginning Cluster, finish off: 24 Clusters.

Rnd 4: With **right** side facing, join Blue with slip st in first ch-2 sp; ch 3, (dc, ch 2, 2 dc) in same sp, † 2 dc in each of next 5 ch-1 sps, (3 dc, 2 tr, ch 3, 2 tr, 3 dc) in next ch-3 sp, 2 dc in each of next 5 ch-1 sps †, (2 dc, ch 2, 2 dc) in next ch-2 sp, repeat from † to † once; join with slip st to first dc: 68 sts and 4 sps.
Rnd 5: Ch 3, dc in next dc, † (dc, ch 2, dc) in next ch-2 sp, dc in next 17 sts, (2 dc, 2 tr, ch 2, 2 tr, 2 dc) in next ch-3 sp †, dc in next 17 sts, repeat from † to † once, dc in last 15 sts; join with slip st to first dc, finish off: 88 sts and 4 sps.

DIAMOND B (Make 25)

With Maroon in place of Blue, work same as Diamond A.

ASSEMBLY

Following Placement Diagram as a guide and using matching colors as desired, with **wrong** sides together and working through **inside** loops only, whipstitch Diamonds together *(Fig. 30b, page 139)*, securing seam at each corner.

Using Blue, add 6" long tassels *(Figs. 32a & b, page 139)* in each point across each end of afghan.

PLACEMENT DIAGRAM

Soft and inviting, this cover-up portrays the beauty of a daisy garden on a gentle spring morning. Each square features a "blossom" with cluster-stitch petals and a lacy border. To make the afghan fast to finish, we used a join-as-you-go method.

Finished Size: 48" x 63"

MATERIALS

Worsted Weight Brushed Acrylic Yarn:
    White - 27 ounces, (770 grams, 1,710 yards)
    Blue - 15 ounces, (430 grams, 950 yards)
    Yellow - 5 ounces, (140 grams, 315 yards)
    Crochet hook, size I (5.50 mm) **or** size needed for gauge

GAUGE: Each Square = 5"

Gauge Swatch: 4" square
Work same as Square through Rnd 4.

STITCH GUIDE

BEGINNING CLUSTER
Ch 2, ★ YO, insert hook in st indicated, YO and pull up a loop, YO and draw through 2 loops on hook; repeat from ★ once **more**, YO and draw through all 3 loops on hook *(Figs. 10a & b, page 134)*.
CLUSTER
★ YO, insert hook in st indicated, YO and pull up a loop, YO and draw through 2 loops on hook; repeat from ★ 2 times **more**, YO and draw through all 4 loops on hook.

FIRST SQUARE

With Yellow, ch 4; join with slip st to form a ring.
Rnd 1 (Right side)**:** Ch 1, 12 sc in ring; join with slip st to first sc.
Note: Loop a short piece of yarn around any stitch to mark Rnd 1 as **right** side.
Rnd 2: Ch 1, sc in each sc around; join with slip st to first sc, finish off.
Rnd 3: With **right** side facing, join White with slip st in any sc; work beginning Cluster, ch 3, (work Cluster in next sc, ch 3) around; join with slip st to top of beginning Cluster, finish off: 12 Clusters.
Rnd 4: With **right** side facing, join Blue with slip st in any ch-3 sp; ch 3, (2 dc, ch 2, 3 dc) in same sp, 3 hdc in each of next 2 ch-3 sps, ★ (3 dc, ch 2, 3 dc) in next ch-3 sp, 3 hdc in each of next 2 ch-3 sps; repeat from ★ around; join with slip st to top of beginning ch-3, finish off: 48 sts and 4 ch-2 sps.
Rnd 5: With **right** side facing, join White with slip st in any corner ch-2 sp; ch 1, ★ (sc, ch 6, sc) in corner ch-2 sp, (ch 4, skip next 3 sts, sc in sp **before** next st) 3 times *(Fig. 23, page 136)*, ch 4; repeat from ★ around; join with slip st to first sc, finish off: 20 loops.

REMAINING SQUARES

Work same as First Square through Rnd 4.
Work One-Sided or Two-Sided Joining to form 9 vertical strips of 12 Squares each.
Note: When working into corner loop that has been previously joined, work into joining slip st.

ONE-SIDED JOINING

Rnd 5: With **right** side facing, join White with slip st in any corner ch-2 sp; ch 1, sc in same sp, (ch 4, skip next 3 sts, sc in sp **before** next st) 3 times, ch 4, ★ (sc, ch 6, sc) in next corner ch-2 sp, (ch 4, skip next 3 sts, sc in sp **before** next st) 3 times, ch 4; repeat from ★ once **more**, sc in next corner ch-2 sp, ch 3, with **wrong** sides together, slip st in corresponding corner loop on **previous Square** *(Fig. 29, page 138)*, ch 3, sc in same sp on **new Square**, ch 2, slip st in next ch-4 sp on **previous Square**, ch 2, (skip next 3 sts on **new Square**, sc in sp **before** next st, ch 2, slip st in next ch-4 sp on **previous Square**, ch 2) 3 times, sc in same sp as first sc, ch 3, slip st in next corner loop on **previous Square**, ch 3; join with slip st to first sc, finish off.

TWO-SIDED JOINING

Rnd 5: With **right** side facing, join White with slip st in any corner ch-2 sp; ch 1, sc in same sp, (ch 4, skip next 3 sts, sc in sp **before** next st) 3 times, ch 4, (sc, ch 6, sc) in next corner ch-2 sp, (ch 4, skip next 3 sts, sc in sp **before** next st) 3 times, ch 4, ★ sc in next corner ch-2 sp, ch 3, with **wrong** sides together, slip st in corresponding corner loop on **previous Square**, ch 3, sc in same sp on **new Square**, ch 2, slip st in next ch-4 sp on **previous Square**, ch 2, (skip next 3 sts on **new Square**, sc in sp **before** next st, ch 2, slip st in next ch-4 sp on **previous Square**, ch 2) 3 times; repeat from ★ once **more**, sc in same sp as first sc, ch 3, slip st in next corner loop on **previous Square**, ch 3; join with slip st to first sc, finish off.

EDGING

Rnd 1: With **right** side facing, join White with slip st in any corner loop; ch 1, ★ sc in corner loop, ch 3, (dc, ch 3, dc) in each ch-4 sp and in both corner loops at each joining across to next corner loop, ch 3; repeat from ★ around; join with slip st to first sc.
Rnd 2: Slip st in first ch-3 sp, ch 6, slip st in second ch from hook, ch 1, dc in same sp, ★ dc in next ch-3 sp, ch 3, slip st in second ch from hook, ch 1, dc in same sp; repeat from ★ around; join with slip st to third ch of beginning ch-6, finish off.

Quick LUXURIOUS RIPPLE

Added as an elegant finishing touch, strips of raised clusters lend luxurious texture to our classic ripple pattern. Sophisticated colors provide pleasant contrast.

Finished Size: 50" x 63"

MATERIALS
Worsted Weight Brushed Acrylic Yarn:
Sage - 29 ounces, (820 grams, 1,835 yards)
Off-White - 13 ounces, (370 grams, 825 yards)
Lavender - 13 ounces, (370 grams, 825 yards)
Crochet hook, size N (9.00 mm) **or** size needed for gauge

GAUGE: In pattern, 1 repeat (16 sts) and 5 rows = 5"

Gauge Swatch: 10"w x 6"h
With Sage, ch 35 **loosely.**
Work same as afghan through Row 6.
Finish off.

STITCH GUIDE

SHELL
(2 Dc, ch 1, 2 dc) in st indicated.

BEGINNING DECREASE (uses first 3 sts)
Ch 3, turn; ★ YO, insert hook in **next** dc, YO and pull up a loop, YO and draw through 2 loops on hook; repeat from ★ once **more**, YO and draw through all 3 loops on hook **(counts as one dc)**.

DECREASE (uses next 5 sts)
★ YO, insert hook in **next** dc, YO and pull up a loop, YO and draw through 2 loops on hook; repeat from ★ 4 times **more**, YO and draw through all 6 loops on hook **(counts as one dc)**.

END DECREASE (uses last 3 sts)
★ YO, insert hook in **next** dc, YO and pull up a loop, YO and draw through 2 loops on hook; repeat from ★ 2 times **more**, YO and draw through all 4 loops on hook **(counts as one dc)**.

CLUSTER
Ch 3, ★ YO twice, insert hook in st indicated, YO and pull up a loop, (YO and draw through 2 loops on hook) twice; repeat from ★ 3 times **more**, YO and draw through all 5 loops on hook *(Figs. 10a & b, page 134)*.

COLOR SEQUENCE
2 Rows each Sage *(Fig. 28a, page 138)*, ★ Off-White, Lavender, Sage; repeat from ★ throughout.

BODY
With Sage, ch 163 **loosely.**
Row 1: YO, insert hook in fourth ch from hook, YO and pull up a loop, YO and draw through 2 loops on hook, YO, insert hook in next ch, YO and pull up a loop, YO and draw through 2 loops on hook, YO and draw through all 3 loops on hook **(counts as first dc)**, dc in next 5 chs, work Shell in next ch, dc in next 5 chs, ★ decrease, dc in next 5 chs, work Shell in next ch, dc in next 5 chs; repeat from ★ across to last 3 chs, work end decrease.
Row 2 (Right side): Working in Back Loops Only *(Fig. 21, page 136)*, work beginning decrease, dc in next 5 dc, work Shell in next ch, dc in next 5 dc, ★ decrease, dc in next 5 dc, work Shell in next ch, dc in next 5 dc; repeat from ★ across to last 3 dc, work end decrease.
Note: Loop a short piece of yarn around any stitch to mark Row 2 as **right** side.
Row 3: Working in Front Loops Only, repeat Row 2.
Repeat Rows 2 and 3 for pattern until afghan measures 63", ending by working 2 Sage rows; finish off.

CLUSTER STRIPES
With **right** side facing and working from bottom edge to top edge, join Sage with slip st in same beginning ch as first Shell on Row 1; work Cluster in same st, slip st in free loop of ch at top of same Shell *(Fig. 22a, page 136)*, ★ work Cluster in same st, slip st in free loop of ch on Shell in next row; repeat from ★ to top edge; finish off.
Repeat along each row of Shells.

Using Sage, add 9" long tassels *(Figs. 32a & b, page 139)* to each point across each end of afghan.

A romantic touch for a lady's bedroom, this lacy cover is incredibly soft and feminine. Created with simple stitches, the airy motifs are joined as you go and complemented by long, graceful tassels.

Finished Size: 45" x 55"

MATERIALS

Worsted Weight Yarn:
  50 ounces, (1,420 grams, 3,165 yards)
Crochet hook, size I (5.50 mm) **or** size needed for gauge

GAUGE SWATCH: 5" square
Work same as First Motif.

FIRST MOTIF

Ch 7; join with slip st to form a ring.

Rnd 1 (Right side): Ch 1, 16 sc in ring; join with slip st to first sc.

Note: Loop a short piece of yarn around any stitch to mark Rnd 1 as **right** side.

Rnd 2: Ch 1, sc in same st, ch 2, skip next sc, (sc in next sc, ch 2, skip next sc) around; join with slip st to first sc: 8 ch-2 sps.

Rnd 3: Slip st in first ch-2 sp, ch 1, (sc, 3 dc, sc) in same sp, ch 1, ★ (sc, 3 dc, sc) in next ch-2 sp, ch 1; repeat from ★ around; join with slip st to first sc: 8 petals.

Rnd 4: Slip st in next 2 dc, ch 1, sc in same st, ★ † ch 3, (hdc, ch 1, hdc) in next ch-1 sp (between petals), ch 3, sc in center dc of next 3-dc group †, ch 4, sc in center dc of next 3-dc group; repeat from ★ 2 times **more**, then repeat from † to † once, ch 2, hdc in first sc to form last sp.

Rnd 5: Ch 3, 2 dc in same sp, ch 4, skip next ch-3 sp, sc in next 3 sts, ch 4, ★ skip next ch-3 sp, (3 dc, ch 3, 3 dc) in next ch-4 sp, ch 4, skip next ch-3 sp, sc in next 3 sts, ch 4; repeat from ★ 2 times **more**, skip next ch-3 sp, 3 dc in same sp as beginning ch-3, ch 3; join with slip st to top of beginning ch-3.

Rnd 6: Ch 3, dc in next 2 dc, ★ † ch 5, slip st in next sc, ch 5, sc in fourth ch from hook, ch 1, skip next sc, slip st in next sc, ch 5, dc in next 3 dc, ch 6, sc in fourth ch from hook, ch 2 †, dc in next 3 dc; repeat from ★ 2 times **more**, then repeat from † to † once; join with slip st to top of beginning ch-3, finish off.

REMAINING MOTIFS

Work same as First Motif through Rnd 5.
Work One-Sided or Two-Sided Joining to form 9 vertical strips of 11 Motifs each.

Note: When working into corner loop that has been previously joined, work into same ch.

ONE-SIDED JOINING

Rnd 6: Ch 3, dc in next 2 dc, ★ † ch 5, slip st in next sc, ch 5, sc in fourth ch from hook, ch 1, skip next sc, slip st in next sc, ch 5, dc in next 3 dc †, ch 6, sc in fourth ch from hook, ch 2, dc in next 3 dc; repeat from ★ once **more**, then repeat from † to † once, ch 2, with **wrong** sides together, slip st in center ch of corresponding corner on **previous Motif** (*Fig. 29, page 138*), ch 2, dc in next 3 dc on **new Motif**, ch 1, slip st in second ch of next ch-5 on **previous Motif**, ch 3, skip next ch-4 sp on **new Motif**, slip st in next sc, ch 1, slip st in center ch of next ch-3 on **previous Motif**, ch 1, skip next sc on **new Motif**, slip st in next sc, ch 3, slip st in fourth ch of next ch-5 on **previous Motif**, ch 1, dc in next 3 dc on **new Motif**, ch 2, slip st in center ch of next corner on **previous Motif**, ch 2; join with slip st to top of beginning ch-3, finish off.

TWO-SIDED JOINING

Rnd 6: Ch 3, dc in next 2 dc, † ch 5, slip st in next sc, ch 5, sc in fourth ch from hook, ch 1, skip next sc, slip st in next sc, ch 5, dc in next 3 dc †, ch 6, sc in fourth ch from hook, ch 2, dc in next 3 dc, repeat from † to † once, ch 2, with **wrong** sides together, slip st in center ch of corresponding corner on **previous Motif**, ch 2, ★ dc in next 3 dc on **new Motif**, ch 1, slip st in second ch of next ch-5 on **previous Motif**, ch 3, skip next ch-4 sp on **new Motif**, slip st in next sc, ch 1, slip st in center ch of next ch-3 on **previous Motif**, ch 1, skip next sc on **new Motif**, slip st in next sc, ch 3, slip st in fourth ch of next ch-5 on **previous Motif**, ch 1, dc in next 3 dc on **new Motif**, ch 2, slip st in center ch of next corner on **previous Motif**, ch 2; repeat from ★ once **more**; join with slip st to top of beginning ch-3, finish off.

Add 8" long tassels (*Figs. 32a & b, page 139*) in each corner and in each joining across each end of afghan.

all through the house

If you're searching for new ways to spruce up your home decor, you'll love this intriguing collection of crocheted items. From the living room, where a quartet of floral doilies offers seasonal touches, to the kitchen's lighthearted blue and white charmers, these interior accessories present you with a wealth of ideas for enhancing your living spaces. "Redecorating" is simpler than you think with these delightful pieces to inspire you!

IN THE LIVING ROOM

*L*et the beauty of these thread crochet doilies accentuate your home with each passing season. (Below) Spring buds excite our spirits as they unfold in the warmth of a sunny day. Here, cheery tulips playfully complement a vase of fresh florals. When fields of summer flowers are in bloom, they beckon us to stop and pick a colorful bouquet. (Opposite) For this charming doily, we gathered a profusion of beautiful blue and white blossoms.

As green leaves redress themselves in brilliant autumn hues, we take time to be thankful — especially for those we hold dear. (Below) Pineapple motifs, traditional symbols of hospitality, beautify this gracious doily. (Opposite) Our stunning poinsettia is a lovely reminder of winter's icy beauty.

WINTER LACE DOILY

Shown on page 27.
Finished Size: 11" in diameter

MATERIALS

Cotton Crochet Thread (size 40), 175 yards
Steel crochet hook, size 12 (1.00 mm) **or** size needed for gauge

GAUGE SWATCH: 2¹/₂" in diameter
Work same as doily through Rnd 7.

STITCH GUIDE

V-ST
(Dc, ch 1, dc) in st or sp indicated.
CLUSTER
★ YO, insert hook in sp indicated, YO and pull up a loop, YO and draw through 2 loops on hook; repeat from ★ 2 times **more**, YO and draw through all 4 loops on hook *(Figs. 10a & b, page 134)*.
DECREASE
YO, insert hook in **same** dc, † YO and pull up a loop, YO and draw through 2 loops on hook †, YO, skip next ch-1 sp, insert hook in **next** dc, repeat from † to † once, YO and draw through all 3 loops on hook **(counts as one dc)**.
SHELL
(2 Dc, ch 3, 2 dc) in st or sp indicated.
PICOT
Ch 3, slip st in third ch from hook.

Ch 8; join with slip st to form a ring.
Rnd 1 (Right side)**:** Ch 1, 16 sc in ring; join with slip st to first sc.
Rnd 2: Ch 4, dc in same st, (ch 5, skip next sc, work V-St in next sc) around to last sc, ch 2, skip last sc, dc in third ch of beginning ch-4 to form last sp: 16 sps.
Rnd 3: Ch 1, sc in same sp, ch 5, work Cluster in next V-St (ch-1 sp), ch 5, (sc in next ch-5 sp, ch 5, work Cluster in next V-St, ch 5) around; join with slip st to first sc: 8 Clusters.
Rnd 4: Slip st in first 3 chs, ch 1, sc in same sp, ch 7, sc in next sp, ch 5, slip st in third ch from hook, ch 2, ★ sc in next sp, ch 7, sc in next sp, ch 5, slip st in third ch from hook, ch 2; repeat from ★ around; join with slip st to first sc: 16 loops.
Rnd 5: Slip st in first 2 chs, ch 3 **(counts as first dc, now and throughout)**, 4 dc in same loop, ch 9, skip next loop, (5 dc in next ch-7 loop, ch 9, skip next loop) around; join with slip st to first dc: 40 dc.
Rnd 6: Ch 3, dc in next dc, 2 dc in next dc, dc in next 2 dc, ch 3, work V-St in center ch of next loop, ch 3, ★ dc in next 2 dc, 2 dc in next dc, dc in next 2 dc, ch 3, work V-St in center ch of next loop, ch 3; repeat from ★ around; join with slip st to first dc.
Rnd 7: Ch 3, dc in next 5 dc, ch 4, work V-St in next V-St, ch 4, (dc in next 6 dc, ch 4, work V-St in next V-St, ch 4) around; join with slip st to first dc.

Rnd 8: Ch 3, dc in next 5 dc, ch 5, work V-St in next V-St, ch 5, (dc in next 6 dc, ch 5, work V-St in next V-St, ch 5) around; join with slip st to first dc.
Rnd 9: Ch 3, dc in next 5 dc, ch 6, work V-St in next V-St, ch 6, (dc in next 6 dc, ch 6, work V-St in next V-St, ch 6) around; join with slip st to first dc.
Rnd 10: Ch 3, dc in next 5 dc, ch 7, work V-St in next V-St, ch 7, (dc in next 6 dc, ch 7, work V-St in next V-St, ch 7) around; join with slip st to first dc.
Rnd 11: Ch 3, dc in next 5 dc, ch 7, dc in next dc, ch 1, decrease, ch 1, dc in same dc, ch 7, ★ dc in next 6 dc, ch 7, dc in next dc, ch 1, decrease, ch 1, dc in same dc, ch 7; repeat from ★ around; join with slip st to first dc.
Rnd 12: Ch 3, dc in next 5 dc, ch 7, dc in next dc, ch 1, (decrease, ch 1) twice, dc in same dc, ch 7, ★ dc in next 6 dc, ch 7, dc in next dc, ch 1, (decrease, ch 1) twice, dc in same dc, ch 7; repeat from ★ around; join with slip st to first dc.
Rnd 13: Ch 3, dc in next 2 dc, ch 3, dc in next 3 dc, ch 6, dc in next dc, ch 1, (decrease, ch 1) 3 times, dc in same dc, ch 6, ★ dc in next 3 dc, ch 3, dc in next 3 dc, ch 6, dc in next dc, ch 1, (decrease, ch 1) 3 times, dc in same dc, ch 6; repeat from ★ around; join with slip st to first dc.
Rnd 14: Ch 3, dc in next 2 dc, ★ † ch 3, dc in next ch-3 sp, ch 3, dc in next 3 dc and in next loop, ch 6, skip next dc and next ch-1 sp, dc in next dc, ch 1, (decrease, ch 1) twice, dc in same dc, ch 6, skip next ch-1 sp and next dc, dc in next loop †, dc in next 3 dc; repeat from ★ 6 times **more**, then repeat from † to † once; join with slip st to first dc.
Rnd 15: Ch 3, dc in next dc, ★ † ch 3, skip next dc and next ch-3 sp, work Shell in next dc, ch 3, skip next ch-3 sp and next dc, dc in next 3 dc and in next loop, ch 6, skip next dc and next ch-1 sp, dc in next dc, ch 1, decrease, ch 1, dc in same dc, ch 6, skip next ch-1 sp and next dc, dc in next loop †, dc in next 3 dc; repeat from ★ 6 times **more**, then repeat from † to † once, dc in last dc; join with slip st to first dc.
Rnd 16: Ch 6, ★ † skip next dc, dc in next ch-3 sp and in next dc, ch 3, skip next dc, dc in next ch-3 sp, ch 3, skip next dc, dc in next dc and in next ch-3 sp, ch 3, skip next dc, dc in next 3 dc and in next loop, ch 6, skip next dc and next ch-1 sp, work V-St in next dc, ch 6, skip next ch-1 sp and next dc, dc in next loop †, dc in next 3 dc, ch 3; repeat from ★ 6 times **more**, then repeat from † to † once, dc in last 2 dc; join with slip st to third ch of beginning ch-6.
Rnd 17: Slip st in first 3 chs, ch 3, dc in next dc, ★ † ch 3, skip next dc, work Shell in next dc, ch 3, skip next ch-3 sp and next dc, dc in next dc and in next ch-3 sp, ch 3, skip next dc, dc in next 3 dc and in next loop, ch 6, (sc, work Picot, sc) in next V-St, ch 6, dc in next loop and in next 3 dc, ch 3 †, dc in next ch-3 sp and in next dc; repeat from ★ 6 times **more**, then repeat from † to † once; join with slip st to first dc.

Rnd 18: Ch 7, skip first ch-3 sp, ★ † 2 dc in next Shell (ch-3 sp), (ch 3, 2 dc) twice in same sp, ch 4, skip next ch-3 sp and next dc, dc in next dc and in next ch-3 sp, ch 3, skip next dc, dc in next 3 dc, 2 dc in next ch-6 loop, ch 6, skip next 2 sc, 2 dc in next ch-6 loop, dc in next 3 dc, ch 3, skip next dc, dc in next ch-3 sp †, dc in next dc, ch 4; repeat from ★ 6 times **more**, then repeat from † to † once; join with slip st to third ch of beginning ch-7.

Rnd 19: Slip st in first 6 sts and in next ch-3 sp, ch 3, (dc, ch 3, 2 dc) in same sp, ★ † ch 3, work Shell in next ch-3 sp, ch 5, skip next ch-4 sp and next dc, dc in next dc and in next ch-3 sp, ch 3, skip next 2 dc, dc in next 3 dc, 6 dc in next ch-6 loop, dc in next 3 dc, ch 3, skip next 2 dc, dc in next ch-3 sp and in next dc, ch 5 †, skip next ch-4 sp, work Shell in next ch-3 sp; repeat from ★ 6 times **more**, then repeat from † to † once; join with slip st to first dc.

Rnd 20: Slip st in next dc and in next ch-3 sp, ch 3, (dc, ch 3, 2 dc) in same sp, ★ † ch 1, work Shell in next ch-3 sp, ch 1, work Shell in next Shell, ch 5, skip next ch-5 sp and next dc, dc in next dc and in next ch-3 sp, ch 4, skip next 2 dc, dc in next 8 dc, ch 4, skip next 2 dc, dc in next ch-3 sp and in next dc, ch 5 †, work Shell in next Shell; repeat from ★ 6 times **more**, then repeat from † to † once; join with slip st to first dc.

Rnd 21: Slip st in next dc and in next ch-3 sp, ch 3, (dc, ch 3, 2 dc) in same sp, ★ † ch 2, (3 dc, ch 3, 3 dc) in next Shell, ch 2, work Shell in next Shell, ch 7, skip next ch-5 sp and next dc, dc in next dc and in next ch-4 sp, ch 5, skip next 2 dc, dc in next 4 dc, ch 5, skip next 2 dc, dc in next ch-4 sp and in next dc, ch 7 †, work Shell in next Shell; repeat from ★ 6 times **more**, then repeat from † to † once; join with slip st to first dc.

Rnd 22: Slip st in next dc and in next ch-3 sp, ch 3, (dc, ch 3, 2 dc) in same sp, ★ † ch 2, skip next ch-2 sp, dc in next 3 dc, 5 dc in next ch-3 sp, dc in next 3 dc, ch 2, work Shell in next Shell, work Shell in center ch of next loop, ch 3, skip next dc, dc in next dc and in next ch-5 sp, ch 5, skip next dc, dc in next 2 dc, ch 5, skip next dc, dc in next ch-5 sp and in next dc, ch 3, work Shell in center ch of next loop †, work Shell in next Shell; repeat from ★ 6 times **more**, then repeat from † to † once; join with slip st to first dc.

Rnd 23: Slip st in next dc and in next ch-3 sp, ch 3, (dc, ch 3, 2 dc) in same sp, ch 1, ★ † skip next ch-2 sp, dc in next dc, (ch 1, skip next dc, dc in next dc) twice, (ch 1, dc in next dc) twice, (ch 1, skip next dc, dc in next dc) twice, (ch 1, work Shell in next Shell) twice, ch 4, skip next ch-3 sp and next dc, dc in next dc and in next ch-5 sp, ch 5, skip next 2 dc, dc in next ch-5 sp and in next dc, ch 4 †, (work Shell in next Shell, ch 1) twice; repeat from ★ 6 times **more**, then repeat from † to † once, work Shell in last Shell, ch 1; join with slip st to first dc.

Rnd 24: Slip st in next dc and in next ch-3 sp, ch 1, sc in same sp, ★ † ch 2, skip next 2 dc and next ch-1 sp, work V-St in each of next 7 dc, ch 2, (sc, work Picot, sc) in next Shell, ch 3, work Shell in next Shell, ch 7, skip next ch-4 sp, 2 dc in next ch-5 sp, ch 7, work Shell in next Shell, ch 3 †, (sc, work Picot, sc) in next Shell; repeat from ★ 6 times **more**, then repeat from † to † once, sc in same sp as first sc, work Picot; join with slip st to first sc.

Rnd 25: Slip st in first 3 sts and in next ch-1 sp, ch 7, dc in next V-St, (ch 4, dc in next V-St) 5 times, ★ † ch 6, work Shell in next Shell, (ch 1, work Shell in center ch of next loop) twice, ch 1, work Shell in next Shell, ch 6 †, dc in next V-St, (ch 4, dc in next V-St) 6 times; repeat from ★ 6 times **more**, then repeat from † to † once; join with slip st to third ch of beginning ch-7.

Rnd 26: Ch 7, dc in same st, (dc, ch 4, dc) in each of next 6 dc, ★ † ch 4, work Shell in next Shell, (ch 1, work Shell in next Shell) 3 times, ch 4 †, (dc, ch 4, dc) in each of next 7 dc; repeat from ★ 6 times **more**, then repeat from † to † once; join with slip st to third ch of beginning ch-7.

Rnd 27: Slip st in first 2 chs, ch 9, dc in next ch-4 sp, (ch 6, dc in next ch-4 sp) 5 times, ★ † ch 3, work Shell in next Shell, (ch 1, work Shell in next Shell) 3 times, ch 3, skip next ch-4 sp †, dc in next ch-4 sp, (ch 6, dc in next ch-4 sp) 6 times; repeat from ★ 6 times **more**, then repeat from † to † once; join with slip st to third ch of beginning ch-9.

Rnd 28: Ch 8, dc in same st, ★ † [ch 1, (dc, ch 5, dc) in next dc] 6 times, ch 2, (sc, work Picot, sc) in next Shell, ch 3, work Shell in next Shell, ch 1, work Shell in next Shell, ch 3, (sc, work Picot, sc) in next Shell, ch 2, skip next ch-3 sp †, (dc, ch 5, dc) in next dc; repeat from ★ 6 times **more**, then repeat from † to † once; join with slip st to third ch of beginning ch-8.

Rnd 29: Slip st in first 3 chs, ch 11, (dc in next ch-5 sp, ch 8) 6 times, ★ † work Shell in next Shell, ch 1, work Shell in next Shell, ch 8, skip next 2 sps †, (dc in next ch-5 sp, ch 8) 7 times; repeat from ★ 6 times **more**, then repeat from † to † once; join with slip st to third ch of beginning ch-11.

Rnd 30: Ch 8, slip st in third ch from hook, ch 3, dc in same st as beginning ch, ch 2, sc in next loop, ch 2, [(dc, ch 5, slip st in third ch from hook, ch 3, dc) in next dc, ch 2, sc in next loop, ch 2] 6 times, ★ † (2 dc, ch 5, slip st in third ch from hook, ch 3, 2 dc) in next Shell, ch 1, (2 dc, ch 5, slip st in third ch from hook, ch 3, 2 dc) in next Shell, ch 2, sc in next loop, ch 2 †, [(dc, ch 5, slip st in third ch from hook, ch 3, dc) in next dc, ch 2, sc in next loop, ch 2] 7 times; repeat from ★ 6 times **more**, then repeat from † to † once; join with slip st to third ch of beginning ch-8, finish off.

See Washing and Blocking, page 138.

SPRING BUDS DOILY

Shown on page 24.
Finished Size: 15" in diameter

MATERIALS
Bedspread Weight Cotton Thread (size 10):
    White - 110 yards
    Pink - 45 yards
    Jade - 35 yards
Steel crochet hook, size 7 (1.65 mm) **or** size needed for gauge

GAUGE SWATCH: 2" in diameter
Work same as doily through Rnd 3.

STITCH GUIDE

BEGINNING TR CLUSTER
Ch 3, ★ YO twice, insert hook in **same** st, YO and pull up a loop, (YO and draw through 2 loops on hook) twice; repeat from ★ once **more**, YO and draw through all 3 loops on hook.

TR CLUSTER
★ YO twice, insert hook in st or sp indicated, YO and pull up a loop, (YO and draw through 2 loops on hook) twice; repeat from ★ 2 times **more**, YO and draw through all 4 loops on hook *(Figs. 10a & b, page 134)*.

BEGINNING DTR CLUSTER
Ch 4, ★ YO 3 times, insert hook in **same** st, YO and pull up a loop, (YO and draw through 2 loops on hook) 3 times; repeat from ★ once **more**, YO and draw through all 3 loops on hook.

DTR CLUSTER
★ YO 3 times, insert hook in st indicated, YO and pull up a loop, (YO and draw through 2 loops on hook) 3 times; repeat from ★ 2 times **more**, YO and draw through all 4 loops on hook.

PICOT
Ch 4, slip st in third ch from hook.

With White, ch 8; join with slip st to form a ring.

Rnd 1 (Right side): Ch 1, 16 sc in ring; join with slip st to first sc.

Note: Loop a short piece of thread around any stitch to mark Rnd 1 as **right** side.

Rnd 2: Ch 4 **(counts as first dc plus ch 1)**, dc in same st, ★ ch 5, skip next sc, (dc, ch 1, dc) in next sc; repeat from ★ around to last sc, ch 2, skip last sc, dc in first dc to form last sp: 8 ch-1 sps.

Rnd 3: Ch 1, sc in same sp, ch 5, work tr Cluster in next ch-1 sp, ch 5, (sc in next ch-5 sp, ch 5, work tr Cluster in next ch-1 sp, ch 5) around; join with slip st to first sc.

Rnd 4: Slip st in first 3 chs, ch 1, sc in same sp, ch 7, sc in next ch-5 sp, work Picot, ch 2, ★ sc in next ch-5 sp, ch 7, sc in next ch-5 sp, work Picot, ch 2; repeat from ★ around; join with slip st to first sc, finish off: 8 Picots.

Rnd 5: With **right** side facing, join Jade with slip st in second ch of any ch-7 loop; work beginning tr Cluster, ch 5, (skip next ch, work tr Cluster in next ch, ch 5) twice, ★ work tr Cluster in second ch of next ch-7 loop, ch 5, (skip next ch, work tr Cluster in next ch, ch 5) twice; repeat from ★ around; join with slip st to top of beginning tr Cluster, finish off: 24 tr Clusters.

Rnd 6: With **right** side facing, join Pink with slip st in second ch of first ch-5 sp; work beginning tr Cluster, ★ † ch 5, skip next ch, work tr Cluster in next ch, ch 1, work tr Cluster in second ch of next ch-5 sp, ch 5, skip next ch, work tr Cluster in next ch, ch 5, sc in next ch-5 sp, ch 5 †, work tr Cluster in second ch of next ch-5 sp; repeat from ★ 6 times **more**, then repeat from † to † once; join with slip st to top of beginning tr Cluster, finish off: 32 tr Clusters.

Rnd 7: With **right** side facing, join White with slip st in first ch-5 sp; ch 1, sc in same sp, ch 11, skip next ch-1 sp, sc in next ch-5 sp, ch 11, skip next 2 ch-5 sps, ★ sc in next ch-5 sp, ch 11, skip next ch-1 sp, sc in next ch-5 sp, ch 11, skip next 2 ch-5 sps; repeat from ★ around; join with slip st to first sc: 16 loops.

Rnd 8: Slip st in first 2 chs, ch 1, (sc, ch 5, sc) in same loop, ★ ch 6, (sc, ch 5, sc) in next loop; repeat from ★ around, ch 3, dc in first sc to form last loop: 32 loops.

Rnd 9: Ch 1, (sc, ch 3, sc) in same loop, ★ ch 7, (sc, ch 3, sc) in next loop; repeat from ★ around, ch 4, dc in first sc to form last loop: 32 loops.

Rnds 10-12: Ch 1, (sc, ch 3, sc) in same loop, ★ ch 7, skip next ch-3 sp, (sc, ch 3, sc) in next loop; repeat from ★ around, ch 4, skip last ch-3 sp, dc in first sc to form last loop.

Rnd 13: Ch 1, (sc, ch 3, sc) in same loop, ★ ch 8, skip next ch-3 sp, (sc, ch 3, sc) in next loop; repeat from ★ around, ch 4, skip last ch-3 sp, tr in first sc to form last loop.

Rnd 14: Ch 1, (sc, ch 3, sc) in same loop, ch 9, skip next ch-3 sp, ★ (sc, ch 3, sc) in next loop, ch 9, skip next ch-3 sp; repeat from ★ around; join with slip st to first sc, finish off.

Rnd 15: With **right** side facing, skip first ch-3 sp and join Jade with slip st in next loop; ch 1, sc in same loop, ch 3, skip next ch-3 sp, work dtr Cluster in second ch of next loop, (ch 7, skip next ch, work dtr Cluster in next ch) 3 times, ch 3, skip next ch-3 sp, ★ sc in next loop, ch 3, skip next ch-3 sp, work dtr Cluster in second ch of next loop, (ch 7, skip next ch, work dtr Cluster in next ch) 3 times, ch 3, skip next ch-3 sp; repeat from ★ around; join with slip st to first sc, finish off: 64 dtr Clusters.

Rnd 16: With **right** side facing, skip first ch-3 sp and join Pink with slip st in third ch of next loop; work beginning dtr Cluster, ch 5, skip next ch, work dtr Cluster in next ch, (ch 3, work dtr Cluster in third ch of next loop, ch 5, skip next ch, work dtr Cluster in next ch) twice, ch 3, skip next 2 ch-3 sps, ★ (work dtr Cluster in third ch of next loop, ch 5, skip next ch, work dtr Cluster in next ch, ch 3) 3 times, skip next 2 ch-3 sps; repeat from ★ around; join with slip st to top of beginning dtr Cluster, finish off: 96 dtr Clusters.

Rnd 17: With **right** side facing, skip first ch-5 sp and join White with slip st in next ch-3 sp; ch 1, sc in same sp, (ch 5, sc in next sp) around, ch 2, dc in first sc to form last sp: 96 sps.

Rnd 18: Ch 1, sc in same sp, ch 5, (sc in next ch-5 sp, ch 5) around; join with slip st to first sc.

Rnd 19: Slip st in first ch-5 sp, ch 1, 5 sc in same sp and in each ch-5 sp around; join with slip st to first sc.

Rnd 20: Slip st in next 2 sc, ch 1, (sc, ch 3) twice in same st, skip next 4 sc, (2 dc, work Picot, ch 2, 2 dc) in next sc, ch 3, skip next 4 sc, ★ (sc, ch 3) twice in next sc, skip next 4 sc, (2 dc, work Picot, ch 2, 2 dc) in next sc, ch 3, skip next 4 sc; repeat from ★ around; join with slip st to first sc, finish off.

See Washing and Blocking, page 138.

SUMMER FLOWERS DOILY

Shown on page 25.

Finished Size: 21" in diameter

MATERIALS

Bedspread Weight Cotton Thread (size 10):
   Blue - 275 yards
   White - 175 yards
Steel crochet hook, size 7 (1.65 mm) **or** size needed for gauge

GAUGE SWATCH: 3" in diameter
Work same as Body through Rnd 7.

STITCH GUIDE

BEGINNING CLUSTER
Ch 4, ★ YO 3 times, insert hook in sp indicated, YO and pull up a loop, (YO and draw through 2 loops on hook) 3 times; repeat from ★ 2 times **more**, YO and draw through all 4 loops on hook *(Figs. 10a & b, page 134)*.

CLUSTER
★ YO 3 times, insert hook in sp indicated, YO and pull up a loop, (YO and draw through 2 loops on hook) 3 times; repeat from ★ 3 times **more**, YO and draw through all 5 loops on hook.

TRIPLE PICOT
(Ch 3, slip st, ch 5, slip st, ch 3, slip st) in side of st just worked *(Fig. 27, page 138)*.

PICOT
Ch 3, slip st in side of st just worked.

DECREASE (uses 2 sps)
★ YO twice, insert in **next** sp, YO and pull up a loop, (YO and draw through 2 loops on hook) twice; repeat from ★ once **more**, YO and draw through all 3 loops on hook.

2-TR CLUSTER
★ YO twice, insert hook in st indicated, YO and pull up a loop, (YO and draw through 2 loops on hook) twice; repeat from ★ once **more**, YO and draw through all 3 loops on hook.

BODY

With White, ch 6; join with slip st to form a ring.

Rnd 1 (Right side): Ch 1, 16 sc in ring; join with slip st to first sc.
Note: Loop a short piece of thread around any stitch to mark Rnd 1 as **right** side.

Rnd 2: Ch 6 **(counts as first dc plus ch 3)**, skip next sc, (dc in next sc, ch 3, skip next sc) around; join with slip st to first dc, finish off: 8 ch-3 sps.

Rnd 3: With **right** side facing, join Blue with slip st in any ch-3 sp; ch 1, (sc, hdc, 3 dc, hdc, sc) in same sp and in each ch-3 sp around; join with slip st to first sc: 8 petals.

Rnd 4: Working **behind** petals, slip st in first unworked dc on Rnd 2, ch 1, sc in same st, ch 4, (sc in next unworked dc on Rnd 2, ch 4) around; join with slip st to first sc: 8 ch-4 sps.

Rnd 5: Slip st in first ch-4 sp, ch 1, (sc, hdc, 5 dc, hdc, sc) in same sp and in each ch-4 sp around; join with slip st to first sc: 8 petals.

Rnd 6: Working **behind** petals, slip st in first unworked sc on Rnd 4, ch 1, sc in same st, ch 5, (sc in next unworked sc on Rnd 4, ch 5) around; join with slip st to first sc, finish off: 8 ch-5 sps.

Rnd 7: With **right** side facing, join White with slip st in any ch-5 sp; work (beginning Cluster, ch 5, Cluster) in same sp, ch 5, (work Cluster, ch 5) twice in each ch-5 sp around; join with slip st to top of beginning Cluster, finish off: 16 Clusters.

Rnd 8: With **right** side facing, join Blue with slip st in any ch-5 sp; ch 1, work (sc, hdc, 3 dc, Triple Picot, 3 dc, hdc, sc) in same sp and in each ch-5 sp around; join with slip st to first sc, finish off.

Rnd 9: With **right** side facing, join White with sc in center ch of any Triple Picot *(see Joining With Sc, page 136)*; (ch 4, dc in fourth ch from hook) twice, ★ sc in center ch of next Triple Picot, (ch 4, dc in fourth ch from hook) twice; repeat from ★ around; join with slip st to first sc.

Rnd 10: Slip st in next 2 chs, ch 8, tr in fifth ch from hook, work Picot, ch 5, tr in fifth ch from hook, ★ decrease, ch 5, tr in fifth ch from hook, work Picot, ch 5, tr in fifth ch from hook; repeat from ★ around, tr in last sp; join with slip st to third ch of beginning ch-8.

Rnd 11: Slip st in next 2 chs, ch 1, sc in same sp, ch 7, (sc in next sp, ch 7) around; join with slip st to first sc, finish off: 32 ch-7 loops.

Rnd 12: With **right** side facing, join Blue with slip st in any loop; ch 1, work (sc, hdc, 4 dc, Triple Picot, 4 dc, hdc, sc) in same loop and in each loop around; join with slip st to first sc, finish off.

Rnd 13: Repeat Rnd 9.

Rnd 14: Slip st in next 2 chs, ch 7, dc in fourth ch from hook, work Picot, ch 4, dc in fourth ch from hook, ★ decrease, ch 4, dc in fourth ch from hook, work Picot, ch 4, dc in fourth ch from hook; repeat from ★ around, tr in last sp; join with slip st to third ch of beginning ch-7.

Rnds 15-17: Repeat Rnds 10-12: 64 Triple Picots.

Rnd 18: With **right** side facing, join White with sc in center ch of any Triple Picot; (ch 7, sc in center ch of next Triple Picot) around; ch 3, tr in first sc to form last loop.

Rnd 19: Ch 1, sc in same loop, ★ † work Picot, (ch 7, sc in next loop, work Picot) twice, ch 5, work (2-tr Cluster, ch 14, 2-tr Cluster) in center ch of next loop, ch 5 †, sc in next loop; repeat from ★ 14 times **more**, then repeat from † to † once; join with slip st to first sc, finish off: 16 ch-14 loops.

SCALLOP

Row 1: With **right** side facing, join Blue with sc in any ch-14 loop; (hdc, 3 dc, hdc, sc) 5 times in same loop: 5 petals.

Row 2: Ch 4, turn; working in **front** of petals, sc around post of next sc *(Fig. 15, page 135)*, (ch 4, sc around post of next sc) across: 5 ch-4 sps.

Row 3: Ch 1, turn; (sc, hdc, 5 dc, hdc, sc) in each ch-4 sp across: 5 petals.

Row 4: Ch 5, turn; working in **front** of petals, skip first unworked sc on Row 2, sc in next sc, (ch 5, sc in next unworked sc on Row 2) across; finish off: 5 ch-5 sps.

Row 5: With **right** side facing, join White with slip st in first ch-5 sp; work (beginning Cluster, ch 5, Cluster) in same sp, (ch 5, work Cluster) twice in each ch-5 sp across; finish off: 9 ch-5 sps.

Repeat for remaining 15 ch-14 loops.

EDGING

With **right** side facing, join Blue with slip st in first ch-5 sp on any Scallop; ch 1, (sc, hdc, 5 dc, hdc, sc) in same sp, ★ † work (sc, hdc, 3 dc, Triple Picot, 3 dc, hdc, sc) in each of next 7 ch-5 sps †, (sc, hdc, 5 dc, hdc, sc) in next ch-5 sp, ch 5, skip next Picot on Rnd 19, sc in next Picot, ch 5, (sc, hdc, 3 dc) in first ch-5 sp on next Scallop, sc in center dc of last group worked on **previous Scallop**, (2 dc, hdc, sc) in same sp on **new Scallop**; repeat from ★ 14 times **more**, then repeat from † to † once, (sc, hdc, 3 dc) in next ch-5 sp, sc in center dc of first group worked on **first Scallop**, (2 dc, hdc, sc) in same sp on **new Scallop**, ch 5, skip next Picot on Rnd 19, sc in next Picot, ch 5; join with slip st to first sc, finish off.

See Washing and Blocking, page 138.

FALL PINEAPPLES DOILY

Shown on page 26.
Finished Size: 12" square

MATERIALS

Bedspread Weight Cotton Thread (size 10), 185 yards
Steel crochet hook, size 7 (1.65 mm) **or** size needed for gauge

GAUGE SWATCH: 3" in diameter
Work same as doily through Rnd 4.

STITCH GUIDE

SHELL
(3 Dc, ch 3, 3 dc) in sp or loop indicated.
PICOT
Ch 3, slip st in side of st just worked *(Fig. 27, page 138)*.
DECREASE (uses 2 Shells)
★ YO twice, insert hook in **next** Shell, YO and pull a loop, (YO and draw through 2 loops on hook) twice; repeat from ★ once **more**, YO and draw through all 3 loops on hook **(counts as one tr)**.

Ch 10; join with slip st to form a ring.

Rnd 1: Ch 3 **(counts as first dc, now and throughout)**, 23 dc in ring; join with slip st to first dc: 24 dc.

Rnd 2: Ch 1, sc in same st, (ch 7, skip next 2 dc, sc in next dc) around to last 2 dc, ch 3, skip last 2 dc, tr in first sc to form last loop: 8 loops.

Rnd 3: Ch 3, 2 dc in same loop, ch 3, (dc, ch 5, dc) in center ch of next loop, ch 3, ★ work Shell in next loop, ch 3, (dc, ch 5, dc) in center ch of next loop, ch 3; repeat from ★ around, 3 dc in same loop as first dc, ch 2, sc in first dc to form last sp: 4 Shells.

Rnd 4: Ch 3, 2 dc in same sp, ch 3, skip next ch-3 sp, 9 dc in next ch-5 sp, ch 3, skip next ch-3 sp, ★ work Shell in next Shell (ch-3 sp), ch 3, skip next ch-3 sp, 9 dc in next ch-5 sp, ch 3, skip next ch-3 sp; repeat from ★ around, 3 dc in same sp as first dc, ch 2, sc in first dc to form last sp.

Rnd 5: Ch 3, 2 dc in same sp, ch 3, skip next ch-3 sp, dc in next dc, (ch 1, dc in next dc) 8 times, ch 3, ★ work Shell in next Shell, ch 3, skip next ch-3 sp, dc in next dc, (ch 1, dc in next dc) 8 times, ch 3; repeat from ★ around, 3 dc in same sp as first dc, ch 2, sc in first dc to form last sp.

Rnd 6: Ch 3, 2 dc in same sp, ch 3, skip next ch-3 sp, dc in next dc, (ch 2, dc in next dc) 8 times, ch 3, ★ work Shell in next Shell, ch 3, skip next ch-3 sp, dc in next dc, (ch 2, dc in next dc) 8 times, ch 3; repeat from ★ around, 3 dc in same sp as first dc, ch 2, sc in first dc to form last sp.

Rnd 7: Ch 3, 2 dc in same sp, ch 3, ★ † skip next ch-3 sp, sc in next ch-2 sp, (ch 5, sc in next ch-2 sp) 7 times, ch 3 †, (3 dc, ch 3) 3 times in next Shell; repeat from ★ 2 times **more**, then repeat from † to † once, work Shell in same sp as first dc, ch 2, sc in first dc to form last sp.

Rnd 8: Ch 3, 2 dc in same sp, ★ † ch 3, skip next ch-3 sp, sc in next ch-5 sp, (ch 5, sc in next ch-5 sp) 6 times, ch 3, skip next ch-3 sp, work Shell in next ch-3 sp, ch 5 †, work Shell in next ch-3 sp; repeat from ★ 2 times **more**, then repeat from † to † once, 3 dc in same sp as first dc, ch 2, sc in first dc to form last sp.

Rnd 9: Ch 3, 2 dc in same sp, ★ † ch 3, skip next ch-3 sp, sc in next ch-5 sp, (ch 5, sc in next ch-5 sp) 5 times, ch 3, work Shell in next Shell, ch 3, (sc, work Picot, ch 5, sc, work Picot) in next ch-5 sp, ch 3 †, work Shell in next Shell; repeat from ★ 2 times **more**, then repeat from † to † once, 3 dc in same sp as first dc, ch 2, sc in first dc to form last sp.

Rnd 10: Ch 3, 2 dc in same sp, ★ † ch 3, skip next ch-3 sp, sc in next ch-5 sp, (ch 5, sc in next ch-5 sp) 4 times, ch 3, work Shell in next Shell, ch 5, (sc, work Picot, ch 5, sc, work Picot) in next ch-5 sp, ch 5 †, work Shell in next Shell; repeat from ★ 2 times **more**, then repeat from † to † once, 3 dc in same sp as first dc, ch 2, sc in first dc to form last sp.

Rnd 11: Ch 3, 2 dc in same sp, ★ † ch 3, skip next ch-3 sp, sc in next ch-5 sp, (ch 5, sc in next ch-5 sp) 3 times, ch 3, work Shell in next Shell, ch 7, skip next ch-5 sp, (sc, work Picot, ch 5, sc, work Picot) in next ch-5 sp, ch 7 †, work Shell in next Shell; repeat from ★ 2 times **more**, then repeat from † to † once, 3 dc in same sp as first dc, ch 2, sc in first dc to form last sp.

Rnd 12: Ch 3, 2 dc in same sp, ★ † ch 3, skip next ch-3 sp, sc in next ch-5 sp, (ch 5, sc in next ch-5 sp) twice, ch 3, work Shell in next Shell, ch 9, skip next loop, dc in next ch-5 sp, work Picot, ch 1, dc) 5 times in same sp, work Picot, ch 9 †, work Shell in next Shell; repeat from ★ 2 times **more**, then repeat from † to † once, 3 dc in same sp as first dc, ch 2, sc in first dc to form last sp.

Rnd 13: Ch 3, 2 dc in same sp, ch 3, ★ † skip next ch-3 sp, sc in next ch-5 sp, ch 5, sc in next ch-5 sp, (ch 3, 3 dc) 3 times in next Shell, ch 9, skip next loop, (dc in next ch-1 sp, work Picot, ch 3) twice, (dc, work Picot, ch 5, dc, work Picot) in next ch-1 sp, (ch 3, dc in next ch-1 sp, work Picot) twice, ch 9 †, (3 dc, ch 3) 3 times in next Shell; repeat from ★ 2 times **more**, then repeat from † to † once, work Shell in same sp as first dc, ch 2, sc in first dc to form last sp.

Rnd 14: Ch 3, 2 dc in same sp, ★ † ch 4, skip next ch-3 sp, sc in next ch-5 sp, ch 4, skip next ch-3 sp, work Shell in next ch-3 sp, ch 3, work Shell in next ch-3 sp, ch 9, skip next loop, dc in next ch-3 sp, work Picot, ch 5) twice, (dc, work Picot, ch 5, dc, work Picot) in next ch-5 sp, (ch 5, dc in next ch-3 sp, work Picot) twice, ch 9, skip next loop, work Shell in next ch-3 sp, ch 3 †, work Shell in next ch-3 sp; repeat from ★ 2 times **more**, then repeat from † to † once, 3 dc in same sp as first dc, ch 2, sc in first dc to form last sp.

Rnd 15: Ch 3, 2 dc in same sp, ★ † ch 4, sc in next sc, ch 4, work Shell in next Shell, ch 3, dc in next ch-3 sp, ch 3, work Shell in next Shell, ch 9, skip next loop, (dc in next ch-5 sp, work Picot, ch 5) twice, (dc, work Picot, ch 5, dc, work Picot) in next ch-5 sp, (ch 5, dc in next ch-5 sp, work Picot) twice, ch 9, work Shell in next Shell, ch 3, dc in next ch-3 sp, ch 3 †, work Shell in next Shell; repeat from ★ 2 times **more**, then repeat from † to † once, 3 dc in same sp as first dc, ch 2, sc in first dc to form last sp.

Rnd 16: Ch 3, 2 dc in same sp, ★ † skip next 2 ch-4 sps, work Shell in next Shell, ch 3, (dc in next ch-3 sp, ch 3) twice, work Shell in next Shell, ch 9, skip next loop, (dc in next ch-5 sp, work Picot, ch 5) twice, (dc, work Picot, ch 5, dc, work Picot) in next ch-5 sp, (ch 5, dc in next ch-5 sp, work Picot) twice, ch 9, work Shell in next Shell, ch 3, (dc in next ch-3 sp, ch 3) twice †, work Shell in next Shell; repeat from ★ 2 times **more**, then repeat from † to † once, 3 dc in same sp as first dc, ch 2, sc in first dc to form last sp.

Rnd 17: Ch 3, tr in next Shell, ★ † ch 3, skip next ch-3 sp, (tr in next dc, ch 3) twice, tr in next Shell, ch 3, tr in third ch of next loop, ch 3, skip next 3 chs, tr in next ch, (ch 3, tr in center ch of next ch-5 sp) 3 times, (ch 3, tr) 3 times in same st, (ch 3, tr in center ch of next ch-5 sp) twice, ch 3, tr in third ch of next loop, ch 3, skip next 3 chs, tr in next ch, ch 3, tr in next Shell, (ch 3, tr in next dc) twice, ch 3 †, decrease; repeat from ★ 2 times **more**, then repeat from † to † once, skip beginning ch-3 and join with slip st to first tr.

Rnd 18: Ch 1, sc in same st, 4 sc in next ch-3 sp, (sc in next tr, 4 sc in next ch-3 sp) around; join with slip st to first sc.

Rnd 19: Ch 1, sc in same st, (ch 5, skip next 4 sc, sc in next sc) around to last 4 sc, ch 4, skip last 4 sc, sc in first sc to form last sp: 76 sps.

Rnd 20: Ch 5, ★ (4 dc in next ch-5 sp, ch 2) across to next corner ch-5 sp, (4 dc, ch 2) twice in corner ch-5 sp; repeat from ★ 3 times **more**, (4 dc in next ch-5 sp, ch 2) across, 3 dc in same sp as beginning ch-5; join with slip st to third ch of beginning ch-5.

Rnd 21: Ch 1, ★ † sc in next ch-2 sp and in next dc, ch 3, skip next dc, dc in next dc, work Picot, ch 3 †, repeat from † to † across to next corner ch-2 sp, (sc, ch 3, dc) in corner ch-2 sp, work Picot, ch 3, sc in next dc, ch 3, skip next dc, dc in next dc, work Picot, ch 3; repeat from ★ 3 times **more**, then repeat from † to † across; join with slip st to first sc, finish off.

See Washing and Blocking, page 138.

FOR THE BEDROOM

Awaken to roses every morning when you decorate your boudoir with these floral delights. (Below) Worked over a metal ring, the enchanting wreath features tiny blossoms that are stitched separately and then attached. (Opposite) This lavish rose-covered afghan allows you to sleep beneath pretty petals every night. A lacy "trellis" runs between the squares.

ROSE AFGHAN

Finished Size: 48" x 67"

MATERIALS

Worsted Weight Yarn:
    Natural - 31 ounces, (880 grams, 2,125 yards)
    Rose - 13 ounces, (370 grams, 890 yards)
    Green - 6 ounces, (170 grams, 410 yards)
Crochet hook, size I (5.50 mm) **or** size needed for gauge

GAUGE: Each Square = 9½"

Gauge Swatch: 3" square
Work same as First Square through Rnd 2.

STITCH GUIDE

> **BEGINNING POPCORN**
> Ch 3, 3 dc in sp indicated, drop loop from hook, insert hook in top of beginning ch-3, hook dropped loop and draw through *(Fig. 12a, page 134)*.
> **POPCORN**
> 4 Dc in sp indicated, drop loop from hook, insert hook in first dc of 4-dc group, hook dropped loop and draw through.
> **V-ST**
> (Dc, ch 1, dc) in st or sp indicated.

FIRST SQUARE

With Rose, ch 4; join with slip st to form a ring.
Rnd 1 (Right side)**:** Work beginning Popcorn in ring, ch 3, (work Popcorn in ring, ch 3) 3 times; join with slip st to top of beginning Popcorn: 4 ch-3 sps.
Rnd 2: Slip st in first ch-3 sp, ch 1, work (sc, dc, 2 tr, dc, sc, slip st, ch 1) twice in each ch-3 sp around; join with slip st to first sc: 8 petals.
Rnd 3: Ch 5, working **behind** petals on Rnd 2, (slip st in next ch-1 sp, ch 5) around; join with slip st to first st: 8 ch-5 sps.
Rnd 4: Slip st in first ch-5 sp, ch 1, work (sc, dc, 5 tr, dc, sc, ch 1) in same sp and in each ch-5 sp around; join with slip st to first sc: 8 petals.
Rnd 5: Ch 5, working **behind** petals on Rnd 4, (slip st in next ch-1 sp, ch 5) around; join with slip st to first st, finish off: 8 ch-5 sps.
Rnd 6: With **right** side facing, join Green with slip st in any ch-5 sp; ch 4 **(counts as first dc plus ch 1, now and throughout)**, in same sp work [dc, (ch 1, dc) twice, ch 3, (dc, ch 1) 4 times], (dc, ch 1) twice in next ch-5 sp, ★ in next ch-5 sp work [dc, (ch 1, dc) 3 times, ch 3, (dc, ch 1) 4 times], (dc, ch 1) twice in next ch-5 sp; repeat from ★ around; join with slip st to first dc, finish off: 40 dc.

Rnd 7: With **right** side facing, join Natural with slip st in any corner ch-3 sp; ch 4, (dc, ch 3, work V-St) in same sp, ch 1, ★ skip next ch-1 sp, (work V-St in next ch-1 sp, ch 1, skip next ch-1 sp) 4 times, work (V-St, ch 3, V-St) in next corner ch-3 sp, ch 1; repeat from ★ 2 times **more**, skip next ch-1 sp, (work V-St in next ch-1 sp, ch 1, skip next ch-1 sp) across; join with slip st to first dc: 24 V-Sts.
Rnd 8: Turn; slip st in first ch-1 sp, ch 4, dc in same sp, ch 1, ★ skip next V-St, (work V-St in next ch-1 sp, ch 1, skip next V-St) across to next corner ch-3 sp, work (V-St, ch 3, V-St) in corner ch-3 sp, ch 1; repeat from ★ 3 times **more**, skip last V-St; join with slip st to first dc: 28 V-Sts.
Rnd 9: Turn; slip st in first ch-1 sp, ch 4, dc in same sp, skip next V-St, work (V-St, ch 3, V-St) in next corner ch-3 sp, ★ (skip next V-St, work V-St in next ch-1 sp) 6 times, skip next V-St, work (V-St, ch 3, V-St) in next corner ch-3 sp; repeat from ★ 2 times **more**, skip next V-St, (work V-St in next ch-1 sp, skip next V-St) across; join with slip st to first dc: 32 V-Sts.
Rnd 10: Do not turn; slip st in first ch-1 sp, ch 3 **(counts as first dc)**, 2 dc in same sp, 3 dc in next V-St (ch-1 sp), ★ (2 dc, ch 3, 2 dc) in next corner ch-3 sp, 3 dc in each V-St across; repeat from ★ around; join with slip st to first dc: 112 dc.
Rnd 11: Slip st in next 2 dc and in sp **before** next dc *(Fig. 23, page 136)*, ch 1, sc in same sp, ch 5, skip next 3 dc, sc in sp **before** next dc, ch 5, ★ † (sc, ch 5) twice in next corner ch-3 sp, skip next 2 dc, sc in sp **before** next dc †, ch 5, (skip next 3 dc, sc in sp **before** next dc, ch 5) across to within 2 dc of next corner ch-3 sp; repeat from ★ 2 times **more**, then repeat from † to † once, (ch 5, skip next 3 dc, sc in sp **before** next dc) across, ch 2, dc in first sc to form last sp: 44 sps.
Rnd 12: Ch 1, sc in same sp, ch 5, ★ (sc in next ch-5 sp, ch 5) across to next corner ch-5 sp, (sc, ch 5) twice in corner ch-5 sp; repeat from ★ 3 times **more**, (sc in next ch-5 sp, ch 5) across; join with slip st to first sc, finish off: 48 ch-5 sps.

ADDITIONAL SQUARES

Work same as First Square through Rnd 11.
Work One-Sided or Two-Sided Joining to form 5 vertical strips of 7 Squares each.
Note: When working into corner sp that has been previously joined, work into joining slip st.

ONE-SIDED JOINING

Rnd 12: Ch 1, sc in same sp, ch 5, (sc in next ch-5 sp, ch 5) twice, ★ (sc, ch 5) twice in next corner ch-5 sp, (sc in next ch-5 sp, ch 5) across to next corner ch-5 sp; repeat from ★ once **more**, sc in corner ch-5 sp, ch 2, with **wrong** sides together, slip st in corner sp on **previous Square** *(Fig. 29, page 138)*, ch 2, sc in same sp on **new Square**, (ch 2, slip st in next ch-5 sp on **previous Square**, ch 2, sc in next ch-5 sp on **new Square** 11 times, ch 2, slip st in corner sp on **previous Square**, ch 2, sc in same sp on **new Square**, ch 5, (sc in next ch-5 sp, ch 5) across; join with slip st to first sc, finish off.

TWO-SIDED JOINING

Rnd 12: Ch 1, sc in same sp, (ch 5, sc in next ch-5 sp) twice, (ch 5, sc) twice in next corner ch-5 sp, (ch 5, sc in next ch-5 sp) 11 times, ch 2, with **wrong** sides together, slip st in corner sp on **previous Square**, ch 2, sc in same sp on **new Square**, ★ (ch 2, slip st in next ch-5 sp on **previous Square**, ch 2, sc in next ch-5 sp on **new Square**) 11 times, ch 2, slip st in corresponding corner on **previous Square**, ch 2, sc in same sp on **new Square**; repeat from ★ once **more**, ch 5, (sc in next ch-5 sp, ch 5) across; join with slip st to first sc, finish off.

ROSE WREATH

Finished Size: 8¹⁄₂" in diameter

MATERIALS
Bedspread Weight Cotton Thread (size 10):
- Cream - 90 yards
- Rose - 40 yards
- Green - 11 yards

Steel crochet hook, size 6 (1.80 mm) **or** size needed for gauge
5" metal ring
Tapestry needle
Spray starch
1 yard of ³⁄₈" wide ribbon
Translucent nylon thread

GAUGE: 8 sts = 1"

Gauge Swatch: 1" square
Ch 10 **loosely**.

Row 1: Dc in fourth ch from hook **(3 skipped chs count as first dc)** and in each ch across: 8 dc.

Rows 2-4: Ch 3 **(counts as first dc)**, turn; dc in next dc and in each dc across.
Finish off.

STITCH GUIDE

> **CLUSTER**
> Ch 7, YO, insert hook in seventh ch from hook, † YO and pull up a loop, YO and draw through 2 loops on hook †, YO, insert hook in **same** ch, repeat from † to † once, YO and draw through all 3 loops on hook *(Figs. 10a & b, page 134)*.
>
> **EXTENDED SC** *(abbreviated Ex sc)*
> Working **around** ring, insert hook in ch at base of next Cluster, YO and pull up a loop, YO and draw through one loop on hook, YO and draw through both loops on hook.
>
> **PICOT**
> Ch 4, slip st in third ch from hook.

WREATH

Inner Trim (Right side)**:** With Cream, work 36 Clusters; being careful not to twist Clusters, join with slip st to bottom of first Cluster.

Foundation: Hold metal ring between loop on hook and thread, ch 2, 5 sc in ring, with **right** side of Clusters facing, (work Ex sc, 5 sc in ring) around; join with slip st to top of beginning ch-2: 216 sts.

Rnd 1 (Eyelet rnd): Ch 6, skip next 3 sc, (dc in next sc, ch 3, skip next 3 sc) around; join with slip st to third ch of beginning ch-6: 54 ch-3 sps.

Rnd 2: Slip st in first ch-3 sp, ch 1, sc in same sp, 6 dc in next ch-3 sp, (sc in next ch-3 sp, 6 dc in next ch-3 sp) around; join with slip st to first sc: 27 sc.

Rnd 3: Ch 3 **(counts as first dc, now and throughout)**, skip next 3 dc, 5 dc in sp **before** next dc *(Fig. 23, page 136)*, skip next 3 dc, ★ dc in next sc, skip next 3 dc, 5 dc in sp **before** next dc, skip next 3 dc; repeat from ★ around; join with slip st to first dc.

Rnd 4: Ch 3, 6 dc in same st, skip next 2 dc, sc in next dc, skip next 2 dc, ★ 7 dc in next dc, skip next 2 dc, sc in next dc, skip next 2 dc; repeat from ★ around; join with slip st to first dc.

Rnd 5: Slip st in next 3 dc, ch 1, sc in same st, ch 5, skip next 3 dc, 3 tr in next sc, ch 5, skip next 3 dc, ★ sc in next dc, ch 5, skip next 3 dc, 3 tr in next sc, ch 5, skip next 3 dc; repeat from ★ around; join with slip st to first sc: 54 ch-5 sps.

Rnd 6: Ch 3, 2 dc in same st, (3 dc, work Picot, ch 1, 3 dc) in next ch-5 sp, skip next tr, (sc, ch 3, sc) in next tr, (3 dc, work Picot, ch 1, 3 dc) in next ch-5 sp, ★ 3 dc in next sc, (3 dc, work Picot, ch 1, 3 dc) in next ch-5 sp, skip next tr, (sc, ch 3, sc) in next tr, (3 dc, work Picot, ch 1, 3 dc) in next ch-5 sp; repeat from ★ around; join with slip st to first dc, finish off.

ROSE (Make 6)

Rnd 1 (Right side): With Rose, ch 2, in second ch from hook work (sc, ch 2, hdc, dc, hdc, ch 2) 3 times; join with slip st to first sc: 3 petals.

Rnd 2: Ch 3, working **behind** petals, (slip st in next sc, ch 3) twice; join with slip st to base of first ch-3 sp: 3 ch-3 sps.

Rnd 3: Slip st in first ch-3 sp, ch 1, (sc, ch 2, dc, tr, dc, ch 2, sc, ch 1) twice in same sp and in each ch-3 sp around; join with slip st to first sc: 6 petals.

Rnd 4: Ch 1, **turn**; working in **front** of petals, slip st in first ch-1 sp, ch 2, (slip st in next ch-1 sp, ch 2) around; join with slip st to first slip st: 6 ch-2 sps.

Rnd 5: Turn; slip st in first ch-2 sp, ch 1, (sc, ch 2, dc, tr, dc, ch 2, sc) in same sp and in each ch-2 sp around; join with slip st to first sc, finish off leaving a long end for sewing: 6 petals.

Continued on page 47.

FOR THE BATH

You'll bring Victorian elegance to your bath when you accessorize with this charming collection. Designed for decorative use, the lacy washcloth is fashioned with size 10 cotton thread. (Opposite) Pamper your guests with plush towels embellished with scalloped trim. Satin ribbon adds a fancy finishing touch to the towels, as well as to the coordinating curtain edging.

SCALLOPED CURTAIN EDGING

Finished Size: 3¼" wide

MATERIALS

Bedspread Weight Cotton Thread (size 10),
  4 yards per **each** inch
Steel crochet hook, size 6 (1.80 mm) **or** size needed for gauge
⅜" wide satin ribbon equal to desired length of Edging plus 1"
Curtain
Pins
Sewing needle and thread

GAUGE SWATCH: 3¼"w x 2"h
Work same as Edging through Row 7.

EDGING

Ch 29.

Row 1: Dc in eighth ch from hook, ch 3, skip next 2 chs, sc in next ch, ch 3, skip next 2 chs, dc in next ch, ch 5, skip next 5 chs, dc in next ch, ch 3, skip next 2 chs, sc in next ch, ch 3, skip next 2 chs, dc in next ch, ch 5, skip next 2 chs, slip st in last ch.

Row 2 (Right side): Ch 3, turn; 9 dc in first ch-5 sp, ch 5, skip next 2 ch-3 sps, dc in next dc, ch 3, skip next 2 chs, sc in next ch, ch 3, dc in next dc, ch 5, skip next 2 ch-3 sps, dc in next dc, ch 2, skip next 2 chs, dc in next ch.

Note: Loop a short piece of thread around any stitch to mark Row 2 as **right** side.

Row 3: Ch 5 **(counts as first dc plus ch 2, now and throughout)**, turn; dc in next dc, ch 3, skip next 2 chs, sc in next ch, ch 3, dc in next dc, ch 5, skip next 2 ch-3 sps, dc in next dc, ch 3, skip next 2 chs, sc in next ch, ch 3, (dc in next dc, ch 1) 9 times, dc in top of turning ch.

Row 4: Ch 3, turn; sc in first ch-1 sp, (ch 3, sc in next ch-1 sp) 8 times, ch 8, skip next 2 ch-3 sps, dc in next dc, ch 3, skip next 2 chs, sc in next ch, ch 3, dc in next dc, ch 5, skip next 2 ch-3 sps, dc in next dc, ch 2, dc in last dc.

Row 5: Ch 5, turn; dc in next dc, ch 3, skip next 2 chs, sc in next ch, ch 3, dc in next dc, ch 5, skip next 2 ch-3 sps, dc in next dc, ch 3, skip next 2 chs, sc in next ch, ch 3, skip next 2 chs, dc in next ch, ch 5, skip next ch-3 sp, sc in next ch-3 sp, leave remaining sps unworked.

Row 6: Ch 3, turn; 9 dc in first ch-5 sp, ch 5, skip next 2 ch-3 sps, dc in next dc, ch 3, skip next 2 chs, sc in next ch, ch 3, dc in next dc, ch 5, skip next 2 ch-3 sps, dc in next dc, ch 2, dc in last dc.

Row 7: Ch 5, turn; dc in next dc, ch 3, skip next 2 chs, sc in next ch, ch 3, dc in next dc, ch 5, skip next 2 ch-3 sps, dc in next dc, ch 3, skip next 2 chs, sc in next ch, ch 3, (dc in next dc, ch 1) 9 times, dc in top of turning ch, skip next ch-3 sp on previous scallop, sc in next ch-3 sp.

Repeat Rows 4-7 for pattern until Edging is desired length, ending by working Row 7.

Edging: Ch 3, turn; sc in first ch-1 sp, (ch 3, sc in next ch-1 sp) 8 times, ch 5, skip next 2 ch-3 sps, sc in next dc, ch 2, sc in next ch-5 sp, ch 2, sc in next dc, ch 5, skip next 2 ch-3 sps, sc in next dc, ch 2, sc in last dc, ch 1; (sc, ch 3, sc) in end of first row and in each row across; finish off.

FINISHING

See Washing and Blocking, page 138.
Using photo as a guide for placement, weave ribbon through spaces on each row. Turn ribbon ends under ¼" and sew in place.
Pin Edging to curtain; sew in place.

Quick SCALLOPED TOWEL EDGING

Finished Size: 2⅜" wide

MATERIALS

Bedspread Weight Cotton Thread (size 10),
  3 yards per **each** inch
Steel crochet hook, size 6 (1.80 mm) **or** size needed for gauge
⅜" wide satin ribbon equal to desired length of Edging plus 1"
Purchased towel
Pins
Sewing needle and thread

GAUGE SWATCH: 2⅜"w x 2"h
Work same as Edging through Row 7.

EDGING

Ch 20.

Row 1: Dc in eighth ch from hook, ch 3, skip next 2 chs, sc in next ch, ch 3, skip next 2 chs, dc in next ch, ch 2, skip next 2 chs, dc in next ch, ch 5, skip next 2 chs, slip st in last ch.

Row 2 (Right side): Ch 3, turn; 9 dc in first ch-5 sp, ch 2, skip next ch-2 sp, dc in next dc, ch 5, skip next 2 ch-3 sps, dc in next dc, ch 2, skip next 2 chs, dc in next ch.

Note: Loop a short piece of thread around any stitch to mark Row 2 as **right** side.

Row 3: Ch 5 **(counts as first dc plus ch 2, now and throughout)**, turn; dc in next dc, ch 3, skip next 2 chs, sc in next ch, ch 3, dc in next dc, ch 2, (dc in next dc, ch 1) 9 times, dc in top of turning ch.

Row 4: Ch 3, turn; sc in first ch-1 sp, (ch 3, sc in next ch-1 sp) 8 times, ch 5, skip next ch-2 sp, dc in next dc, ch 5, skip next 2 ch-3 sps, dc in next dc, ch 2, dc in last dc.

Row 5: Ch 5, turn; dc in next dc, ch 3, skip next 2 chs, sc in next ch, ch 3, dc in next dc, ch 2, skip next 2 chs, dc in next ch, ch 5, skip next ch-3 sp, sc in next ch-3 sp, leave remaining sps unworked.

Row 6: Ch 3, turn; 9 dc in first ch-5 sp, ch 2, skip next ch-2 sp, dc in next dc, ch 5, skip next 2 ch-3 sps, dc in next dc, ch 2, dc in last dc.

Row 7: Ch 5, turn; dc in next dc, ch 3, skip next 2 chs, sc in next ch, ch 3, dc in next dc, ch 2, (dc in next dc, ch 1) 9 times, dc in top of turning ch, skip next ch-3 sp on previous scallop, sc in next ch-3 sp.

Repeat Rows 4-7 for pattern until Edging is desired length, ending by working Row 7.

Edging: Ch 3, turn; sc in first ch-1 sp, (ch 3, sc in next ch-1 sp) 8 times, ch 2, skip next ch-2 sp, sc in next dc, ch 5, skip next 2 ch-3 sps, sc in next dc, ch 2, sc in last dc, ch 1; (sc, ch 3, sc) in end of first row and in each row across; finish off.

FINISHING

See Washing and Blocking, page 138.

Using photo as a guide for placement, weave ribbon through spaces on each row. Turn ribbon ends under ¼" and sew in place. Pin Edging to towel; sew in place.

Quick VICTORIAN WASHCLOTH

Finished Size: 10½" square

MATERIALS

Bedspread Weight Cotton Thread (size 10), 155 yards
Steel crochet hook, size 6 (1.80 mm) **or** size needed for gauge

GAUGE SWATCH: 2½" square
Work same as Cloth through Rnd 5.

STITCH GUIDE

BEGINNING CLUSTER
Ch 3, ★ YO, insert hook in st or sp indicated, YO and pull up a loop, YO and draw through 2 loops on hook; repeat from ★ once **more**, YO and draw through all 3 loops on hook *(Figs. 10a & b, page 134)*.

CLUSTER
★ YO, insert hook in st or sp indicated, YO and pull up a loop, YO and draw through 2 loops on hook; repeat from ★ 2 times **more**, YO and draw through all 4 loops on hook.

DECREASE (uses next 2 sc)
Pull up a loop in next 2 sc, YO and draw through all 3 loops on hook **(counts as one sc)**.

CLOTH

Ch 4; join with slip st to form a ring.

Rnd 1 (Right side)**:** Ch 3 **(counts as first dc, now and throughout)**, 11 dc in ring; join with slip st to first dc: 12 dc.
Note: Loop a short piece of thread around any stitch to mark Rnd 1 as **right** side.

Rnd 2: Work beginning Cluster in same st, (ch 1, work Cluster in next dc) twice, ch 5, ★ work Cluster in next dc, (ch 1, work Cluster in next dc) twice, ch 5; repeat from ★ around; join with slip st to top of beginning Cluster: 12 Clusters.

Rnd 3: Slip st in first ch-1 sp, work beginning Cluster in same sp, ch 1, work Cluster in next ch-1 sp, ch 3, skip next 2 chs, (tr, ch 5, tr) in next ch, ch 3, ★ work Cluster in next ch-1 sp, ch 1, work Cluster in next ch-1 sp, ch 3, skip next 2 chs, (tr, ch 5, tr) in next ch, ch 3; repeat from ★ around; join with slip st to top of beginning Cluster: 8 Clusters.

Rnd 4: Slip st in first ch-1 sp, work beginning Cluster in same sp, ch 2, dc in next ch-3 sp, ch 2, (dc, ch 2) 4 times in next corner ch-5 sp, dc in next ch-3 sp, ch 2, ★ work Cluster in next ch-1 sp, ch 2, dc in next ch-3 sp, ch 2, (dc, ch 2) 4 times in next corner ch-5 sp, dc in next ch-3 sp, ch 2; repeat from ★ around; join with slip st to top of beginning Cluster: 28 ch-2 sps.

Rnd 5: Ch 1, sc in same st, (2 sc in next ch-2 sp, sc in next dc) 3 times, 3 sc in next corner ch-2 sp, ★ sc in next dc, (2 sc in next ch-2 sp, sc in next st) 6 times, 3 sc in next corner ch-2 sp; repeat from ★ 2 times **more**, (sc in next dc, 2 sc in next ch-2 sp) 3 times; join with slip st to first sc: 88 sc.

Rnd 6: Slip st in next sc, ch 4 **(counts as first dc plus ch 1, now and throughout)**, (skip next sc, dc in next sc, ch 1) 4 times, skip next sc, (dc, ch 3, dc) in next sc, ch 1, ★ (skip next sc, dc in next sc, ch 1) 10 times, skip next sc, (dc, ch 3, dc) in next sc, ch 1; repeat from ★ 2 times **more**, (skip next sc, dc in next sc, ch 1) 5 times, skip last sc; join with slip st to first dc: 48 sps.

Rnds 7 and 8: Ch 4, ★ (dc in next dc, ch 1) across to next corner ch-3 sp, (dc, ch 3, dc) in corner ch-3 sp, ch 1; repeat from ★ 3 times **more**, (dc in next dc, ch 1) across; join with slip st to first dc: 64 sps.

Rnd 9: Ch 1, sc in same st, ★ sc in each ch-1 sp and in each dc across to next corner ch-3 sp, 5 sc in corner ch-3 sp, sc in next dc; repeat from ★ 3 times **more**, sc in each ch-1 sp and in each dc across; join with slip st to first sc: 144 sc.

Rnd 10: Slip st in next sc, ch 6 **(counts as first dc plus ch 3, now and throughout)**, (skip next 3 sc, dc in next sc, ch 3) 3 times, skip next 3 sc, (dc, ch 3) twice in next sc, ★ (skip next 3 sc, dc in next sc, ch 3) 8 times, skip next 3 sc, (dc, ch 3) twice in next sc; repeat from ★ 2 times **more**, (skip next 3 sc, dc in next sc, ch 3) 4 times, skip last 3 sc; join with slip st to first dc: 40 sps.

Continued on page 47.

IN THE KITCHEN

*F*ashioned in a classic mix of blue and white, this quick-and-easy kitchen collection proves that you don't have to make big changes to update your decor! (Below) Shells and flowers are worked into this pretty pair of dishcloths. Crocheted with cotton worsted weight yarn, these handy projects will help you breeze through kitchen chores! (Opposite) The set also includes miniature hat magnets that are ideal for perking up the refrigerator. A coordinating towel holder has a plastic canvas circle sewn to the back from which the towel is hung.

HAT MAGNETS

Finished Size: Hat #1 - 2³/₄" in diameter
Hat #2 - 3¹/₂" in diameter
Hat #3 - 2" in diameter

MATERIALS

Bedspread Weight Cotton Thread (size 10),
   20 yards **each**
Steel crochet hook, size 6 (1.80 mm)
Glue
Craft flowers
¹/₄" wide ribbon
Cardboard
Magnetic strips
Starching materials: Commercial fabric stiffener, blocking
   board, plastic wrap, resealable plastic bag, terry towel,
   paper towels, and stainless steel pins

Note: Gauge is not important. Hats can be larger or smaller without changing the overall effect.

HAT #1

Ch 5; join with slip st to form a ring.

Rnd 1 (Right side)**:** Ch 2, 11 hdc in ring; join with slip st to top of beginning ch-2: 12 sts.

Rnds 2 and 3: Ch 3, dc in same st, 2 dc in next st and in each st around; join with slip st to top of beginning ch-3: 48 sts.

Rnd 4: Ch 3, skip next dc, (hdc in next dc, ch 1, skip next dc) around; join with slip st to second ch of beginning ch-3: 24 ch-1 sps.

Rnd 5: Slip st in first ch-1 sp, ch 3, dc in same sp, ch 1, skip next ch-1 sp, (2 dc in next ch-1 sp, ch 1, skip next ch-1 sp) around; join with slip st to top of beginning ch-3: 12 ch-1 sps.

Rnd 6: Slip st in next dc and in next ch-1 sp, ch 1, sc in same sp, ch 4, (sc in next ch-1 sp, ch 4) around; join with slip st to first sc: 12 ch-4 sps.

Rnd 7: Slip st in first ch-4 sp, ch 3, 5 dc in same sp, 6 dc in next ch-4 sp and in each ch-4 sp around; join with slip st to top of beginning ch-3: 72 sts.

Rnd 8: Ch 1, sc in same st, 2 dc in each of next 4 dc, (sc in next 2 dc, 2 dc in each of next 4 dc) around to last dc, sc in last dc; join with slip st to first sc, finish off.

FINISHING

See Starching and Blocking, page 140.
Using photo as a guide for placement, glue bow and flower to Hat.
Cut cardboard slightly larger than opening and glue in place.
Glue magnetic strip to cardboard.

HAT #2

Ch 5; join with slip st to form a ring.

Rnd 1 (Right side)**:** Ch 3, 11 dc in ring; join with slip st to top of beginning ch-3: 12 sts.

Rnds 2 and 3: Ch 3, dc in same st, 2 dc in next dc and in each dc around; join with slip st to top of beginning ch-3: 48 sts.

Rnd 4: Ch 3, skip next dc, (hdc in next dc, ch 1, skip next dc) around; join with slip st to second ch of beginning ch-3: 24 ch-1 sps.

Rnd 5 (Eyelet rnd)**:** Slip st in first ch-1 sp, ch 5, skip next ch-1 sp, (dc in next ch-1 sp, ch 2, skip next ch-1 sp) around; join with slip st to third ch of beginning ch-5: 12 ch-2 sps.

Rnd 6: Slip st in first ch-2 sp, ch 1, sc in same sp, (ch 5, sc in next ch-2 sp) around, ch 2, dc in first sc to form last sp.

Rnd 7: Ch 1, sc in same sp, (ch 6, sc in next ch-5 sp) around, ch 3, dc in first sc to form last loop.

Rnd 8: Ch 1, sc in same loop, ch 7, (sc in next ch-6 loop, ch 7) around; join with slip st to first sc.

Rnd 9: Slip st in first loop, ch 1, sc in same loop, (ch 3, sc) 4 times in same loop, ★ sc in next loop, (ch 3, sc) 4 times in same loop; repeat from ★ around; join with slip st to first sc, finish off.

FINISHING

See Starching and Blocking, page 140.
Weave ribbon through Eyelet rnd and tie in a bow.
Using photo as a guide for placement, glue flower to Hat above bow.
Cut cardboard slightly larger than opening and glue in place.
Glue magnetic strip to cardboard.

HAT #3

Work same as Hat #2 through Rnd 4: 24 ch-1 sps.

Rnd 5: Slip st in first ch-1 sp, ch 1, sc in same sp and in each ch-1 sp around; join with slip st to first sc: 24 sc.

Rnd 6: Ch 1, 2 sc in same st and in each sc around; join with slip st to first sc: 48 sc.

Rnds 7-11: Ch 1, sc in each sc around; join with slip st to first sc. Finish off.

FINISHING

See Starching and Blocking, page 140.
Glue edge of brim to side of Hat.
Using photo as a guide for placement, glue bow and flower to Hat.
Cut cardboard slightly larger than opening and glue in place.
Glue magnetic strip to cardboard.

HAT TOWEL HOLDER

Finished Size: 6" in diameter

MATERIALS

100% Cotton Worsted Weight Yarn:
    White - 3 ounces, (90 grams, 135 yards)
    Blue - 15 yards
Crochet hook, size H (5.00 mm) **or** size needed for gauge
6" plastic canvas circle
7 mesh plastic canvas - 6" x 1"
Polyester fiberfill
Tapestry needle
Craft glue
¼" wide ribbon bow
Craft flowers

GAUGE SWATCH: 2½" in diameter
Work same as Hat through Rnd 2.

STITCH GUIDE

> **DECREASE** (uses next 2 dc)
> ★ YO, insert hook in **next** dc, YO and pull up a loop, YO and draw through 2 loops on hook; repeat from ★ once **more**, YO and draw through all 3 loops on hook (**counts as one dc**).

HAT

Rnd 1 (Right side)**:** With White, ch 4, 11 dc in fourth ch from hook; join with slip st to top of beginning ch: 12 sts.
Note: Loop a short piece of yarn around any stitch to mark Rnd 1 as **right** side.
Rnd 2: Ch 3 (**counts as first dc, now and throughout**), dc in same st, 2 dc in next dc and in each dc around; join with slip st to first dc: 24 dc.
Rnd 3: Ch 3, dc in same st and in next dc, (2 dc in next dc, dc in next dc) around; join with slip st to first dc: 36 dc.
Rnd 4: Ch 3, dc in next 3 dc, decrease, (dc in next 4 dc, decrease) around; join with slip st to first dc: 30 dc.
Rnd 5: Ch 3, working in Front Loops Only *(Fig. 21, page 136)*, dc in same st and in next dc, (2 dc in next dc, dc in next dc) around; join with slip st to first dc: 45 dc.
Rnd 6: Ch 3, working in both loops, dc in same st and in next 2 dc, (2 dc in next dc, dc in next 2 dc) around; join with slip st to first dc, finish off: 60 dc.
Rnd 7: With **right** side facing, join Blue with slip st in any dc; ch 1, sc in each dc around; join with slip st to first sc, finish off.

TIE

With Blue, ch 75; with **right** side of Hat facing, join with slip st in any sc on Rnd 7; slip st in next sc; ch 75; finish off.

BAND

With Blue, ch 100; finish off.

FINISHING

TOWEL BAR

Place a 6" x 1" piece of plastic canvas on circle, ½" from center. Sew pieces together along edges; trim corners to match circle.

Stuff crown of Hat with polyester fiberfill.
With Towel Bar at back and bottom edge, place **wrong** side of Hat on plastic circle, with Tie centered at top edge. With Blue and working through all thicknesses, sew pieces together. Center Band over Rnd 4 of Hat; tie in a bow on opposite side from Tie. Glue in place.
Glue ribbon bow and flowers above crocheted bow.

FLOWER DISHCLOTH

Finished Size: 11½" square

MATERIALS

100% Cotton Worsted Weight Yarn,
    2 ounces, (60 grams, 90 yards)
Crochet hook, size F (3.75 mm) **or** size needed for gauge

GAUGE SWATCH: 2¾" square
Work same as Dishcloth through Rnd 2.

STITCH GUIDE

> **CLUSTER**
> ★ YO twice, insert hook in sp indicated, YO and pull up a loop, (YO and draw through 2 loops on hook) twice; repeat from ★ 3 times **more**, YO and draw through all 5 loops on hook *(Figs. 10a & b, page 134)*.
> **SHELL**
> (2 Dc, ch 2, 2 dc) in sp indicated.
> **PICOT**
> Ch 3, sc in third ch from hook.

Ch 5; join with slip st to form a ring.
Rnd 1: Ch 1, (sc in ring, ch 3) 6 times; join with slip st to first sc.
Rnd 2: Ch 7, work Cluster in first ch-3 sp, ch 3, (tr in next sc, ch 3, work Cluster in next ch-3 sp, ch 3) around; join with slip st to fourth ch of beginning ch-7: 6 Clusters.
Rnd 3: Slip st in first ch-3 sp, ch 1, sc in same sp, (ch 5, sc in next ch-3 sp) around, ch 2, dc in first sc to form last sp: 12 sps.
Rnd 4: Ch 1, sc in same sp, ch 5, sc in next ch-5 sp, (ch 5, work Cluster) twice in next ch-5 sp, ★ (ch 5, sc in next ch-5 sp) twice, (ch 5, work Cluster) twice in next ch-5 sp; repeat from ★ around, ch 2, dc in first sc to form last sp: 8 Clusters.

Rnd 5: Ch 1, sc in same sp, (ch 5, sc in next ch-5 sp) twice, (ch 5, sc) twice in next ch-5 sp, ★ (ch 5, sc in next ch-5 sp) 3 times, (ch 5, sc) twice in next ch-5 sp; repeat from ★ around, ch 2, dc in first sc to form last sp: 20 sps.

Rnd 6: Ch 1, sc in same sp, (ch 5, sc in next ch-5 sp) 3 times, (ch 5, sc) twice in next ch-5 sp, ★ (ch 5, sc in next ch-5 sp) 4 times, (ch 5, sc) twice in next ch-5 sp; repeat from ★ around, ch 2, dc in first sc to form last sp: 24 sps.

Rnd 7: Ch 4, dc in same sp, ch 1, (dc, ch 1) twice in each of next 4 ch-5 sps, (dc, ch 1, dc) in next ch-5 sp, ch 3, (dc, ch 1) twice in same sp, ★ (dc, ch 1) twice in each of next 5 ch-5 sps, (dc, ch 1, dc) in next ch-5 sp, ch 3, (dc, ch 1) twice in same sp; repeat from ★ around; join with slip st to third ch of beginning ch-4.

Rnd 8: Slip st in first ch-1 sp, ch 3 **(counts as first dc, now and throughout)**, (dc, ch 2, 2 dc) in same sp, ch 2, skip next ch-1 sp, sc in next ch-1 sp, ch 2, ★ † skip next ch-1 sp, work Shell in next ch-1 sp, ch 2, skip next ch-1 sp, sc in next ch-1 sp, ch 2 †, repeat from † to † across to next corner ch-3 sp, work Shell in corner ch-3 sp, ch 2, sc in next ch-1 sp, ch 2; repeat from ★ around, skip last ch-1 sp; join with slip st to first dc: 16 Shells.

Rnd 9: Slip st in next dc and in next ch-2 sp, ch 3, (dc, ch 2, 2 dc) in same sp, ch 2, sc in next ch-2 sp, ch 5, sc in next ch-2 sp, ch 2, ★ † work Shell in next Shell (ch-2 sp), ch 2, sc in next ch-2 sp, ch 5, sc in next ch-2 sp, ch 2 †, repeat from † to † across to next corner Shell, (2 dc, ch 2) 3 times in corner Shell, sc in next ch-2 sp, ch 5, sc in next ch-2 sp, ch 2; repeat from ★ around; join with slip st to first dc.

Rnd 10: Slip st in next dc and in next ch-2 sp, ch 3, (dc, ch 2, 2 dc) in same sp, ch 2, skip next ch-2 sp, sc in next ch-5 sp, ch 2, (work Shell in next Shell, ch 2, skip next ch-2 sp, sc in next ch-5 sp, ch 2) twice, ★ † skip next ch-2 sp, work Shell in next ch-2 sp, ch 3, work Shell in next ch-2 sp, ch 2, skip next ch-2 sp, sc in next ch-5 sp, ch 2 †, (work Shell in next Shell, ch 2, skip next ch-2 sp, sc in next ch-5 sp, ch 2) 3 times; repeat from ★ 2 times **more**, then repeat from † to † once; join with slip st to first dc.

Rnd 11: Slip st in next dc and in next ch-2 sp, ch 3, (dc, work Picot, 2 dc) in same sp, ch 2, ★ † sc in next ch-2 sp, work Picot, sc in next ch-2 sp, ch 2, (2 dc, work Picot, 2 dc) in next Shell, ch 2 †, repeat from † to † across to next corner ch-3 sp, (sc, work Picot, sc) in corner ch-3 sp, ch 2, (2 dc, work Picot, 2 dc) in next Shell, ch 2; repeat from ★ around to last 2 sps, sc in next sp, work Picot, sc in last sp, ch 2; join with slip st to first dc, finish off.

LACY SHELLS DISHCLOTH

Quick

Finished Size: 11" x 12"

MATERIALS
100% Cotton Worsted Weight Yarn:
    Blue - 1¾ ounces, (50 grams, 80 yards)
    White - 7 yards
Crochet hook, size F (3.75 mm) **or** size needed for gauge

GAUGE SWATCH: 4"w x 2"h
Ch 18.
Work same as Body for 4 rows.
Finish off.

STITCH GUIDE

PICOT
Ch 3, sc in third ch from hook.

BODY
With Blue, ch 32.

Row 1 (Right side): Dc in fourth ch from hook **(3 skipped chs count as first dc)**, ★ ch 3, skip next 2 chs, (sc, work Picot, sc) in next ch, ch 3, skip next 2 chs, dc in next 2 chs; repeat from ★ across: 8 ch-3 sps.

Note: Loop a short piece of yarn around any stitch to mark Row 1 as **right** side.

Row 2: Ch 1, turn; sc in first dc, ch 1, skip next dc, ★ sc in next ch-3 sp, ch 6, skip next Picot, sc in next ch-3 sp, ch 1; repeat from ★ across, skip next dc, sc in last dc: 4 ch-6 loops.

Row 3: Ch 1, turn; sc in first sc and in next ch-1 sp, ★ (3 dc, ch 2, 3 dc) in next loop, sc in next ch-1 sp; repeat from ★ across, sc in last sc: 4 ch-2 sps.

Row 4: Ch 3 **(counts as first dc)**, turn; dc in same st, ch 3, (sc, work Picot, sc) in next ch-2 sp, ch 3, ★ 2 dc in next sc, ch 3, (sc, work Picot, sc) in next ch-2 sp, ch 3; repeat from ★ across to last 2 sc, skip next sc, 2 dc in last sc.

Rows 5-20: Repeat Rows 2-4, 5 times, then repeat Row 2 once **more**; do **not** finish off.

EDGING

Rnd 1: Ch 1, turn; skip first sc, sc in next ch-1 sp and in next sc, (5 sc in next ch-6 loop, sc in next sc and in next ch-1 sp, sc in next sc) across; work 34 sc evenly spaced across end of rows; work 34 sc evenly spaced across working in ch-2 sps and in free loops of beginning ch *(Fig. 22b, page 136)*; work 34 sc evenly spaced across end of rows; join with slip st to first sc: 136 sc

Rnd 2: Ch 1, (sc, ch 5) 3 times in same st, (skip next sc, sc in next sc, ch 5) 16 times, ★ skip next sc, (sc, ch 5) 4 times in next sc, (skip next sc, sc in next sc, ch 5) 16 times; repeat from ★ around to last sc, skip last sc, sc in same st as first sc, ch 2, dc in first sc to form last sp: 80 ch-5 sps.

Rnd 3: Ch 1, sc in same sp, (ch 5, sc in next ch-5 sp) around, ch 2, dc in first sc to form last sp.

Rnd 4: Ch 1, sc in same sp, ch 4, sc in third ch from hook, ch 1, (sc in next ch-5 sp, ch 4, sc in third ch from hook, ch 1) around; join with slip st to first sc, finish off.

TRIM

With **right** side facing and working in sps between sc on Rnd 1 of Edging, hold White at back of work, insert hook from **front** to **back** between first 2 sts, YO and pull up a loop, ★ insert hook in next sp, YO and draw through loop on hook; repeat from ★ around; join with slip st to first slip st, finish off.

VICTORIAN WASHCLOTH
Continued from page 41.

Rnd 11: Work beginning Cluster in same st, ch 3, ★ (work Cluster in next dc, ch 3) across to next corner ch-3 sp, work (Cluster, ch 3) twice in corner ch-3 sp; repeat from ★ 3 times **more**, (work Cluster in next dc, ch 3) 5 times; join with slip st to top of beginning Cluster: 48 Clusters.

Rnd 12: Ch 6, ★ (dc in next Cluster, ch 3) across to next corner ch-3 sp, dc in corner ch-3 sp, ch 3; repeat from ★ 3 times **more**, (dc in next Cluster, ch 3) across; join with slip st to first dc: 52 dc.

Rnd 13: Work beginning Cluster in same st, ch 3, ★ (work Cluster in next dc, ch 3) across to next corner dc, (work Cluster, ch 3) twice in corner dc; repeat from ★ 3 times **more**, (work Cluster in next dc, ch 3) 6 times; join with slip st to top of beginning Cluster: 56 Clusters.

Rnd 14: Repeat Rnd 12: 60 dc.

Rnd 15: Ch 5, sc in first ch-3 sp, ch 2, ★ (dc in next dc, ch 2, sc in next ch-3 sp, ch 2) across to next corner dc, (dc, ch 3, dc) in corner dc, ch 2, sc in next ch-3 sp, ch 2; repeat from ★ 3 times **more**, (dc in next dc, ch 2, sc in next ch-3 sp, ch 2) 7 times; join with slip st to third ch of beginning ch-5.

Rnd 16: Ch 6, ★ (dc in next dc, ch 3) across to next corner ch-3 sp, (dc, ch 3) twice in corner ch-3 sp; repeat from ★ 3 times **more**, (dc in next dc, ch 3) 8 times; join with slip st to first dc: 72 sps.

Rnd 17: Ch 5, sc in first ch-3 sp, ch 2, ★ dc in next dc, ch 2, (sc in next ch-3 sp, ch 2, dc in next dc, ch 2) across to next corner ch-3 sp, dc in corner ch-3 sp, ch 2; repeat from ★ 3 times **more**, (sc in next ch-3 sp, ch 2, dc in next dc, ch 2) 9 times; join with slip st to third ch of beginning ch-5.

Rnd 18: Ch 6, ★ (dc in next dc, ch 3) across to next corner dc, (dc, ch 3) twice in corner dc; repeat from ★ 3 times **more**, (dc in next dc, ch 3) 9 times; join with slip st to first dc: 80 dc.

Rnd 19: Ch 1, sc in same st, ch 3, ★ [(sc, ch 5, sc) in next dc, ch 3, (sc in next dc, ch 3) twice] across to next corner ch-3 sp, (sc, ch 5, sc) in corner ch-3 sp, ch 3, (sc in next dc, ch 3) twice; repeat from ★ 3 times **more**, (sc, ch 5, sc) in next dc, [ch 3, (sc in next dc, ch 3) twice, (sc, ch 5, sc) in next dc] twice, ch 3, sc in last dc, ch 3; join with slip st to first sc: 28 ch-5 sps.

Rnd 20: Slip st in first ch-3 sp, ch 1, sc in same sp, ★ † 8 dc in next ch-5 sp, sc in next ch-3 sp, (sc, ch 3, sc) in next ch-3 sp †, sc in next ch-3 sp; repeat from ★ around to last 3 sps, then repeat from † to † once; join with slip st to first sc: 28 8-dc groups.

Rnd 21: Slip st in first dc, ch 4, dc in next dc, (ch 1, dc in next dc) 6 times, sc in next ch-3 sp, ★ dc in next dc, (ch 1, dc in next dc) 7 times, sc in next ch-3 sp; repeat from ★ around; join with slip st to first dc.

Rnd 22: Slip st in first ch-1 sp, ch 1, sc in same sp, (ch 3, sc in next ch-1 sp) 6 times, ★ skip next sc, sc in next ch-1 sp, (ch 3, sc in next ch-1 sp) 6 times; repeat from ★ around; join with slip st to first sc, finish off.

TIE
Make a 15" chain; slip st **loosely** in second ch from hook and in each ch across; finish off.

With **right** side facing and working from **back** to **front**, weave Tie around center sc of Rnd 22 on any corner; tie in a bow.

See Washing and Blocking, page 138.

ROSE WREATH
Continued from page 37.

ROSEBUD (Make 4)
Rnd 1 (Right side)**:** With Green, ch 4, dc in fourth ch from hook **(3 skipped chs count as first dc)**, work Picot, (2 dc in same st, work Picot) 3 times; join with slip st to first dc, finish off: 8 dc.
Note: Mark Rnd 1 as **right** side.

Rnd 2: With **wrong** side facing, join Rose with slip st in any dc; ch 1, working in **front** of Picots, sc in each dc around; join with slip st to first sc: 8 sc.

Rnd 3: Ch 1, sc in each sc around; join with slip st to first sc, finish off leaving a long end for sewing.

Thread needle with end and weave through sts of Rnd 3; gather tightly to close and pull end through center of Rnd 1; secure.

LEAF (Make 7)
With Green, ch 5 **loosely**, sc in second ch from hook, dc in next 2 chs, (sc, ch 2, sc) in last ch; working in free loops of beginning ch *(Fig. 22b, page 136)*, dc in next 2 chs, sc in next ch, ch 2; join with slip st to first sc, finish off leaving a long end for sewing.

FINISHING
Using photo as a guide for placement, sew Roses, Rosebuds, and Leaves to Wreath as desired.
Spray starch on wrong side of Wreath.
Weave ribbon through Eyelet rnd and tie in a bow.
Add translucent nylon thread hanger.

gifts for all

*A handmade present is the most personal way to show someone you care.
To make your gift-giving decisions easier, we've created unique crochet
projects for an anniversary or wedding, Mother's Day, and Father's Day.
We also picked several all-occasion items that you can stitch ahead of
time and keep on hand until a special day arrives. These gifts, made with
your loving stitches, will add cheer to your loved ones' celebrations!*

FILET HEART FRAME

*Whether given as an anniversary remembrance or a surprise for newlyweds,
this sweetheart frame will delight the honored couple. The filet crochet edging is
accented with satin ribbon and then glued to a purchased frame. A thoughtful
keepsake, it's especially charming when presented holding a wedding day photo.*

Finished Size: 3¹/₂" wide, made to fit a 5" x 7" frame

MATERIALS
Cotton Crochet Thread (size 20), 360 yards
Steel crochet hook, size 11 (1.10 mm) **or** size needed for gauge
Tapestry needle
Spray starch
1 yard of ¹/₈" wide ribbon
5" x 7" photo frame (the flat moulding of our frame is
    1¹/₂" wide)
Craft glue

GAUGE: 9 sps and 9 rows = 2"

Gauge Swatch: 3¹/₂"w x 4"h
Work same as Edging, page 50, through Row 18.

CHART

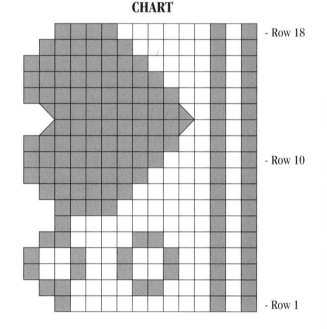

- Row 18

- Row 10

- Row 1

On **right** side rows, follow Chart from **right** to **left**;
on **wrong** side rows, follow Chart from **left** to **right**.

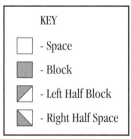

KEY
☐ - Space
▨ - Block
◨ - Left Half Block
◧ - Right Half Space

STITCH GUIDE

BEGINNING BLOCK OVER BLOCK
Ch 3 **(counts as first dc)**, turn; dc in next 3 dc.
BLOCK OVER BLOCK
Dc in next 3 dc.
BLOCK OVER SPACE
2 Dc in next ch-2 sp, dc in next dc.
SPACE OVER BLOCK
Ch 2, skip next 2 dc, dc in next dc.
SPACE OVER SPACE
Ch 2, dc in next dc.
BEGINNING BLOCK INCREASE
Ch 5, turn; dc in back ridge of fourth ch from hook and in next ch *(Fig. 2a, page 133)*, dc in next st.
ENDING BLOCK INCREASE
★ YO, insert in base of last dc worked *(Fig. 24b, page 136)*, YO and pull up a loop, YO and draw through one loop on hook, (YO and draw through 2 loops on hook) twice; repeat from ★ 2 times **more**.
BEGINNING BLOCK DECREASE
Turn; slip st in next 3 dc, ch 3.
ENDING BLOCK DECREASE
Leave last 3 dc unworked.
BEGINNING BLOCK AND A HALF DECREASE
Turn; slip st in next 3 dc, ch 3, ★ YO, insert hook in **next** dc, YO and pull up a loop, YO and draw through 2 loops on hook; repeat from ★ 2 times **more**, YO and draw through all 4 loops on hook **(counts as one dc)**.
ENDING HALF BLOCK INCREASE
(2 Dc, tr) in same dc as dc just worked.
LEFT HALF BLOCK
(Point of heart, Row 12) 2 Dc in same st as last dc worked, dc in next dc.
RIGHT HALF SPACE
(Point of heart, Row 13) Ch 2, ★ YO, insert hook in **next** dc, YO and pull up a loop, YO and draw through 2 loops on hook; repeat from ★ 2 times **more**, YO and draw through all 4 loops on hook.

EDGING

Ch 42.

Row 1 (Right side)**:** Dc in fourth ch from hook and in next 2 chs **(3 skipped chs count as first dc)**, ch 2, skip next 2 chs, dc in next 4 chs, (ch 2, skip next 2 chs, dc in next ch) 8 times, ch 2, skip next 2 chs, dc in last 4 chs: 10 Spaces.
Note: Loop a short piece of thread around any stitch to mark Row 1 as **right** side.
Rows 2-11: Follow Rows 2-11 of Chart, page 48.
Row 12: Work beginning Block and a half decrease, work 8 Blocks, work left half Block, (work Space, work Block) twice.
Row 13: Work beginning Block, work Space, work Block, work Space, work right half Space, work 8 Blocks, work ending half Block increase.
Rows 14-18: Follow Chart.
Rows 19-216: Follow Rows 1-18 of Chart, 11 times: 12 hearts. Finish off, leaving a long end for sewing.

FINISHING

See Washing and Blocking, page 138.
With **wrong** sides together and working through **both** loops of last row and in free loops of beginning ch *(Fig. 22b, page 136)*, whipstitch edges together *(Fig. 30a, page 139)*.

Spray wrong side of Edging with spray starch and let dry.

ASSEMBLY

Placing joining at lower right corner of frame, skip one heart and center next heart on 7" side of frame with first line of blocks and spaces placed over inner edge of frame. Use a small amount of glue or double-stick tape at back of heart to hold in place while positioning Edging, leaving spaces at inner edge of frame free to weave ribbon through.
★ Skip 2 hearts and center next heart on next side of frame; glue back of heart in place; repeat from ★ 2 times **more**.
Using photo as a guide, pleat corners.
Weave ribbon through spaces along inner edge of frame, skipping corner pleats; glue ribbon ends together on wrong side.
After positioning is complete, glue Edging securely in place.
Spray additional starch on back of Edging if needed.

Quick PETITE BASKET

There's no need to wait for a special occasion to share this little fabric-strip basket. Filled with decorative soaps, the pretty container offers a fresh way to say, "I'm thinking of you today." When the soaps are gone, the recipient will still have a petite organizer to use every day.

Finished Size: 4" in diameter x 3" high

MATERIALS
100% Cotton Fabric, 44/45" wide:
    Print - ½ yard
    Off-White - ⅜ yard
Crochet hook, size K (6.50 mm)

Note: Gauge is not important. Basket and Lid can be smaller or larger without changing the overall effect.

Prepare fabric and cut into 1" wide strips *(see Preparing Fabric Strips and Joining Fabric Strips, page 137)*.

BASKET
Rnd 1 (Right side)**:** With Off-White, ch 4 **loosely**, 11 dc in fourth ch from hook; join with slip st to top of beginning ch: 12 sts.

Note: Loop a scrap piece of fabric around any stitch to mark Rnd 1 as **right** side.

Rnd 2: Ch 3 **(counts as first dc, now and throughout)**, dc in same st, 2 dc in next dc and in each dc around; join with slip st to first dc changing to Print: 24 dc.

Rnd 3: Ch 1, sc in Back Loop only of each dc around *(Fig. 21, page 136)*; do **not** join, place marker *(see Markers, page 136)*.

Rnds 4-7: Sc in both loops of each sc around; at end of Rnd 7, slip st in next sc, finish off.

Edging: With bottom of basket facing you and working in free loops of Rnd 2 *(Fig. 22a, page 136)*, join Off-White with slip st in any st; slip st in each st around; join with slip st to first slip st, finish off.

LID
Rnd 1: With Print, ch 4 **loosely**, 11 dc in fourth ch from hook; join with slip st to top of beginning ch: 12 sts.

Rnd 2: Ch 3, dc in same st, 2 dc in next dc and in each dc around; join with slip st to first dc changing to Off-White: 24 dc.

Rnd 3: Ch 1, sc in same st, (ch 2, skip next dc, sc in next dc) around to last dc, ch 1, skip last dc; join with slip st to first sc, finish off: 12 sps.

HANDLE
With Off-White and leaving a long end, ch 8; finish off leaving a long end.

Pull long ends of Handle through center of Lid to **wrong** side; weave ends through sts to secure.

These cute fairies make sending happy birthday wishes even more fun! All created from the same pattern, each doll can be dressed to represent the honoree's birthstone color. Our September fairy wears blue for sapphire, Miss October's gown shimmers with opalescent hues, and April has a white gown to represent the diamond.

Finished Size: 5" tall

MATERIALS

For **each** Fairy:

Sport Weight Yarn:

Peach (Fairy) - 26 yards

White (Wings) - 12 yards

Dress & Panties (see chart for color) - 42 yards

Silver blending filament (Wings) - 12 yards

Steel crochet hooks, sizes 2 (2.25 mm) **and** 6 (1.80 mm) **or** sizes needed for gauge

Polyester fiberfill

Tapestry needle

Soft sculpture needle

Embroidery floss (black and desired hair color)

Pink crayon for cheek color

MONTH	STONE	DRESS & PANTIES COLOR
January	Garnet	Maroon
February	Amethyst	Purple
March	Aquamarine	Aqua
April	Diamond	White
May	Emerald	Green
June	Pearl	Off-white
July	Ruby	Red
August	Peridot	Jade
September	Sapphire	Blue
October	Opal	Ombre
November	Topaz	Topaz
December	Turquoise	Turquoise

GAUGE: With small hook (size 6), 7 sc and 7 rows = 1"

With large hook (size 2), 6 dc and 3 rows = 1"

Gauge Swatch #1: 1" square

With small hook (size 6), ch 8 **loosely**.

Row 1: Sc in second ch from hook and in each ch across: 7 sc

Rows 2-7: Ch 1, turn; sc in each sc across.

Finish off.

Gauge Swatch #2: 1" square

With large hook (size 2), ch 8 **loosely**.

Row 1: Dc in fourth ch from hook **(3 skipped chs count as first dc)** and in each ch across: 6 dc.

Rows 2 and 3: Ch 3 **(counts as first dc)**, turn; dc in next dc and in each dc across.

Finish off.

FAIRY

HEAD AND BODY

Rnd 1 (Right side)**:** With small size hook and Peach, ch 2, 8 sc in second ch from hook; do **not** join, place marker *(see Markers, page 136)*.

Rnd 2: 2 Sc in each sc around: 16 sc.

Rnd 3: (Sc in next sc, 2 sc in next sc) around: 24 sc.

Rnds 4-8: Sc in each sc around.

Rnd 9: (Skip next sc, sc in next 2 sc) around: 16 sc.

Stuff Head firmly with polyester fiberfill.

Rnd 10: (Skip next sc, sc in next sc) around: 8 sc.

Rnds 11 and 12: Sc in each sc around.

Rnd 13: 2 Sc in each sc around: 16 sc.

Rnds 14-21: Sc in each sc around.

Rnd 22: (Skip next sc, sc in next sc) around: 8 sc.

Stuff Body firmly with polyester fiberfill.

Rnd 23: (Skip next sc, sc in next sc) around; slip st in next sc finish off leaving a long end for sewing: 4 sc.

Thread tapestry needle with end and weave through remaining sts; gather tightly and secure.

VIOLET BOUQUET AFGHAN

*O*ne of spring's tiniest companions, violets often hide their colorful heads beneath lush green leaves. But on this pretty Mother's Day afghan, we showcased the beautiful flowers with clusters of oversize blossoms embroidered on our crocheted squares.

Finished Size: 40" x 65"

MATERIALS
Worsted Weight Brushed Acrylic Yarn:
    Off-White - 48 ounces, (1,360 grams, 2,430 yards)
    Violet - 7 ounces, (200 grams, 355 yards)
    Green - 1½ ounces, (40 grams, 75 yards)
    Yellow - ½ ounce, (15 grams, 25 yards)
Crochet hook, size G (4.00 mm) **or** size needed for gauge
Yarn needle
Safety pin

GAUGE: 17 sc and 18 rows = 5"
               Each Square, Rows 1-35 = 9¾"

Gauge Swatch: 5" square
With Off-White, ch 18 **loosely**.
Work same as Square through Row 18: 17 sc.

SQUARE (Make 15)
With Off-White, ch 34 **loosely**.
Row 1 (Right side)**:** Sc in second ch from hook and in each ch across: 33 sc.
Note: Loop a short piece of yarn around any stitch to mark Row 1 as **right** side and bottom edge.
Rows 2-35: Ch 1, turn; sc in each sc across; do **not** finish off.

BORDER
Rnd 1: Ch 3 **(counts as first dc, now and throughout)**, (dc, ch 2, 2 dc) in same st, work 31 dc evenly spaced across end of rows; working in free loops of beginning ch *(Fig. 22b, page 136)*, (2 dc, ch 2, 2 dc) in first ch, dc in each ch across to last ch, (2 dc, ch 2, 2 dc) in last ch; work 31 dc evenly spaced across end of rows; working across last row, (2 dc, ch 2, 2 dc) in first sc, dc in each sc across; join with slip st to first dc: 140 dc.
Rnd 2: Ch 4, skip next dc, (2 dc, ch 2, 2 dc) in next corner ch-2 sp, ★ ch 1, (skip next dc, dc in next dc, ch 1) across to within 1 dc of next corner ch-2 sp, skip next dc, (2 dc, ch 2, 2 dc) in corner ch-2 sp; repeat from ★ 2 times **more**, ch 1, skip next dc, (dc in next dc, ch 1, skip next dc) across; join with slip st to third ch of beginning ch-4.
Rnd 3: Ch 3, dc in next ch-1 sp and in next 2 dc, (2 dc, ch 2, 2 dc) in next corner ch-2 sp, ★ dc in each dc and in each ch-1 sp across to next corner ch-2 sp, (2 dc, ch 2, 2 dc) in corner ch-2 sp; repeat from ★ 2 times **more**, dc in each dc and in each ch-1 sp across; join with slip st to first dc, finish off.

CHAIN
Holding 2 strands of Violet together, chain a 44" length, do **not** finish off, slip loop from hook onto safety pin. Weave beginning end of chain through Rnd 2 of Border, working through ch-1 sps along sides and dc at corners; remove loop from safety pin and slip onto hook; adjust length as needed, join with slip st to first st, finish off.

FINISHING
Work embroidery on 7 Squares following Chart.
With Green, add Cross St leaves *(Fig. 37, page 141)*.
With Yellow, add a French Knot for center of each flower *(Fig. 36, page 141)*.
With 3 strands of Violet, add Straight St flower petals *(Fig. 34, page 141)*.

CHART

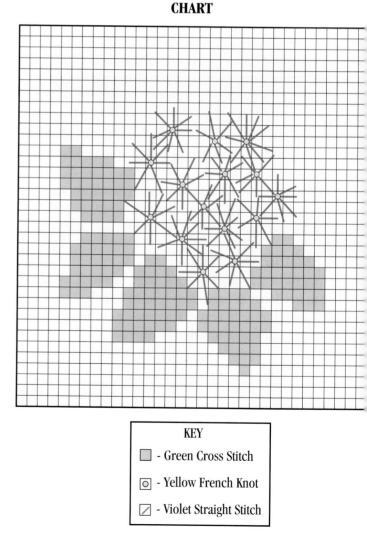

KEY	
▨	- Green Cross Stitch
⊙	- Yellow French Knot
◩	- Violet Straight Stitch

ASSEMBLY

With **wrong** sides together, bottom edges at the same end and Off-White, and working through **both** loops, whipstitch Squares together *(Fig. 30a, page 139)*. Using photo as a guide for placement, form 3 vertical strips of 5 Squares each, alternating plain and cross-stitched Squares. Whipstitch strips together, securing seam at each joining.

EDGING

With **right** side facing, join Off-White with slip st in any corner ch-2 sp; ch 3, (dc, ch 2, 2 dc) in same sp, ★ † dc in each dc across Square, [dc in next ch-2 sp, dc in next joining and in next ch-2 sp, dc in each dc across Square] across to next corner ch-2 sp †, (2 dc, ch 2, 2 dc) in corner ch-2 sp; repeat from ★ 2 times **more**, then repeat from † to † once; join with slip st to first dc, finish off.

Add fringe using 6 strands of Off-White, each 13" long *(Figs. 33a & b, page 139)*; spacing evenly, attach across each end of afghan.

Quick CLASSIC COASTER SET

Our classic coaster set is a wonderful gift for almost any occasion. Crocheted with absorbent cotton thread, the easy-to-make designs will provide a touch of refinement to the table. A wooden Shaker box embellished with wrapping paper, ribbon, and a matching coaster completes your present.

Finished Size: 5¼" in diameter

MATERIALS
Bedspread Weight Cotton Thread (size 10), 200 yards
Steel crochet hook, size 6 (1.80 mm) **or** size needed for gauge
Shaker box (4¾" in diameter)
28" length of ⅝" wide white ribbon
28" length of ⅜" wide blue ribbon
1⅞"w x 16"l decorative paper to cover box
White craft paint and paint brush
Craft glue

GAUGE SWATCH: 1¾" in diameter
Work same as Coaster through Rnd 3.

STITCH GUIDE

2-DC CLUSTER
★ YO, insert hook in dc indicated, YO and pull up a loop, YO and draw through 2 loops on hook; repeat from ★ once **more**, YO and draw through all 3 loops on hook *(Figs. 10a & b, page 134)*.

5-DC CLUSTER
★ YO, insert hook in sp indicated, YO and pull up a loop, YO and draw through 2 loops on hook; repeat from ★ 4 times **more**, YO and draw through all 6 loops on hook.

BEGINNING DECREASE (uses first 6 dc)
Ch 2, ★ YO, insert hook in **next** dc, YO and pull up a loop, YO and draw through 2 loops on hook; repeat from ★ 4 times **more**, YO and draw through all 6 loops on hook.

DECREASE (uses next 6 dc)
★ YO, insert hook in **next** dc, YO and pull up a loop, YO and draw through 2 loops on hook; repeat from ★ 5 times **more**, YO and draw through all 7 loops on hook.

COASTER (Make 5)
Ch 10; join with slip st to form a ring.
Rnd 1 (Right side): Ch 3 **(counts as first dc, now and throughout)**, work 19 dc in ring; join with slip st to first dc: 20 dc.

Rnd 2: Ch 2, dc in same st, ch 5, skip next dc, ★ work 2-dc Cluster in next dc, ch 5, skip next dc; repeat from ★ around; skip beginning ch-2 and join with slip st to first dc: 10 ch-5 sps.

Rnd 3: Slip st in first ch-5 sp, ch 3, 5 dc in same sp, ch 1, (6 dc in next ch-5 sp, ch 1) around; join with slip st to first dc: 60 dc.

Rnd 4: Ch 3, dc in next 2 dc, ch 2, (dc in next 3 dc, ch 2) around; join with slip st to first dc: 20 ch-2 sps.

Rnd 5: Ch 3, dc in next 2 dc, work 5-dc Cluster in next ch-2 sp, dc in next 3 dc, ch 5, ★ dc in next 3 dc, work 5-dc Cluster in next ch-2 sp, dc in next 3 dc, ch 5; repeat from ★ around; join with slip st to first dc: 10 5-dc Clusters.

Rnd 6: Ch 3, dc in next 2 dc, skip next Cluster, dc in next 3 dc, ch 4, sc in next loop, ch 4, ★ dc in next 3 dc, skip next Cluster, dc in next 3 dc, ch 4, sc in next loop, ch 4; repeat from ★ around; join with slip st to first dc.

Rnd 7: Work beginning decrease, (ch 6, sc in next ch-4 sp) twice, ★ ch 6, decrease, (ch 6, sc in next ch-4 sp) twice; repeat from ★ around, ch 2, tr in top of first st to form last loop: 30 loops.

Rnd 8: Ch 1, sc in same loop, ch 7, (sc in next loop, ch 7) around; join with slip st to first sc.

Rnd 9: Slip st in first loop, ch 3, 10 dc in same loop, sc in next loop, ★ 11 dc in next loop, sc in next loop; repeat from ★ around; join with slip st to first dc: 15 sc.

Rnd 10: Ch 1, sc in same st and in next dc, ch 3, (sc in next 3 dc, ch 3) twice, ★ sc in next 6 sts, ch 3, (sc in next 3 dc, ch 3) twice; repeat from ★ around to last 4 sts, sc in last 4 sts; join with slip st to first sc, finish off.

FINISHING
See Washing and Blocking, page 138.
Paint lid of box.
Using photo as a guide, glue decorative paper to side of box.
Glue White ribbon around edge of lid and Blue ribbon centered on top of White ribbon.
Glue wrong side of one Coaster to lid of box.

58

GREEK PUZZLE AFGHAN

*P*lease a special gentleman with our handsome Greek-inspired afghan.
A welcome addition to his favorite easy chair, this bold wrap is crafted in a trio
of masculine colors using single crochets. It's finished with long, generous fringe.

Finished Size: 46" x 63½"

MATERIALS
Worsted Weight Yarn:
Black - 33 ounces, (940 grams, 2,075 yards)
Natural - 15 ounces, (430 grams, 945 yards)
Gray - 12 ounces, (340 grams, 755 yards)
Crochet hook, size I (5.50 mm) **or** size needed for gauge

GAUGE: 15 sc and 15 rows = 4"

Gauge Swatch: 5½"w x 4"h
With Black, ch 21 **loosely**.
Work same as Body through Row 15: 20 sc.
Finish off.

BODY

With Black, ch 174 **loosely**.
Row 1 (Right side)**:** Sc in second ch from hook and in each ch across: 173 sc.
Note: Loop a short piece of yarn around any stitch to mark Row 1 as **right** side.
Row 2: Ch 1, turn; sc in each sc across.
Note: When changing colors *(Fig. 28a, page 138)*, work **over** unused color held on **wrong** side of work with normal tension; do **not** cut yarn until color is no longer needed.
Rows 3-238: Repeat Row 2 for pattern, following Rows 3-28 of Chart once; then follow Rows 1-28, 7 times; then follow Rows 1-14 once **more**; do **not** finish off.

EDGING

Rnd 1: Ch 1, turn; 3 sc in first st, sc in each sc across to last sc skipping 1 sc in middle of row, 3 sc in last sc; sc in end of each row across to next corner; working in free loops of beginning ch *(Fig. 22b, page 136)*, 3 sc in first ch, sc in each ch across to last ch skipping 1 ch in middle of row, 3 sc in last ch; sc in end of each row across; join with slip st to first sc.
Rnd 2: Ch 1, sc in each sc around working 3 sc in each corner sc; join with slip st to first sc.

Rnd 3: Ch 1, sc in same st and in next sc, † (sc, ch 2, sc) in next corner sc, ch 2, skip next 2 sc, (sc in next 2 sc, ch 2, skip next 2 sc) across to next corner sc, (sc, ch 2, sc) in corner sc †, sc in each sc across to next corner sc, repeat from † to † once, sc in each sc across; join with slip st to first sc, finish off.

Add fringe using 10 strands of Black, each 16" long *(Figs. 33a & b, page 139)*; attach in ch-2 sps across each end of afghan.

CHART

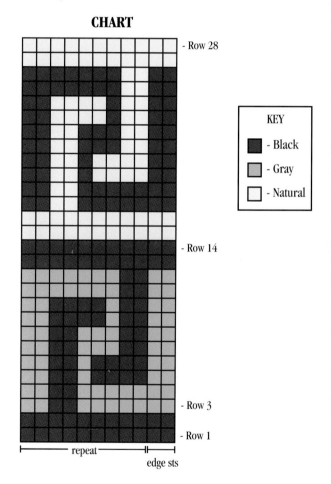

KEY
■ - Black
▨ - Gray
□ - Natural

- Row 28
- Row 14
- Row 3
- Row 1

repeat
edge sts

On **right** side rows, follow Chart from **right** to **left**, working 2 edge sts, then working repeat across.
On **wrong** side rows, follow Chart from **left** to **right**, working repeat across to last 2 sts, then working 2 edge sts.

LACY ACCENT PILLOW

Shallow shells form the lacy design on this sweet accent pillow. Sure to charm a lady on your gift list, the cushion provides a feminine touch for a bed or chair.

Finished Size: 10" square

MATERIALS
Bedspread Weight Cotton Thread (size 10), 320 yards
Steel crochet hook, size 7 (1.65 mm) **or** size needed for gauge
2 pieces of fabric - 8¹/₂" square
Polyester fiberfill
Tapestry needle
Finishing materials: Ribbons, rose, sewing needle, and thread

GAUGE: In pattern, 2 repeats = 2³/₄" and 12 rows = 2¹/₂"

Gauge Swatch: 2³/₄"w x 2¹/₂"h
Ch 26.
Work same as Back for 12 rows.
Finish off.

STITCH GUIDE

SHELL
(2 Dc, ch 1, 2 dc) in st or sp indicated.

BACK
Ch 74.
Row 1 (Right side): Sc in second ch from hook, ★ ch 3, skip next 5 chs, dc in next ch, (ch 1, dc) 4 times in same ch, ch 3, skip next 5 chs, sc in next ch; repeat from ★ across: 12 ch-3 sps.
Note: Loop a short piece of thread around any stitch to mark Row 1 as **right** side.
Row 2: Ch 3 **(counts as first dc, now and throughout)**, turn; 2 dc in same st, ★ † ch 1, skip next ch-3 sp, sc in next ch-1 sp, (ch 3, sc in next ch-1 sp) 3 times, ch 1, skip next ch-3 sp †, work Shell in next sc; repeat from ★ 4 times **more**, then repeat from † to † once, 3 dc in last sc.
Row 3: Ch 3, turn; 2 dc in same st, ★ † ch 2, skip next ch-1 sp, sc in next ch-3 sp, (ch 3, sc in next ch-3 sp) twice, ch 2 †, skip next ch-1 sp, work Shell in next Shell (ch-1 sp); repeat from ★ 4 times **more**, then repeat from † to † once, skip next ch-1 sp and next 2 dc, 3 dc in last dc.
Row 4: Ch 3, turn; 2 dc in same st, ★ † ch 3, skip next ch-2 sp, (sc in next ch-3 sp, ch 3) twice †, skip next ch-2 sp, work Shell in next Shell; repeat from ★ 4 times **more**, then repeat from † to † once, skip next ch-2 sp and next 2 dc, 3 dc in last dc.

Row 5: Ch 1, turn; sc in first dc, ★ † ch 3, skip next ch-3 sp, dc in next ch-3 sp, (ch 1, dc) 4 times in same sp, ch 3 †, skip next ch-3 sp, sc in next Shell; repeat from ★ 4 times **more**, then repeat from † to † once, skip next ch-3 sp and next 2 dc, sc in last dc.
Repeat Rows 2-5 for pattern until piece measures 8¹/₄", ending by working Row 5.
Edging: Ch 1, 2 sc in same st, work 79 sc evenly spaced across end of rows; working in free loops of beginning ch *(Fig. 22b, page 136)*, 3 sc in first ch, work 79 sc evenly spaced across to last ch, 3 sc in last ch; work 79 sc evenly spaced across end of rows; 3 sc in first sc, work 79 sc evenly spaced across, sc in same st as first sc; join with slip st to first sc, finish off: 328 sc.

FRONT
Work same as Back; do **not** finish off.

BORDER
Rnd 1: Ch 3, working in Front Loops Only *(Fig. 21, page 136)*, 2 dc in same st, ★ dc in next sc and in each sc across to next corner sc, 3 dc in corner sc; repeat from ★ 2 times **more**, dc in each sc across; join with slip st to first dc: 336 dc.
Rnd 2: Ch 1, working in both loops, ★ sc in next dc, ch 3, skip next 5 dc, dc in next dc, (ch 1, dc) 4 times in same dc, ch 3, skip next 5 dc; repeat from ★ around; join with slip st to first sc: 28 sc.
Rnd 3: Ch 3, (dc, ch 1, 2 dc) in same st, ch 1, skip next ch-3 sp, sc in next ch-1 sp, (ch 3, sc in next ch-1 sp) 3 times, ch 1, skip next ch-3 sp, ★ work Shell in next sc, ch 1, skip next ch-3 sp, sc in next ch-1 sp, (ch 3, sc in next ch-1 sp) 3 times, ch 1, skip next ch-3 sp; repeat from ★ around; join with slip st to first dc.
Rnd 4: Slip st in next dc and in next ch-1 sp, ch 3, (dc, ch 1, 2 dc) in same sp, ch 2, skip next ch-1 sp, sc in next ch-3 sp, (ch 3, sc in next ch-3 sp) twice, ch 2, skip next ch-1 sp, ★ work Shell in next Shell, ch 2, skip next ch-1 sp, sc in next ch-3 sp, (ch 3, sc in next ch-3 sp) twice, ch 2, skip next ch-1 sp; repeat from ★ around; join with slip st to first dc.
Rnd 5: Slip st in next dc and in next ch-1 sp, ch 3, (dc, ch 1, 2 dc) in same sp, ch 3, skip next ch-2 sp, (sc in next ch-3 sp, ch 3) twice, skip next ch-2 sp, ★ work Shell in next Shell, ch 3, skip next ch-2 sp, (sc in next ch-3 sp, ch 3) twice, skip next ch-2 sp; repeat from ★ around; join with slip st to first dc, finish off.

62

FINISHING

See Washing and Blocking, page 138.
Make pillow form, page 138.

With **wrong** sides together, Back facing, and working through **inside** loops only of sc on Edging, whipstitch Front and Back together, inserting pillow form before closing *(Fig. 30b, page 139)*.

Sew ribbon bow and rose to corner of Pillow as desired.

just for fun

*When there's no particular reason — or season — to crochet,
why not stitch one of these fanciful creations just for the fun
of it! We included a cute watermelon rug, an adorable hooded
towel, cheery kitchen accents, and more. So when you're itching
to start stitching, here's the place to get hooked on crochet!*

CRAYON AFGHAN

*Youngsters will love this brightly colored afghan! Resembling rows of giant crayons, the fun throw
is worked in durable worsted weight yarn to withstand years of playtime and naps. Because
it's crocheted with basic stitches, even beginning stitchers will be drawn to this clever cover-up.*

Finished Size: 43" x 57"

MATERIALS
Worsted Weight Yarn:
  Black - 12 ounces, (340 grams, 680 yards)
  Blue - 5 ounces, (140 grams, 285 yards)
  Red - 5 ounces, (140 grams, 285 yards)
  Green - 5 ounces, (140 grams, 285 yards)
  Yellow - 5 ounces, (140 grams, 285 yards)
  Purple - 5 ounces, (140 grams, 285 yards)
Crochet hook, size I (5.50 mm) **or** size needed for gauge

GAUGE: 12 dc and 7 rows = 4"
     One Strip = 8$\frac{1}{2}$" x 57"

Gauge Swatch: 4" square
Ch 14 **loosely**.
Row 1: Dc in fourth ch from hook **(3 skipped chs count as first dc)** and in each ch across: 12 dc.
Rows 2-6: Ch 3 **(counts as first dc)**, turn; dc in next dc and in each dc across.
Finish off.

STITCH GUIDE

> **ADDING ON DC**
> YO, insert hook in base of last dc worked *(Fig. 24b, page 136)*, YO and pull up a loop, YO and draw through one loop on hook, (YO and draw through 2 loops on hook) twice.

FIRST STRIP

Row 1: With Blue, ch 2, 2 sc in second ch from hook.
Row 2 (Right side): Ch 3 **(counts as first dc, now and throughout)**, turn; dc in same st, 2 dc in last sc: 4 dc.
Note: Loop a short piece of yarn around any stitch to mark Row 2 as **right** side.
Rows 3-10: Ch 3, turn; dc in same st and in each dc across to last dc, 2 dc in last dc: 20 dc.
Row 11: Ch 4 **loosely**, turn; dc in fourth ch from hook **(3 skipped chs count as first dc)** and in each dc across, add on 2 dc: 24 dc.
Row 12: Ch 3, turn; dc in next dc and in each dc across.
Row 13: Ch 3, turn; dc in next dc and in each dc across changing to Black in last dc worked *(Fig. 28a, page 138)*.
Row 14: Ch 1, turn; sc in each dc across.
Row 15: Ch 4, turn; † dc in next sc, hdc in next 3 sc, sc in next 2 sc, hdc in next 3 sc, dc in next sc †, tr in next 2 sc, repeat from † to † once, tr in last sc changing to Blue.

Rows 16 and 17: Ch 1, turn; sc in each st across, changing to Black at end of Row 17.

Row 18: Ch 1, turn; sc in each sc across.

Row 19: Ch 1, turn; sc in first sc, † hdc in next 3 sc, dc in next sc, tr in next 2 sc, dc in next sc, hdc in next 3 sc †, sc in next 2 sc, repeat from † to † once, sc in last sc changing to Blue.

Row 20: Ch 1, turn; sc in each st across.

Rows 21-44: Ch 3, turn; dc in next st and in each st across.

Row 45: Ch 3, turn; dc in next 9 dc changing to Black in last dc worked, do **not** cut yarn, dc in next 4 dc changing to Blue in last dc worked, dc in each dc across.

Row 46: Ch 3, turn; dc in next 8 dc changing to Black in last dc worked, dc in next 6 dc changing to Blue in last dc worked, dc in each dc across.

Rows 47-70: Ch 3, turn; dc in next 7 dc changing to Black in last dc worked, dc in next 8 dc changing to Blue in last dc worked, dc in each dc across.

Row 71: Ch 3, turn; dc in next 8 dc changing to Black in last dc worked, dc in next 6 dc changing to Blue in last dc worked, dc in each dc across.

Row 72: Ch 3, turn; dc in next 9 dc changing to Black in last dc worked, dc in next 4 dc changing to Blue in last dc worked, dc in each dc across; cut Black.

Rows 73-94: Ch 3, turn; dc in next dc and in each dc across.

Rows 95-102: Repeat Rows 13-20.

Rows 103-105: Ch 3, turn; dc in next st and in each st across. Finish off.

EDGING

With **right** side facing, join Black with slip st in first dc; ch 1, 3 sc in same st, sc in each dc across to last dc, 3 sc in last dc; working in end of rows, sc in first row, 2 sc in each of next 2 rows, sc in next 5 rows, 2 sc in next row, sc in next row, work 128 sc evenly spaced across end of rows to next sc row, sc in next 5 rows, 2 sc in next row, sc in next row, 2 sc in each of next 2 rows, sc in next row, 3 sc in base of first dc, sc in base of next dc, sc evenly spaced across end of rows to point; 3 sc in free loop of beginning ch *(Fig. 22b, page 136)*; sc evenly spaced across end of rows to Row 11, sc in base of next dc, 3 sc in base of next dc, sc in same row, 2 sc in each of next 2 rows, sc in next row, 2 sc in next row, sc in next 5 rows, work 128 sc evenly spaced across to next sc row, sc in next row, 2 sc in next row, sc in next 5 rows, 2 sc in each of next 2 rows, sc in last row; join with slip st to first sc, finish off.

REMAINING 4 STRIPS

Work same as first Strip, using Red, Green, Yellow, or Purple in place of Blue.

ASSEMBLY

Join Strips as follows: With **wrong** sides together and working through **inside** loops only, join Black with slip st in bottom right corner sc; slip st in each sc across to corner sc on Row 11; finish off.

Quick WATERMELON RAG RUG

*E*njoy a slice of the good life any time you like by crafting this watermelon rug! Fashioned with cotton fabric strips, the quick-to-make piece is a unique way to celebrate one of nature's summer delights.

Finished Size: 17" x 34"

MATERIALS
100% Cotton Fabric, 44/45" wide:
    Red - 8 yards
    Green - 5 yards
    White - 2 yards
    Black - ¼ yard
Crochet hook, size N (9.00 mm) **or** size needed for gauge

Prepare fabric and tear into 3" wide strips *(see Preparing Fabric Strips and Joining Fabric Strips, page 137)*.

GAUGE: 6 dc = 4" and 3 rows = 4¼"

Gauge Swatch: 4½"h x 7"w
Work same as Rug through Row 2.

RUG

With Red, ch 5 **loosely**.

Row 1: Dc in fourth ch from hook, 6 dc in last ch; working in free loops of beginning ch *(Fig. 22b, page 136)*, dc in next 2 chs: 10 sts.

Note: Loop a short scrap of fabric around any stitch to mark Row 1 as **right** side.

Row 2: Ch 3 **(counts as first dc, now and throughout)**, turn; dc in same st and in next dc, 2 dc in each of next 6 dc, dc in last 2 sts: 17 dc.

Row 3: Ch 3, turn; dc in same st and in next 3 dc, (2 dc in next dc, dc in next dc) 4 times, 2 dc in next dc, dc in last 4 dc: 23 dc.

Row 4: Ch 3, turn; dc in same st and in next 5 dc, 2 dc in next dc, (dc in next 2 dc, 2 dc in next dc) 3 times, dc in last 7 dc: 28 dc.

Row 5: Ch 3, turn; dc in same st and in next dc, (2 dc in next dc, dc in next 5 dc) 3 times, (2 dc in next dc, dc in next 3 dc) twice: 34 dc.

Row 6: Ch 3, turn; dc in same st, dc in next dc changing to Black, dc in next dc changing to Red, dc in next 3 dc, ★ 2 dc in next dc, dc in next 2 dc changing to Black in last dc worked, dc in next dc changing to Red, dc in next 3 dc; repeat from ★ across: 39 dc.

Row 7: Ch 3, turn; dc in same st and in next 4 dc, 2 dc in next dc, dc in next 6 dc, 2 dc in next dc, dc in next 5 dc, (2 dc in next dc, dc in next 6 dc) 3 times: 45 dc.

Row 8: Ch 3, turn; dc in same st and in next 6 dc, 2 dc in next dc, dc in next 7 dc, (2 dc in next dc, dc in next 6 dc) 3 times, 2 dc in next dc, dc in last 8 dc changing to White in last dc worked: 51 dc.

Row 9: Ch 3, turn; dc in same st, (dc in next 7 dc, 2 dc in next dc) twice, (dc in next 8 dc, 2 dc in next dc) 3 times, dc in last 7 dc changing to Green in last dc worked: 57 dc.

Row 10: Ch 3, turn; dc in same st, (dc in next 8 dc, 2 dc in next dc) twice, dc in next 9 dc, 2 dc in next dc, dc in next 7 dc, 2 dc in next dc, dc in next 9 dc, 2 dc in next dc, dc in last 10 dc: 63 dc.

Row 11: Ch 3, turn; dc in same st, (dc in next 10 dc, 2 dc in next dc) twice, dc in next 7 dc, 2 dc in next dc, dc in next 13 dc, 2 dc in next dc, dc in next 6 dc, 2 dc in next dc, dc in last 11 dc; finish off: 69 dc.

You don't have to make a trip to market to pick up this little piggy! Simply work continuous rounds of single crochets, add embroidered features, and she's yours to love before you know it. With a soft, cushy body and curly tail, this petite porker is quite a babe!

Finished Size: 5" tall x 9" long

MATERIALS
Worsted Weight Brushed Acrylic Yarn:
    Pink - 2¼ ounces, (65 grams, 130 yards)
    Black - 12 yards
Crochet hook, size I (5.50 mm)
Polyester fiberfill
Yarn needle

Note: Gauge is not important. Pig can be larger or smaller without changing the overall effect.

STITCH GUIDE

> **DECREASE** (uses next 2 sc)
> Pull up a loop in next 2 sc, YO and draw through all 3 loops on hook (**counts as one sc**).

BODY
With Pink, ch 3; being careful not to twist ch, join with slip st to form a ring.
Rnd 1 (Right side)**:** Ch 1, 2 sc in each ch around; do **not** join, place marker *(see Markers, page 136)*: 6 sc.
Rnd 2: 2 Sc in each sc around: 12 sc.
Rnd 3: (Sc in next sc, 2 sc in next sc) around: 18 sc.
Rnd 4: (Sc in next 2 sc, 2 sc in next sc) around: 24 sc.
Rnd 5: (Sc in next 3 sc, 2 sc in next sc) around: 30 sc.
Rnd 6: (Sc in next 4 sc, 2 sc in next sc) around: 36 sc.
Rnd 7: (Sc in next 5 sc, 2 sc in next sc) around: 42 sc.
Rnds 8-19: Sc in each sc around.
Rnd 20: (Sc in next 5 sc, decrease) around: 36 sc.
Rnd 21: (Sc in next 4 sc, decrease) around: 30 sc.
Rnd 22: (Sc in next 3 sc, decrease) around: 24 sc.
Rnd 23: (Sc in next 2 sc, decrease) around: 18 sc.
Stuff Body with polyester fiberfill.
Rnd 24: (Sc in next sc, decrease) around: 12 sc.
Rnd 25: Decrease around: 6 sc.
Rnd 26: (Skip next st, slip st in next st) 3 times: 3 sts.
Tail: Ch 6 **loosely**; 3 sc in second ch from hook and in each ch across; slip st in next st; finish off.

HEAD
With Pink, ch 3; being careful not to twist ch, join with slip st to form a ring.
Rnd 1 (Right side)**:** Ch 1, 2 sc in each ch around; do **not** join, place marker: 6 sc.
Rnd 2: 2 Sc in each sc around: 12 sc.
Rnd 3: (Sc in next sc, 2 sc in next sc) around: 18 sc.
Rnd 4: (Sc in next 2 sc, 2 sc in next sc) around: 24 sc.
Rnd 5: (Sc in next 3 sc, 2 sc in next sc) around: 30 sc.
Rnd 6: (Sc in next 4 sc, 2 sc in next sc) around: 36 sc.
Rnds 7-11: Sc in each sc around.
Rnd 12: (Sc in next 4 sc, decrease) around: 30 sc.
Rnd 13: (Sc in next 3 sc, decrease) around: 24 sc.
Rnd 14: Sc in each sc around; slip st in next sc, finish off leaving a long end for sewing.

SNOUT
With Pink, ch 3; being careful not to twist ch, join with slip st to form a ring.
Rnd 1 (Right side)**:** Ch 1, 2 sc in each ch around; do **not** join, place marker: 6 sc.
Rnd 2: (2 Sc in next sc, 2 hdc in next sc) around: 12 sts.
Rnd 3: (Sc in next 2 sts, 2 sc in each of next 4 sts) twice: 20 sts.
Rnd 4: Sc in Back Loop Only of each sc around *(Fig. 21, page 136)*.
Rnd 5: Sc in both loops of each sc around; slip st in next sc, finish off leaving a long end for sewing.

EAR (Make 2)
Row 1 (Right side)**:** With Pink, ch 2, 2 sc in second ch from hook.
Note: Loop a short piece of yarn around any stitch to mark Row 1 as **right** side.
Row 2: Ch 1, turn; sc in each sc across.
Row 3: Ch 1, turn; 2 sc in each sc across: 4 sc.
Row 4: Ch 1, turn; 2 sc in first sc, sc in next 2 sc, 2 sc in last sc: 6 sc.
Rows 5 and 6: Ch 1, turn; sc in each sc across.
Edging: Ch 1, turn; 2 sc in first sc, sc in next 4 sc, 3 sc in last sc in end of next 5 rows; 3 sc in free loop of beginning ch *(Fig. 22b, page 136)*; sc in end of each row across; join with slip st to first sc, finish off leaving a long end for sewing: 23 sc.

LEG (Make 4)

With Black, ch 3; being careful not to twist ch, join with slip st to form a ring.

Rnd 1 (Right side)**:** Ch 1, 2 sc in each ch around; do **not** join, place marker: 6 sc.

Rnd 2: 2 Sc in each sc around: 12 sc.

Rnd 3: (Sc in next sc, 2 sc in next sc) around changing to Pink in last sc worked *(Fig. 28a, page 138)*: 18 sc.

Rnds 4-10: Sc in each sc around; at end of Rnd 10, slip st in next sc, finish off leaving a long end for sewing.

FINISHING

Stuff Head and Legs with polyester fiberfill; sew to Body.

Using photo as a guide for placement, sew Ears to top of Head along Rnd 10, placing 4 sts apart.

Sew Snout to Head with increases of Rnd 3 at sides, stuffing with polyester fiberfill before closing.

With Black, add Satin Stitch eyes and nostrils *(Fig. 35b, page 141)*.

Quick PANDA HOODED TOWEL

Here's a bath buddy that will make tub-time more enjoyable for your little one! Bearing a playful grin and large friendly eyes, the cute panda hood is easy to crochet onto a terry towel. This whimsical project also makes a wonderful baby shower gift.

MATERIALS

100% Cotton Worsted Weight Yarn:
 White - 3 ounces, (90 grams, 130 yards)
 Black - 30 yards
Crochet hook, size G (4.00 mm) **or** size needed for gauge
Bath towel
Straight pin
Fabric marking pen
Yarn and tapestry needles
Sewing needle and thread
5/8" Black button (nose)
2 - 20 mm wiggle eyes

GAUGE: 8 sc and 9 rows = 2"

Gauge Swatch: 2" square
Ch 9.
Row 1: Sc in second ch from hook and in each ch across: 8 sc.
Rows 2-9: Ch 1, turn; sc in each sc across.
Finish off.

STITCH GUIDE

> **DECREASE** (uses next 2 sc)
> Pull up a loop in next 2 sc, YO and draw through all 3 loops on hook (**counts as one sc**).

PREPARING TOWEL

Locate the center of one long edge by folding towel in half with right side out and short ends together; mark fold with a straight pin. Unfold towel and use fabric marking pen to place a dot at edge of towel 5" from each side of straight pin; remove pin.

BACK

Row 1 (Right side): With **right** side of towel facing and inserting hook through towel 1/4" from edge, join White with sc at first dot **(see Joining With Sc, page 136)**, work 41 sc evenly spaced across to last dot: 42 sc.
Row 2: Ch 1, turn; sc in each sc across.
Row 3 (Decrease row): Ch 1, turn; decrease, sc in each sc across to last 2 sc, decrease: 40 sc.
Row 4: Ch 1, turn; sc in each sc across.
Rows 5-14: Repeat Rows 3 and 4, 5 times: 30 sc.
Rows 15-24: Repeat Row 3, 10 times; at end of Row 24, finish off: 10 sc.

Edging: With **right** side facing, join White with sc in end of first row; work 21 sc evenly spaced across end of rows; working across last row, sc in next 10 sc; work 22 sc evenly spaced across end of rows; finish off leaving a long end for sewing: 54 sc

FRONT

With White, ch 43.
Row 1 (Right side): Sc in second ch from hook and in each ch across: 42 sc.
Note: Loop a short piece of yarn around any stitch to mark Row 1 as **right** side.
Rows 2-24: Work same as Back: 10 sc.
Edging: Work same as Back; do **not** leave a long end.

MUZZLE

With White, ch 4; join with slip st to form a ring.
Rnd 1 (Right side): Ch 1, 6 sc in ring; join with slip st to first sc.
Note: Mark Rnd 1 as **right** side.
Rnd 2: Ch 1, 2 sc in same st and in each sc around; join with slip st to first sc: 12 sc.
Rnd 3: Ch 1, 2 sc in same st, sc in next sc, (2 sc in next sc, sc in next sc) around; join with slip st to first sc: 18 sc.
Rnd 4: Ch 1, 2 sc in same st, sc in next 2 sc, (2 sc in next sc, sc in next 2 sc) around; join with slip st to first sc: 24 sc.
Rnd 5: Ch 1, 2 sc in same st, sc in next 3 sc, (2 sc in next sc, sc in next 3 sc) around; join with slip st to first sc: 30 sc.
Rnd 6: Ch 1, 2 sc in same st, sc in next 4 sc, (2 sc in next sc, sc in next 4 sc) around; join with slip st to first sc, finish off leaving a long end for sewing: 36 sc.

EAR (Make 2)

BACK

With Black, work same as Muzzle through Rnd 5: 30 sc.
Finish off.

FRONT

With Black, work same as Muzzle through Rnd 5; do **not** finish off: 30 sc.
Rnd 6 (Joining): Ch 1, with **wrong** sides of Front and Back together, Front facing, and working through **both** loops of **both** pieces, sc in each sc around; join with slip st to first sc, finish off leaving a long end for sewing.

EYE PATCH (Make 2)

Rnd 1 (Right side): With Black, ch 8, 3 dc in fourth ch from hook, dc in next 3 chs, 4 dc in last ch; working in free loops of beginning ch *(Fig. 22b, page 136)*, dc in next 3 chs; join with slip st to top of beginning ch: 14 sts.

Note: Mark Rnd 1 as **right** side.

Rnd 2: Ch 1, 2 sc in same st and in each of next 3 dc, sc in next 3 dc, 2 sc in each of next 4 dc, sc in last 3 dc; join with slip st to first sc, finish off leaving a long end for sewing: 22 sc.

FINISHING

Using photo as guide for placement, sew wiggle eyes to Eye Patches and button to Muzzle.

With Black and tapestry needle, work Straight Sts for mouth *(Fig. 34, page 141)*.

Sew **wrong** sides of Muzzle and Eye Patches to **right** side of Front. Sew Ears to Front.

With **wrong** sides together and White, and working through **inside** loops only, whipstitch Front to Back *(Fig. 30b, page 139)*.

Quick "DRESSY" POT HOLDERS

Add fun to the kitchen with these nostalgic pot holders! We stitched the miniature dress and apron accents in cheery red and white, but you can choose colors to complement any decor.

Finished Size: Apron - 6" x 7"
Dress - 6¹/₂"w x 5"h

MATERIALS
Bedspread Weight Cotton Thread (size 10):
Apron
Red - 65 yards
White - 10 yards
Dress
White - 85 yards
Red - 27 yards
Steel crochet hook, size 6 (1.80 mm) **or** size needed for gauge

GAUGE: In pattern, (5-dc group, dc) 3 times = 2"
and 4 rows = 1"

Gauge Swatch: 2¹/₈"w x 1"h
Ch 20 **loosely**.
Row 1: Sc in second ch from hook and in each ch across: 19 sc.
Row 2: Ch 3 **(counts as first dc, now and throughout)**, turn; (skip next 2 sc, 5 dc in next sc, skip next 2 sc, dc in next sc) across: 3 5-dc groups.
Rows 3 and 4: Ch 3, turn; ★ skip next 2 dc, 5 dc in next dc, skip next 2 dc, dc in next dc; repeat from ★ across.
Finish off.

APRON
SKIRT
With Red, ch 31 **loosely**.
Row 1 (Right side): Sc in second ch from hook and in each ch across: 30 sc.
Note: Loop a short piece of thread around any stitch to mark Row 1 as **right** side.
Row 2: Ch 3 **(counts as first dc, now and throughout)**, turn; 2 dc in next sc, (dc in next sc, 2 dc in next sc) across: 45 dc.
Row 3: Ch 5 **(counts as first dc plus ch 2, now and throughout)**, turn; skip next dc, dc in next dc, (ch 2, skip next dc, dc in next dc) across: 22 ch-2 sps.
Row 4: Turn; slip st in first ch-2 sp, ch 3, (5 dc in next ch-2 sp, dc in next ch-2 sp) across to last sp, 6 dc in last sp: 11 dc groups.
Rows 5-14: Ch 3, turn; ★ skip next 2 dc, 5 dc in next dc, skip next 2 dc, dc in next dc; repeat from ★ across.
Row 15: Ch 3, turn; skip next 2 dc, 5 dc in next dc, ★ skip next 2 dc, dc in next dc, skip next 2 dc, 5 dc in next dc; repeat from ★ across to last 3 dc, skip next 2 dc, sc in last dc changing to White *(Fig. 28a, page 138)*.

Row 16: Ch 1, turn; sc in first sc, (ch 5, skip next 2 dc, sc in next dc) across to last 6 dc, skip next 2 dc, pull up a loop in next dc, skip next 2 dc, pull up a loop in last dc, YO and draw through all 3 loops on hook: 21 ch-5 sps.
Row 17: Ch 1, turn; sc in first ch-5 sp, (7 dc in next ch-5 sp, sc in next ch-5 sp) across changing to Red in last sc worked: 81 sts.
Row 18: Ch 1, turn; sc in first sc, ch 2, (sc in next dc, ch 2) 7 times, ★ skip next sc, (sc in next dc, ch 2) 7 times; repeat from ★ across to last sc, sc in last sc; finish off.

WAISTBAND
Row 1: With **right** side facing and working in free loops of beginning ch *(Fig. 22b, page 136)*, join Red with slip st in first ch; ch 5, skip next 2 chs, dc in next ch, (ch 2, skip next ch, dc in next ch) across: 14 ch-2 sps.
Row 2: Ch 1, turn; sc in first dc, (2 sc in next ch-2 sp, sc in next dc) across; finish off: 43 sc.

BIB
Row 1: With **wrong** side facing, skip first 12 sc on Waistband and join Red with slip st in next sc; ch 3, ★ skip next 2 sc, 5 dc in next sc, skip next 2 sc, dc in next sc; repeat from ★ 2 times **more**, leave remaining 12 sc unworked: 3 5-dc groups.
Rows 2-5: Ch 3, turn; ★ skip next 2 dc, 5 dc in next dc, skip next 2 dc, dc in next dc; repeat from ★ across; at end of Row 5, change to White in last dc worked.
Row 6: Ch 1, turn; sc in each dc across; finish off.

STRAP
Foundation: With **right** side facing, join Red with slip st in first sc on Row 6 of Bib; ch 40 **loosely**; being careful not to twist ch, join with slip st to last sc, finish off.
Row 1: With **right** side facing, join Red with slip st in end of first row of Bib; ch 1, sc in same sp, sc evenly across end of rows; sc in each ch across; sc evenly across end of rows; finish off.
Row 2: With **right** side facing, join White with slip st in first sc; ch 1, sc in each sc across; finish off.

DRESS
With White, ch 48 **loosely**; being careful not to twist ch, join with slip st to form a ring.
Rnd 1 (Right side): Ch 3 **(counts as first dc, now and throughout)**, dc in next 2 chs, 2 dc in next ch, (dc in next 3 chs, 2 dc in next ch) around; join with slip st to Back Loop Only of first dc *(Fig. 21, page 136)*: 60 dc.

Note #1: Loop a short piece of thread around any stitch to mark Rnd 1 as **right** side.

Note #2: Work next 4 rnds in Back Loops Only.

Rnd 2: Ch 3, dc in next dc, 2 dc in next dc, (dc in next 2 dc, 2 dc in next dc) around; join with slip st to first dc: 80 dc.

Rnd 3: Ch 3, dc in next 2 dc, 2 dc in next dc, (dc in next 3 dc, 2 dc in next dc) around; join with slip st to first dc: 100 dc.

Rnd 4: Ch 3, dc in next 3 dc, 2 dc in next dc, (dc in next 4 dc, 2 dc in next dc) around; join with slip st to first dc: 120 dc.

Rnd 5: Ch 1, sc in same st and in next 29 dc, skip next 30 dc (armhole), sc in next 30 dc, skip next 30 dc (armhole); join with slip st to both loops of first sc: 60 sc.

Rnd 6: Ch 4 **(counts as first dc plus ch 1, now and throughout)**, working in both loops, skip next sc, (dc in next sc, ch 1, skip next sc) around; join with slip st to first dc: 30 ch-1 sps.

Rnd 7: Slip st in first ch-1 sp, ch 3, 5 dc in next ch-1 sp, (dc in next ch-1 sp, 5 dc in next ch-1 sp) around; join with slip st to first dc: 15 5-dc groups.

Rnds 8 and 9: Ch 3, skip next 2 dc, 5 dc in next dc, skip next 2 dc, ★ dc in next dc, skip next 2 dc, 5 dc in next dc, skip next 2 dc; repeat from ★ around; join with slip st to first dc.

Rnds 10-12: Ch 4, skip next 2 dc, 5 dc in next dc, ch 1, skip next 2 dc, ★ dc in next dc, ch 1, skip next 2 dc, 5 dc in next dc, ch 1, skip next 2 dc; repeat from ★ around; join with slip st to first dc.

Rnds 13-15: Ch 5 **(counts as first dc plus ch 2, now and throughout)**, skip next 2 dc, 5 dc in next dc, ch 2, skip next 2 dc, ★ dc in next dc, ch 2, skip next 2 dc, 5 dc in next dc, ch 2, skip next 2 dc; repeat from ★ around; join with slip st to first dc changing to Red at end of Rnd 15 *(Fig. 28b, page 138)*.

Rnd 16: Ch 5, dc in same st, skip next 2 dc, (3 dc, ch 2, 3 dc) in next dc, skip next 2 dc, ★ (dc, ch 2, dc) in next dc, skip next 2 dc, (3 dc, ch 2, 3 dc) in next dc, skip next 2 dc; repeat from ★ around; join with slip st to first dc: 30 ch-2 sps.

Rnd 17: Slip st in first ch-2 sp, ch 1, sc in same sp, 10 dc in next ch-2 sp, (sc in next ch-2 sp, 10 dc in next ch-2 sp) around; join with slip st to Back Loop Only of first sc changing to White: 15 10-dc groups.
Rnd 18: Ch 1, working in Back Loops Only, sc in same st, ch 3, (sc in next st, ch 3) around; join with slip st to first sc, finish off.

BODICE RUFFLE

With **right** side of back facing and top of Dress toward you, join Red with slip st in free loop of first st on Rnd 4 **(Fig. 22a,**

page 136); ch 1, sc in same st, ch 3, (sc in next st, ch 3) around; join with slip st to first sc, finish off.

NECK EDGING

Fold Dress flat with armholes even at sides.
With **right** side of front facing and working through **both** thicknesses, join Red with slip st in first free loop of beginning ch **(Fig. 22b, page 136)**; ch 1, sc in same st and in next 23 chs; ch 10 (hanger); being careful not to twist ch, slip st in same st as last sc worked; finish off.

TIC-TAC-TOE GAME

This oversize tic-tac-toe game is a great way to beat the rainy day ho-hums. Crafted with sunny yellow and black worsted weight yarns, it allows youngsters to enjoy a classic pastime. Best of all, the entire set rolls up, so it's easy to take along!

Finished Size: 24¹/₂" square

MATERIALS
Worsted Weight Yarn:
    Yellow - 8 ounces, (230 grams, 525 yards)
    Black - 7 ounces, (200 grams, 460 yards)
Crochet hook, size I (5.50 mm) **or** size needed for gauge
Bobbin
1 yard of black felt
Sewing needle and thread
Glue

GAUGE: 7 sc and 7 rows = 2"

Gauge Swatch: 2" square
Ch 8 **loosely.**
Row 1: Sc in second ch from hook and in each ch across: 7 sc.
Rows 2-7: Ch 1, turn; sc in each sc across.
Finish off.

BOARD

Note: Wind a small amount of Black onto a bobbin. Work each stripe with separate yarn. Always keep the unused yarn to the wrong side of work.
With Yellow, ch 84 **loosely.**
Row 1 (Right side): Working in back ridge of chs **(Fig. 2a, page 133)**, sc in second ch from hook and in next 24 chs changing to Black in last sc worked **(Fig. 28a, page 138)**, do **not** cut yarn, sc in next 4 chs changing to Yellow in last sc worked, sc in next 25 chs changing to Black in last sc worked, sc in next 4 chs changing to Yellow in last sc worked, sc in each ch across: 83 sc.
Note: Loop a short piece of yarn around any stitch to mark Row 1 as **right** side.

Row 2: Ch 1, turn; sc in first 25 sc changing to Black in last sc worked, sc in next 4 sc changing to Yellow in last sc worked, sc in next 25 sc changing to Black in last sc worked, sc in next 4 sc changing to Yellow in last sc worked, sc in each sc across.
Rows 3-25: Repeat Row 2, 23 times; at end of Row 25, change to Black.
Rows 26-29: Ch 1, turn; sc in each sc across; at end of Row 29, change to Yellow.
Rows 30-54: Repeat Row 2, 25 times; at end of Row 54, change to Black.
Rows 55-83: Repeat Rows 26-54; do **not** finish off.

EDGING

Rnd 1: Ch 1, do **not** turn; sc evenly around working 3 sc in each corner; join with slip st to first sc.
Rnd 2: Ch 1, sc in each sc around working 3 sc in each corner sc; join with slip st to first sc, finish off.

X's (Make 5)

Holding 2 strands of Black together, ch 5 **loosely.**
Row 1 (Right side): Sc in second ch from hook and in each ch across: 4 sc.
Note: Mark Row 1 as **right** side.
Rows 2-16: Ch 1, turn; sc in each sc across.
Finish off.

FIRST SIDE

Row 1: With **right** side facing, join 2 strands of Black with sc in end of Row 7 **(see Joining With Sc, page 136)**; sc in end of next 3 rows: 4 sc.
Rows 2-6: Ch 1, turn; sc in each sc across.
Finish off.

SECOND SIDE

Row 1: With **right** side facing, join 2 strands of Black with sc in end of Row 10; sc in end of next 3 rows: 4 sc.

Rows 2-6: Ch 1, turn; sc in each sc across.

Edging: Ch 1, turn; slip st evenly around working (slip st, ch 1, slip st) in each corner; join with slip st to first slip st, finish off.

O's (Make 5)

Rnd 1 (Right side): Holding 2 strands of Yellow together, ch 4, 11 dc in fourth ch from hook; join with slip st to top of beginning ch: 12 sts.

Note: Mark Rnd 1 as **right** side.

Rnd 2: Ch 3, dc in same st, 2 dc in next dc and in each dc around; join with slip st to top of beginning ch-3 changing to Black: 24 sts.

Rnd 3: Ch 3, dc in same st, 2 dc in next dc and in each dc around; join with slip st to top of beginning ch-3: 48 sts.

Edging: Slip st in next dc and in each dc around; join with slip st to first st, finish off.

FINISHING

Cut a piece of felt same size as Board and sew to wrong side. Cut pieces of felt same size as X's and O's; glue to wrong side.

Pint-size partygoers will be delighted when you favor them with these comical clown keepsakes!
Sporting big felt smiles and polka-dot bow ties, they'll make funny reminders of a happy day.

Finished Size: 2½"w x 4"h

MATERIALS

Bedspread Weight Cotton Thread (size 10):

Clown #1

White - 17 yards
Pastel Variegated - 8 yards
Yellow - 19 yards
Violet - 10 yards

Clown #2

White - 17 yards
Pastel Variegated - 8 yards
Blue - 19 yards
Rose - 11 yards

Clown #3

White - 17 yards
Pastel Variegated - 8 yards
Green - 19 yards
Rose - 10 yards

Steel crochet hook, size 6 (1.80 mm)
Pink felt
Tapestry needle
Polyester fiberfill
Glue

Note: Gauge is not important. Clowns can be larger or smaller without changing the overall effect.

STITCH GUIDE

DECREASE (uses next 2 sc)
Pull up a loop in next 2 sc, YO and draw through all 3 loops on hook **(counts as one sc)**.

CLOWN #1

HEAD (Make 2)

Rnd 1 (Right side)**:** With White, ch 2, 10 hdc in second ch from hook; join with slip st to first hdc.
Note: Loop a short piece of thread around any stitch to mark Rnd 1 as **right** side.
Rnd 2: Ch 2 **(counts as first hdc, now and throughout)**, hdc in same st, 2 hdc in next hdc and in each hdc around; join with slip st to first hdc: 20 hdc.
Rnd 3: Ch 2, hdc in same st and in next hdc, (2 hdc in next hdc, hdc in next hdc) around; join with slip st to first hdc: 30 hdc.
Rnd 4: Ch 2, hdc in same st and in next 2 hdc, (2 hdc in next hdc, hdc in next 2 hdc) around; join with slip st to first hdc: 40 hdc.

Rnd 5: Ch 2, hdc in same st and in next 4 hdc, (2 hdc in next hdc hdc in next 4 hdc) around; join with slip st to first hdc: 48 hdc.
Rnd 6: Ch 1, sc in each hdc around; join with slip st to first sc, finish off leaving a long end for sewing on one piece.

NOSE

Rnd 1 (Right side)**:** With Pastel Variegated, ch 2, 6 sc in second ch from hook; do **not** join, place marker *(see Markers, page 136)*.
Rnd 2: 2 Sc in each sc around: 12 sc.
Rnd 3: Sc in each sc around.
Rnd 4: (Decrease, sc in next sc) 4 times; slip st in next sc, finish off leaving a long end for sewing: 8 sc.

EYE (Make 2)

With Violet, ch 2, 8 sc in second ch from hook; join with slip st to first sc, finish off leaving a long end for sewing.

HAT (Make 2)

With Yellow, ch 16 **loosely**.
Row 1: Sc in second ch from hook and in each ch across: 15 sc.
Row 2 (Right side)**:** Ch 1, turn; sc in each sc across.
Note: Mark Row 2 as **right** side.
Row 3: Ch 1, turn; decrease, sc in each sc across to last 2 sc, decrease: 13 sc.
Rows 4-9: Repeat Rows 2 and 3, 3 times: 7 sc.
Edging: Ch 1, turn; sc in each sc across; ch 1, sc in end of each row across; ch 1, working in free loops of beginning ch *(Fig. 22b, page 136)*, sc in each ch across; ch 1, sc in end of each row across, ch 1; join with slip st to first sc, finish off: 40 sc.

BUTTON (Make 2)

Rnd 1 (Right side)**:** With Violet, ch 2, 4 sc in second ch from hook; do **not** join, place marker.
Rnd 2: 2 Sc in each sc around; slip st in next sc, finish off leaving a long end for sewing: 8 sc.

BOW TIE

With Violet, ch 21 **loosely**.
Row 1 (Right side)**:** Hdc in third ch from hook and in each ch across: 20 sts.
Note: Mark Row 1 as **right** side.
Rows 2-6: Ch 2, turn; hdc in next hdc and in each st across. Finish off.
Edging: With **right** side facing, join Yellow with slip st in first hdc; ch 1, sc in each hdc across; sc in end of each row; sc in free loop of each ch across; sc in end of each row across; join with slip st to first sc, finish off: 52 sc.

BAND

With Yellow, ch 11 **loosely**.

Row 1: Sc in second ch from hook and in each ch across: 10 sc.

Rows 2 and 3: Ch 1, turn; sc in each sc across.

Finish off leaving a long end for sewing.

POLKA DOTS (Make 6)

With Yellow, ch 2, 8 sc in second ch from hook; join with slip st to first sc, finish off leaving a long end for sewing.

FINISHING

With **wrong** sides together and White, and working through **both** loops, whipstitch Head together *(Fig. 30a, page 139)*, stuffing lightly with polyester fiberfill before closing.

Using 3 strands of Pastel Variegated, each 1½" long, add fringe to sc at top of Head as desired for bangs *(Figs. 33a & b, page 139)*. Using 3 strands of Pastel Variegated, each 3" long, add fringe to sc at sides of Head.

Sew Buttons to **right** side of Hat, stuffing lightly with polyester fiberfill before closing.

With **wrong** sides together, whipstitch sides and top of Hat together. Stuff Hat lightly with polyester fiberfill; sew to top of Head.

Stuff Nose lightly with polyester fiberfill; sew to center of Head.

Sew Eyes to Head.

Using patterns, cut cheeks and mouth from felt and glue to Head.

Sew Polka Dots to Bow Tie.

Gather center of Bow Tie; place Band around gathered area and sew ends together.

Sew Bow Tie to bottom edge of Head.

CLOWN #2

Using the following colors, work same as Clown #1.

    Head - White

    Nose and Hair - Pastel Variegated

    Eyes, Hat, and Bow Tie - Blue

    Buttons, Bow Tie Edging, Band, and Polka Dots - Rose

Cheek (cut 2)

Mouth

CLOWN #3

Using the following colors, work same as Clown #1.

    Head - White

    Nose and Hair - Pastel Variegated

    Eyes, Buttons, and Bow Tie - Rose

    Hat, Bow Tie Edging, Band, and Polka Dots - Green

rock-a-bye collection

Showering a little one with sweet surprises is a joy few of us can resist, and handmade treasures are especially nice for showing your love. In this selection of darling baby accessories, you'll discover a snuggly bunting, keepsake bibs, adorable afghans, and an exquisite christening set to please parents and baby. How do we love babies — let us stitch the ways!

HEIRLOOM CHRISTENING SET

With baby dressed from head to toe in an heirloom christening set, memories of a momentous day will last a lifetime. This exquisite ensemble, crocheted with size 10 cotton thread, includes a bonnet, a gown, and booties. Each piece is embellished with satin ribbon and tiny ribbon rosebuds.

Finished Size: Newborn

MATERIALS

Bedspread Weight Cotton Thread (size 10):
   Complete Set - 1,540 yards
   Gown - 1,390 yards
   Bonnet - 70 yards
   Booties - 80 yards
Steel crochet hook, size 7 (1.65 mm) **or** size needed for gauge
Tapestry needle
Sewing needle and thread
1/8" wide ribbon:
   Gown - 3 yards
   Bonnet - 1¼ yards
   Booties - 1 yard
3/4" Ribbon rosebuds:
   Gown - 3
   Bonnet - 3
   Booties - 2
3 - 3/8" buttons for Gown

GAUGE: 18 dc and 8 rows = 2"
15 V-Sts and 16 rows = 4"

Gauge Swatch: 2" square
Ch 20 **loosely**.
Row 1: Dc in fourth ch from hook **(3 skipped chs count as first dc)** and in each ch across: 18 dc.
Rows 2-8: Ch 3 **(counts as first dc)**, turn; dc in next dc and in each dc across.
Finish off.

STITCH GUIDE

> **V-ST**
> (Dc, ch 1, dc) in st or sp indicated.
> **BEGINNING CLUSTER**
> Ch 2, (YO, insert hook in same sp, YO and pull up a loop, YO and draw through 2 loops on hook) twice, YO and draw through all 3 loops on hook *(Figs. 10a & b, page 134)*.
> **CLUSTER**
> ★ YO, insert hook in sp indicated, YO and pull up a loop, YO and draw through 2 loops on hook; repeat from ★ 2 times **more**, YO and draw through all 4 loops on hook.

GOWN

YOKE

Ch 89 **loosely**.

Row 1 (Right side)**:** Dc in fourth ch from hook and in next 5 chs, 3 dc in next ch, (dc in next 11 chs, 3 dc in next ch) 6 times, dc in last 7 chs: 101 sts.

Note: Loop a short piece of thread around any stitch to mark Row 1 as **right** side.

Row 2: Ch 3 **(counts as first dc, now and throughout)**, turn; dc in same st and in next 14 dc, 3 dc in next dc, (dc in next 13 dc, 3 dc in next dc) 5 times, dc in next 14 dc, 2 dc in last st: 115 dc.

Row 3: Ch 3, turn; dc in same st and in each dc across to last dc, 2 dc in last dc: 117 dc.

Row 4: Ch 3, turn; dc in next 9 dc, 3 dc in next dc, (dc in next 15 dc, 3 dc in next dc) 6 times, dc in last 10 dc: 131 dc.

Row 5: Ch 3, turn; dc in same st and in next 19 dc, 3 dc in next dc, (dc in next 17 dc, 3 dc in next dc) 5 times, dc in next 19 dc, 2 dc in last dc: 145 dc.

Row 6 (Eyelet row)**:** Ch 3, turn; dc in same st and in next 2 dc, ch 1, ★ skip next dc, dc in next dc, ch 1; repeat from ★ across to last 4 dc, skip next dc, dc in next 2 dc, 2 dc in last dc: 77 dc and 70 ch-1 sps.

Row 7: Ch 3, turn; working in each dc and in each ch-1 sp across, dc in next 12 sts, 3 dc in next dc, (dc in next 19 sts, 3 dc in next dc) 6 times, dc in last 13 sts: 161 dc.

Row 8: Ch 3, turn; dc in same st and in next 24 dc, 3 dc in next dc, (dc in next 21 dc, 3 dc in next dc) 5 times, dc in next 24 dc, 2 dc in last dc: 175 dc.

Row 9: Ch 3, turn; dc in same st and in next 14 dc, 3 dc in next dc, (dc in next 23 dc, 3 dc in next dc) 6 times, dc in next 14 dc, 2 dc in last dc: 191 dc.

Row 10: Ch 3, turn; dc in same st and in next 29 dc, 3 dc in next dc, (dc in next 25 dc, 3 dc in next dc) 5 times, dc in next 29 dc, 2 dc in last dc: 205 dc.

Note: Begin working in rounds.

Rnd 1: Ch 3, turn; dc in next 17 dc, 3 dc in next dc, (dc in next 27 dc, 3 dc in next dc) 6 times, dc in next 17 dc, 2 dc in last dc; join with slip st to first dc: 220 dc.

Rnd 2: Ch 1, do **not** turn; sc in first 28 dc, ch 33 **loosely**, skip next 55 dc (armhole), sc in next 55 dc, ch 33 **loosely**, skip next 55 dc (armhole), sc in last 27 dc; join with slip st to first sc, do **not** finish off: 110 sc.

SKIRT

Rnd 1 (Eyelet rnd)**:** Ch 4 **(counts as first dc plus ch 1, now and throughout)**, working in each sc and in each ch around, skip next sc, ★ dc in next st, ch 1, skip next st; repeat from ★ around; join with slip st to first dc: 88 ch-1 sps.

Rnd 2: Ch 4, dc in same st, work V-St in next 2 ch-1 sps, ★ work V-St in next dc, work V-St in next 2 ch-1 sps; repeat from ★ around; join with slip st to first dc: 132 V-Sts.

Rnd 3: Slip st in first ch-1 sp, ch 4, dc in same sp, work V-St in each V-St (ch-1 sp) around; join with slip st to first dc. Repeat Rnd 3 until Skirt measures 14", do **not** finish off.

EDGING

Rnd 1: Slip st in first ch-1 sp, ch 6, dc in same sp, ch 2, skip next V-St, sc in next V-St, ch 2, skip next V-St, ★ (dc, ch 3, dc) in next V-St, ch 2, skip next V-St, sc in next V-St, ch 2, skip next V-St; repeat from ★ around; join with slip st to third ch of beginning ch-6: 33 sc.

Rnd 2: Slip st in first ch-3 sp, work beginning Cluster in same sp, ch 2, (work Cluster, ch 2) twice in same sp, skip next 2 ch-2 sps, ★ (work Cluster, ch 2) 3 times in next ch-3 sp, skip next 2 ch-2 sps; repeat from ★ around; join with slip st to top of beginning Cluster: 99 Clusters.

Rnd 3: Slip st in first ch-2 sp, work (beginning Cluster, ch 2, Cluster) in same sp, (ch 2, work Cluster) twice in next ch-2 sp, ch 1, skip next ch-2 sp, ★ (work Cluster, ch 2) twice in next ch-2 sp, work (Cluster, ch 2, Cluster) in next ch-2 sp, ch 1, skip next ch-2 sp; repeat from ★ around; join with slip st to top of beginning Cluster.

Rnd 4: Slip st in first ch-2 sp, ch 1, (sc, ch 3, sc) in same sp and in each sp around; join with slip st to first sc, finish off.

SLEEVE

Rnd 1: With **right** side facing and working in skipped dc on Yoke and in free loops of ch at underarm *(Fig. 22b, page 136)* skip first 7 ch-1 sps and join thread with slip st in next ch; ch 1, sc in same st and in each sp and each ch across, sc in same dc as Skirt, sc in each dc across Yoke, sc in same dc as Skirt, sc in next st and in each sp and each st around; join with slip st to first sc: 90 sc.

Rnd 2: Ch 4, dc in same st, skip next 2 sc, work V-St in next sc, skip next sc, ★ work V-St in next sc, skip next 2 sc, work V-St in next sc, skip next sc; repeat from ★ around; join with slip st to first dc: 36 V-Sts.

Rnd 3: Slip st in first ch-1 sp, ch 4, dc in same sp, work V-St in next V-St and in each V-St around; join with slip st to first dc.

Rnds 4-12: Repeat Rnd 3, 9 times.

Rnd 13 (Eyelet rnd)**:** Slip st in first ch-1 sp, ch 4, (dc in next V-St, ch 1) around; join with slip st to first dc: 36 ch-1 sps.

Rnd 14: Slip st in first ch-1 sp, ch 6, dc in same sp, ch 2, skip next ch-1 sp, sc in next ch-1 sp, ch 2, skip next ch-1 sp, ★ (dc, ch 3, dc) in next ch-1 sp, ch 2, skip next ch-1 sp, sc in next ch-1 sp, ch 2, skip next ch-1 sp; repeat from ★ around; join with slip st to third ch of beginning ch-6: 9 sc.

Rnds 15-17: Work same as Skirt Edging Rnds 2-4.
Repeat for second Sleeve.

BUTTONHOLE BAND

Row 1: With **right** side facing and working in end of rows, join thread with slip st in first row of right back Yoke; ch 1, work 23 sc evenly spaced across.

Row 2 (Buttonhole row)**:** Ch 1, turn; sc in first 2 sc, ch 3, (skip next 3 sc, sc in next 5 sc, ch 3) twice, skip next 3 sc, sc in last 2 sc.

Row 3: Ch 1, turn; sc in first 2 sc, 3 sc in next ch-3 sp, (sc in next 5 sc, 3 sc in next ch-3 sp) twice, sc in last 2 sc; finish off: 23 sc.

BUTTON BAND

Row 1: With **right** side facing and working in end of rows, join thread with slip st in first row of left back Yoke; ch 1, work 23 sc evenly spaced across.

Rows 2 and 3: Ch 1, turn; sc in each sc across. Finish off.

FINISHING

Overlapping Buttonhole Band over Button Band, sew lower edges together.

Sew buttons to Button Band.

Beginning at back opening, weave a 22" length of ribbon through Eyelet row of Yoke; sew ends to wrong side of back.

Sew a ribbon rosebud to ribbon at center front.

Beginning at front, weave a 1½ yards length of ribbon through Eyelet rnd of Skirt and tie in a bow.

Beginning at top of each Sleeve, weave a 16" length of ribbon through Eyelet rnd and tie in a bow.

Sew a ribbon rosebud above bow on each Sleeve.

BONNET

BACK

Ch 6; join with slip st to form a ring.

Rnd 1 (Right side)**:** Ch 3 (**counts as first dc, now and throughout**), 2 dc in ring, ch 2, (3 dc in ring, ch 2) 5 times; join with slip st to first dc: 18 dc.

Note: Loop a short piece of thread around any stitch to mark Rnd 1 as **right** side.

Rnd 2: Slip st in next dc, ch 3, dc in same st and in next dc, 2 dc in next ch-2 sp, ch 2, skip next dc, ★ 2 dc in next dc, dc in next dc, 2 dc in next ch-2 sp, ch 2, skip next dc; repeat from ★ around; join with slip st to first dc: 30 dc.

Rnds 3-9: Slip st in next dc, ch 3, dc in same st and in each dc across to next ch-2 sp, 2 dc in ch-2 sp, ch 2, skip next dc, ★ 2 dc in next dc, dc in each dc across to next ch-2 sp, 2 dc in ch-2 sp, ch 2, skip next dc; repeat from ★ around; join with slip st to first dc: 114 dc.

Rnd 10: Ch 1, (sc in each dc across to next ch-2 sp, 2 sc in ch-2 sp) around; join with slip st to first sc, do **not** finish off: 126 sc.

CROWN

Row 1 (Right side)**:** Slip st in next 4 sc, ch 3, skip next sc, work V-St in next sc, (skip next 2 sc, work V-St in next sc) across to last 8 sc, skip next sc, dc in next sc, leave remaining 6 sc unworked: 38 V-Sts.

Rows 2-11: Ch 3, turn; work V-St in each V-St across to last dc, dc in last dc.

Row 12 (Eyelet row)**:** Ch 4, turn; (dc in next V-St, ch 1) across to last dc, dc in last dc: 39 sps.

Row 13: Ch 1, turn; sc in first dc, ch 2, skip next ch-1 sp, (dc, ch 3, dc) in next ch-1 sp, ch 2, ★ skip next ch-1 sp, sc in next ch-1 sp, ch 2, skip next ch-1 sp, (dc, ch 3, dc) in next ch-1 sp, ch 2; repeat from ★ across to last sp, skip next ch, sc in next ch: 11 sc.

Row 14: Ch 3, turn; skip first ch-2 sp, work Cluster in next ch-3 sp, (ch 2, work Cluster) twice in same sp, ★ skip next 2 ch-2 sps, (ch 2, work Cluster) 3 times in next ch-3 sp; repeat from ★ across to last ch-2 sp, skip next ch-2 sp, dc in last sc: 30 Clusters.

Row 15: Ch 3, turn; (work Cluster, ch 2) twice in next ch-2 sp, work (Cluster, ch 2, Cluster) in next ch-2 sp, ★ ch 1, skip next ch-2 sp, (work Cluster, ch 2) twice in next ch-2 sp, work (Cluster, ch 2, Cluster) in next ch-2 sp; repeat from ★ across, dc in last dc; do **not** finish off: 40 Clusters.

EDGING

Row 1: Ch 1, work 29 sc evenly spaced across end of rows to unworked sts on Back; sc in next 5 sc, 2 sc in next sc, sc in next 4 sts; work 29 sc evenly spaced across end of rows: 69 sc.

Row 2 (Eyelet row)**:** Ch 4, turn; skip next sc, dc in next sc, (ch 1, skip next sc, dc in next sc) across: 34 sps.

Trim: Turn; slip st in first ch-1 sp, (sc, ch 3, sc) in same sp and in each ch-1 sp across to last sp, (sc, ch 3, sc) twice in last sp, (sc, ch 3, sc) in each sp across Row 15 of Crown, (sc, ch 3, sc) in same sp as first sc; join with slip st to first sc, finish off.

FINISHING

Weave a 12" length of ribbon through Eyelet row of Crown; sew ends to wrong side.

Weave a 33" length of ribbon through Eyelet row of Edging. Sew a ribbon rosebud to first ribbon at each corner and at center of Bonnet.

Continued on page 85.

Fashioned with soft brushed acrylic yarn, this adorable baby bunting will keep Jack Frost from nipping at the nose of a precious little one. The cozy chill-chaser features an attached hood and zippered front opening to make dressing baby easy. Created in soft yellow, it's a sweet shower gift for a little boy or girl.

Finished Size: Newborn to 6 months

MATERIALS

Worsted Weight Brushed Acrylic Yarn,
  15 ounces, (430 grams, 950 yards)
Crochet hooks, sizes F (3.75 mm) **and** H (5.00 mm) **or**
  sizes needed for gauge
18" zipper
Yarn needle
Sewing needle and thread

GAUGE: In pattern, with large size hook (size H),
  3 pattern repeats = 4"
  In ribbing pattern, with small size hook (size F),
  4 sc and 3 rows = 1"

Gauge Swatch: $4^1/_2$"w x $3^1/_2$"h
With large size hook, ch 16 **loosely**.
Row 1: Sc in second ch from hook and in each ch across: 15 sc.
Row 2: Ch 3 **(counts as first dc, now and throughout)**, turn; dc in next sc, skip next sc, work V-St in next sc, (skip next sc, dc in next sc, skip next sc, work V-St in next sc) twice, skip next sc, dc in last 2 sc: 3 V-Sts.
Rows 3-6: Work same as Body Rows 9 and 10, twice. Finish off.

STITCH GUIDE

V-ST
(Dc, ch 3, dc) in st or sp indicated.
PUFF ST
(YO, insert hook in sp indicated, YO and pull up a loop **even** with loop on hook) 4 times *(Fig. 13, page 134)*, YO and draw through all 9 loops on hook.

YOKE

With large size hook, ch 10 **loosely**.
Row 1: Sc in second ch from hook and in each ch across: 9 sc.
Note: Work in Back Loops Only throughout Yoke *(Fig. 21, page 136)*.
Row 2: Ch 1, turn; sc in each sc across.
Row 3: Ch 1, turn; sc in first 7 sc, leave remaining 2 sc unworked: 7 sc.
Row 4: Ch 1, turn; sc in each sc across.
Row 5: Ch 1, turn; sc in each sc across, sc in next 2 unworked sc on second row below previous row: 9 sc.

Rows 6-66: Repeat Rows 2-5, 15 times, then repeat Row 2 once **more**; do **not** finish off.

BODY

Row 1 (Right side)**:** Ch 1, working in end of rows, 2 sc in first row, sc in each row across: 67 sc.
Row 2: Ch 5, turn; skip next sc, dc in next sc, ★ ch 2, skip next sc, dc in next sc; repeat from ★ across: 33 sps.
Row 3 (Ruffle)**:** Ch 3, turn; skip first dc, (sc, ch 3) 4 times around post of next dc and around each dc across to beginning ch-5 *(Fig. 15, page 135)*, skip next 2 chs, slip st in next ch.
Row 4: Ch 1, turn; working in sts and sps on Row 2, sc in same st and in first ch-2 sp, sc in next dc, (2 sc in next ch-2 sp, sc in next dc) across: 99 sc.
Row 5: Ch 1, turn; slip st in each sc across.
Row 6: Ch 3 **(counts as first dc, now and throughout)**, turn; working in sc on Row 4, dc in next sc, ★ skip next sc, work V-St in next sc, skip next sc, dc in next sc; repeat from ★ across to last sc, dc in last sc: 24 V-Sts.
Row 7: Ch 3, turn; † dc in next dc, [work (Puff St, ch 3, Puff St) in next V-St (ch-3 sp), dc in next dc] 4 times †, ch 7 **loosely**, skip next 4 V-Sts (armhole), dc in next dc, [work (Puff St, ch 3, Puff St) in next V-St, dc in next dc] 8 times, ch 7 **loosely**, skip next 4 V-Sts (armhole), repeat from † to † once, dc in last dc: 32 Puff Sts.
Row 8: Ch 3, turn; dc in next dc, (work V-St in next ch-3 sp, dc in next dc) 4 times, † skip next ch, work V-St in next ch, skip next ch, dc in next ch, skip next ch, work V-St in next ch, skip next ch, dc in next dc †, (work V-St in next ch-3 sp, dc in next dc) 8 times, repeat from † to † once, (work V-St in next ch-3 sp, dc in next dc) 4 times, dc in last dc: 20 V-Sts.
Row 9: Ch 3, turn; ★ dc in next dc, work (Puff St, ch 3, Puff St) in next V-St; repeat from ★ across to last 2 dc, dc in last 2 dc.
Row 10: Ch 3, turn; (dc in next dc, work V-st in next ch-3 sp) across to last 2 dc, dc in last 2 dc.
Repeat Rows 9 and 10 for pattern until piece measures 17" from beginning, ending by working Row 10, do **not** finish off.
Note: Begin working in rounds.
Rnd 1: Ch 3, turn; ★ dc in next dc, work (Puff St, ch 3, Puff St) in next V-St; repeat from ★ across to last 2 dc, dc in last 2 dc; join with slip st to first dc.

Rnd 2: Ch 3, turn; skip next 2 dc, work V-st in next ch-3 sp, (dc in next dc, work V-St in next ch-3 sp) around to last dc, skip last dc; join with slip st to first dc: 20 V-Sts.

Rnd 3: Ch 3, turn; work (Puff St, ch 3, Puff St) in next V-St, ★ dc in next dc, work (Puff St, ch 3, Puff St) in next V-St; repeat from ★ around; join with slip st to first dc.

Rnd 4: Ch 5, turn; dc in next ch-3 sp, ch 2, (dc in next dc, ch 2, dc in next ch-3 sp, ch 2) around; join with slip st to third ch of beginning ch-5: 40 ch-2 sps.

Rnd 5 (Ruffle): Ch 1, turn; (sc, ch 3) 4 times around beginning ch and around post of each dc around; join with slip st to first sc.

Rnd 6: Turn; slip st in top of beginning ch on Rnd 4, ch 3, working in dc on Rnd 4, work V-St in next dc, (dc in next dc, work V-St in next dc) around; join with slip st to first dc: 20 V-Sts.

Rnd 7: Repeat Rnd 3.

Rnd 8: Ch 3, turn; work V-St in next ch-3 sp, (dc in next dc, work V-St in next ch-3 sp) around; join with slip st to first dc.

Rnd 9: Repeat Rnd 3; finish off.

BOTTOM

Row 1: With **wrong** side facing and large size hook, skip 4 ch-3 sps to **right** of joining and join yarn with slip st in next dc; ch 3, (work V-St in next ch-3 sp, dc in next dc) 8 times, leave remaining 12 ch-3 sps unworked: 8 V-Sts.

Row 2: Ch 3, turn; ★ work (Puff St, ch 3, Puff St) in next V-St, dc in next dc; repeat from ★ across.

Row 3: Ch 3, turn; (work V-St in next ch-3 sp, dc in next dc) across.

Rows 4 and 5: Repeat Rows 2 and 3.
Finish off.
Sew bottom seam.

SLEEVE

Rnd 1: With **right** side facing and large size hook, join yarn with slip st in free loop of center ch at underarm *(Fig. 22b, page 136)*; ch 3, work (Puff St, ch 3, Puff St) in sp after next V-St, dc in same st as next dc, [work (Puff St, ch 3, Puff St) in next V-St, dc in next dc] 4 times, work (Puff St, ch 3, Puff St) in sp before next V-St; join with slip st to first dc: 6 ch-3 sps.

Rnd 2: Ch 3, turn; work V-St in next ch-3 sp, (dc in next dc, work V-St in next ch-3 sp) around; join with slip st to first dc: 6 V-Sts.

Rnd 3: Ch 3, turn; work (Puff St, ch 3, Puff St) in next V-St, ★ dc in next dc, work (Puff St, ch 3, Puff St) in next V-St; repeat from ★ around; join with slip st to first dc.

Rnds 4-6: Repeat Rnds 2 and 3 once, then repeat Rnd 2 once **more**.

Rnd 7: Ch 1, turn; sc in same st, 2 sc in next V-St, (sc in next dc, 2 sc in next V-St) around; join with slip st to first sc, do **not** finish off: 18 sc.

RIBBING

Change to small size hook.

Ch 11 **loosely**.

Row 1: Sc in sixth ch from hook and in next 5 chs, slip st in first 2 sc on Rnd 7 of Sleeve: 6 sc.

Row 2: Turn; skip first 2 slip sts, sc in Back Loop Only of each sc across: 6 sc.

Row 3: Ch 5, turn; sc in Back Loop Only of each sc across, slip st in next 2 sc on Rnd 7 of Sleeve.

Repeat Rows 2 and 3 around, ending by working Row 2; finish off leaving a long end for sewing.

Sew seam.

Repeat for second Sleeve.

YOKE EDGING

With **right** side facing and large size hook, skip first 4 ribs and join yarn with slip st in next rib; ch 1, sc in end of next 23 ribs, slip st in next rib, leave remaining 4 ribs unworked; finish off.

HOOD

RIBBING

With small size hook, ch 11 **loosely**.

Row 1: Sc in sixth ch from hook and in next 5 chs: 6 sc.

Row 2: Ch 1, turn; sc in Back Loop Only of each sc across.

Row 3: Ch 5, turn; sc in Back Loop Only of each sc across.

Rows 4-47: Repeat Rows 2 and 3, 22 times; do **not** finish off.

SIDES

Change to large size hook.

Row 1: Ch 5, working in end of rows, skip first 2 rows, dc in next row, (ch 2, skip next row, dc in next row) across: 23 sps.

Row 2 (Right side - Ruffle): Ch 3, turn; skip first dc, (sc, ch 3) 4 times around post of next dc and around each dc across to beginning ch-5, skip next 2 chs, slip st in next ch.

Row 3: Turn; working in ch-2 sps of Row 1, slip st in first sp, ch 3, (work V-St in next ch-2 sp, dc in next ch-2 sp) across: 11 V-Sts.

Row 4: Ch 3, turn; ★ work (Puff St, ch 3, Puff St) in next V-St, dc in next dc; repeat from ★ across.

Row 5: Ch 3, turn; (work V-St in next ch-3 sp, dc in next dc) across.

Rows 6-9: Repeat Rows 4 and 5, twice.

Row 10: Ch 3, turn; [work (Puff St, ch 3, Puff St) in next V-St, dc in next dc] twice, [work (Puff St, ch 3, Puff St) in next V-St, dc in next V-St] 3 times, [work (Puff St, ch 3, Puff St) in next V-St, dc in next dc] 3 times; finish off leaving a long end for sewing: 8 ch-3 sps.

Fold Hood in half along last row and sew back seam.

NECK EDGING

Row 1: With **right** side of Hood facing, large size hook, and working in free loops of beginning ch on Ribbing and across end of rows, join yarn with slip st in first st; ch 1, sc in same st, work 33 sc evenly spaced across: 34 sc.

Row 2 (Eyelet row): Ch 4, turn; skip first 3 sc, hdc in next sc, ch 2, skip next 2 sc, hdc in next sc) across: 11 sps.

Row 3: Ch 1, turn; sc in each hdc and in each ch-2 sp across to last sp, sc in last sp and in next ch; finish off leaving a long end for sewing: 23 sc.

With **wrong** sides together, matching sc on Neck Edging of Hood and Yoke Edging, and working through **both** loops, whipstitch pieces together *(Fig. 30a, page 139)*.

CORD

With large size hook, make a 24" chain, slip st **loosely** in second ch from hook and in each ch across; finish off. Weave cord through Eyelet row on Neck Edging. Add fringe to each end of cord using 4 strands, each 6" long *(Figs. 33a & b, page 139)*.

Sew zipper into front opening.

HEIRLOOM CHRISTENING SET

Continued from page 81.

BOOTIES

SOLE

Ch 26 **loosely**.

Rnd 1 (Right side): (Dc, work 2 V-Sts) in fifth ch from hook (4 skipped chs count as first dc plus ch 1), (skip next 2 chs, work V-St in next ch) 6 times, skip next 2 chs, work 3 V-Sts in last ch; working in free loops of beginning ch *(Fig. 22b, page 136)*, (skip next 2 chs, work V-St in next ch) 6 times, skip remaining chs; join with slip st to first dc: 18 ch-1 sps.

Note: Loop a short piece of thread around any stitch to mark Rnd 1 as **right** side.

Rnd 2: Slip st in first ch-1 sp, ch 4 **(counts as first dc plus ch 1, now and throughout)**, (dc, work V-St) in same sp, work 2 V-Sts in each of next 2 V-Sts (ch-1 sp), work V-St in next 6 V-Sts, work 2 V-Sts in each of next 3 V-Sts, work V-St in last 6 V-Sts; join with slip st to first dc: 24 V-Sts.

Rnd 3: Slip st in first ch-1 sp, ch 4, (dc, work V-St) in same sp, (work V-St in next V-St, work 2 V-Sts in next V-St) twice, work V-St in next 7 V-Sts, work 2 V-Sts in next V-St, (work V-St in next V-St, work 2 V-Sts in next V-St) twice, work V-St in last 7 V-Sts; join with slip st to first dc: 30 V-Sts.

Rnds 4-6: Slip st in first ch-1 sp, ch 4, dc in same sp, work V-St in each V-St around; join with slip st to first dc, do **not** finish off.

INSTEP

Row 1: Slip st in first ch-1 sp, work V-St in next 4 V-Sts, slip st in next V-St, ch 3, slip st in next V-St: 4 V-Sts.

Rows 2-4: Turn; work V-St in next 4 V-Sts, slip st in next V-St on Rnd 6 of Sole, ch 3, slip st in next V-St.

Row 5: Turn; work V-St in next 4 V-Sts, slip st in next V-St on Sole; do **not** finish off.

CUFF

Rnd 1: Ch 4, do **not** turn; dc in same sp, work V-St in next 16 V-Sts on Sole, work V-St in same sp as previous slip st, work V-St in next 4 V-Sts on Instep; join with slip st to first dc: 22 V-Sts.

Rnd 2 (Eyelet rnd): Slip st in first ch-1 sp, ch 4, (dc in next V-St, ch 1) around; join with slip st to first dc: 22 ch-1 sps.

Rnd 3: Ch 1, sc in same st and in next ch-1 sp, sc in next dc, (2 sc in next ch-1 sp, sc in next dc) around to last ch-1 sp, sc in last ch-1 sp; join with slip st to first sc: 64 sc.

Rnd 4: Slip st in next 2 sc, ch 1, sc in same st, ch 2, skip next 3 sc, (dc, ch 3, dc) in next sc, ch 2, ★ skip next 3 sc, sc in next sc, ch 2, skip next 3 sc, (dc, ch 3, dc) in next sc, ch 2; repeat from ★ around; join with slip st to first sc: 8 sc.

Rnd 5: Slip st in next 3 sts and in next ch-3 sp, work beginning Cluster in same sp, ch 2, (work Cluster, ch 2) twice in same sp, skip next 2 ch-2 sps, ★ (work Cluster, ch 2) 3 times in next ch-3 sp, skip next 2 ch-2 sps; repeat from ★ around; join with slip st to top of beginning Cluster: 24 Clusters.

Rnd 6: Slip st in first ch-2 sp, work (beginning Cluster, ch 2, Cluster) in same sp, (ch 2, work Cluster) twice in next ch-2 sp, ch 1, skip next ch-2 sp, ★ (work Cluster, ch 2) twice in next ch-2 sp, work (Cluster, ch 2, Cluster) in next ch-2 sp, ch 1, skip next ch-2 sp; repeat from ★ around; join with slip st to top of beginning Cluster: 32 Clusters.

Rnd 7: Slip st in first ch-2 sp, ch 1, (sc, ch 3, sc) in same sp and in each sp around; join with slip st to first sc, finish off.

Beginning at front, weave an 18" length of ribbon through Eyelet rnd on Cuff and tie in a bow.
Sew ribbon rosebud to center of Instep at base of Cuff.

Destined to become keepsakes, these beautiful bibs are ideal for birthdays or other occasions. They're made from handkerchief linen and finished with fine edgings worked in cluster and picot stitches.

Finished Size: Edging #1: 7³/4" x 8¹/2"
Edging #2: 6³/4" x 7¹/2"

MATERIALS
Cotton Crochet Thread (size 30):
   Edging #1 - 56 yards
   Edging #2 - 32 yards
Steel crochet hook, size 10 (1.30 mm) **or** size needed for gauge
Typing paper
Pins
Sewing needle and thread
2 - 12" length of ¹/8" wide ribbon **each**
Handkerchief linen - 8" square **each**

GAUGE: 10 sc and 8 rows = 1"

Gauge Swatch: 2" square
Ch 21 **loosely.**
Row 1: Sc in second ch from hook and in each ch across: 20 sc.
Row 2-16: Ch 1, turn; sc in each sc across.
Finish off.

EDGING #1
STITCH GUIDE

CLUSTER (uses next 3 dc)
★ YO, insert hook in **next** dc, YO and pull up a loop, YO and draw through 2 loops on hook; repeat from ★ 2 times **more**, YO and draw through all 4 loops on hook (*Figs. 11a & b, page 134*).
PICOT
Ch 3, slip st in side of st just worked (*Fig. 27, page 138*).

Ch 243; being careful not to twist ch, join with slip st to form a ring.
Rnd 1 (Right side): 2 Sc in first ch, sc in next 9 chs, 3 sc in next ch, sc in next 65 chs, 3 sc in next ch, sc in next 53 chs, 3 sc in next ch, sc in next 65 chs, 3 sc in next ch, sc in next 9 chs, 3 sc in next ch, sc in last 36 chs, sc in same st as first sc; join with slip st to first sc: 255 sc.
Note: Loop a short piece of thread around any stitch to mark Rnd 1 as **right** side.
Rnd 2: Ch 1, sc in same st and in each sc across to next corner sc, (5 sc in corner sc, sc in each sc across to next corner sc) 4 times, 3 sc in corner sc, sc in each sc across, 2 sc in same st as first sc; join with slip st to first sc: 275 sc.

Rnd 3: Ch 4, ★ skip next sc, (hdc in next sc, ch 2, skip next sc) across to next corner sc, (hdc, ch 2) 3 times in corner sc; repeat from ★ 3 times **more**, skip next sc, hdc in next sc, (ch 2, skip next sc, hdc in next sc) 6 times, 2 sc in next sc, sc in each sc across to last sc, 2 sc in last sc; join with slip st to second ch of beginning ch-4: 124 ch-2 sps.
Note: Begin working in rows.
Row 1: Ch 3, (3 dc in next hdc, dc in next hdc) around to last hdc, leave remaining sts unworked: 62 3-dc groups.
Row 2: Ch 4, **turn**; work Cluster, ch 1, (dc in next dc, ch 1, work Cluster, ch 1) twice, (dc in next dc, ch 3, work Cluster, ch 3) twice, ★ (dc in next dc, ch 1, work Cluster, ch 1) across to within 4 dc of next corner dc, (dc in next dc, ch 3, work Cluster, ch 3) twice; repeat from ★ 2 times **more**, dc in next dc, (ch 1, work Cluster, ch 1, dc in next dc) 3 times: 62 Clusters.
Row 3: Ch 1, turn; sc in first dc, ch 3, dc in next Cluster, work Picot, ch 3, (sc in next dc, ch 3, dc in next Cluster, work Picot, ch 3) twice, (sc in next dc, ch 5, dc in next Cluster, work Picot, ch 5) twice, ★ (sc in next dc, ch 3, dc in next Cluster, work Picot, ch 3) across to within one dc of next corner dc, (sc in next dc, ch 5, dc in next Cluster, work Picot, ch 5) twice; repeat from ★ 2 times **more**, sc in next dc, (ch 3, dc in next Cluster, work Picot, ch 3, sc in next dc) 3 times; finish off.

EDGING #2
STITCH GUIDE

PICOT
Ch 4, slip st in side of st just worked (*Fig. 27, page 138*).

Ch 245; being careful not to twist ch, join with slip st to form a ring.
Rnd 1 (Right side): Sc in first 11 chs, 3 sc in next ch, sc in next 65 chs, 3 sc in next ch, sc in next 53 chs, 3 sc in next ch, sc in next 65 chs, 3 sc in next ch, sc in next 10 chs, 3 sc in next ch, sc in last 36 chs, 2 sc in same st as first sc; join with slip st to first sc: 257 sc.
Note: Loop a short piece of thread around any stitch to mark Rnd 1 as **right** side.
Rnd 2: Ch 7, skip next 3 sc, dc in next 8 sc, (dc, ch 4, dc) in next corner sc, dc in next 8 sc, ★ (ch 4, skip next 3 sc, dc in next 9 sc) across to next corner, ch 4, dc in same corner sc, dc in next 8 sc; repeat from ★ 2 times **more**, ch 4, skip next 3 sc, dc in next sc, 2 sc in next sc, sc in each sc across to last sc, 2 sc in last sc; join with slip st to third ch of beginning ch-7: 20 sps.

Rnd 3: Ch 1, sc in same st, ch 2, sc in next sp, work Picot, ch 2, sc in next dc, ★ ch 2, skip next 3 dc, dc in next dc, work Picot, (ch 1, dc in same dc, work Picot) 4 times, ch 2, skip next 3 dc, sc in next dc, ch 2, sc in next ch-4 sp, work Picot, ch 2, sc in next dc; repeat from ★ around to next sc, ch 1, (slip st in next sc, ch 1) across; join with slip st to first sc, finish off.

FINISHING

Wash, dry, and press fabric. Trace pattern, page 142, onto typing paper; cut out traced pattern. Pin pattern to linen on fold; cut out Bib. Press edges of Bib ⅛" to wrong side; press ⅛" to wrong side again and hem. Pin Edging on right side along hemmed edge and sew in place.

Sew ribbon to corner of neck edge of Bib for ties.

DELIGHTFULLY DELICATE WRAP

Snuggle a "beary" special someone in this delicate afghan! Featuring a variety of cluster stitches, the softly colored wrap is worked in squares using sport weight yarn and completed with a sweet picot edging.

Finished Size: 37" x 50"

MATERIALS

Sport Weight Yarn:
   White - 18 ounces, (510 grams, 1,818 yards)
   Variegated - 2 ounces, (60 grams, 165 yards)
Crochet hook, size F (3.75 mm) **or** size needed for gauge
Yarn needle

GAUGE: Each Square = 6½"

Gauge Swatch: 3" in diameter
Work same as Square through Rnd 2.

STITCH GUIDE

BEGINNING TR CLUSTER

Ch 3, ★ YO twice, insert hook in sp indicated, YO and pull up a loop, (YO and draw through 2 loops on hook) twice; repeat from ★ once **more**, YO and draw through all 3 loops on hook *(Figs. 10a & b, page 134)*.

TR CLUSTER

★ YO twice, insert hook in sp indicated, YO and pull up a loop, (YO and draw through 2 loops on hook) twice; repeat from ★ 2 times **more**, YO and draw through all 4 loops on hook.

DC CLUSTER

★ YO, insert hook in sp indicated, YO and pull up a loop, YO and draw through 2 loops on hook; repeat from ★ 2 times **more**, YO and draw through all 4 loops on hook.

PICOT

Ch 3, slip st in third ch from hook.

SQUARE (Make 35)

With Variegated, ch 4; join with slip st to form a ring.

Rnd 1 (Right side): Work beginning tr Cluster in ring, ch 3, (work tr Cluster in ring, ch 3) 7 times; join with slip st to top of beginning tr Cluster, finish off: 8 ch-3 sps.

Note: Loop a short piece of yarn around any stitch to mark Rnd 1 as **right** side.

Rnd 2: With **right** side facing, join White with slip st in any tr Cluster; ch 3 **(counts as first dc, now and throughout)**, 5 dc in next ch-3 sp, (dc in next tr Cluster, 5 dc in next ch-3 sp) around; join with slip st to first dc: 48 dc.

Rnd 3: Ch 1, sc in same st, ★ ch 3, skip next dc, sc in next dc; repeat from ★ around to last dc, ch 1, skip last dc, hdc in first sc to form last sp: 24 sps.

Rnd 4: Ch 1, sc in same sp, ch 6, sc in next ch-3 sp, ★ (ch 3, sc in next ch-3 sp) 5 times, ch 6, sc in next ch-3 sp; repeat from ★ 2 times **more**, (ch 3, sc in next ch-3 sp) 4 times, ch 1, hdc in first sc to form last sp.

Rnd 5: Ch 5, ★ † work (dc Cluster, ch 3, tr Cluster, ch 3, dc Cluster) in next loop, ch 2, dc in next ch-3 sp, ch 2, hdc in next ch-3 sp, ch 2, sc in next ch-3 sp, ch 2, hdc in next ch-3 sp, ch 2 †, dc in next ch-3 sp, ch 2; repeat from ★ 2 times **more**, then repeat from † to † once; join with slip st to third ch of beginning ch-5: 32 sps.

Rnd 6: Slip st in first ch-2 sp, ch 3, dc in same sp, ★ † dc in next dc Cluster, 3 dc in next ch-3 sp, 3 dc in next tr Cluster and in next ch-3 sp, dc in next dc Cluster, 2 dc in each of next 3 ch-2 sps, dc in next sc †, 2 dc in each of next 3 ch-2 sps; repeat from ★ 2 times **more**, then repeat from † to † once, 2 dc in each of last 2 ch-2 sps; join with slip st to first dc: 96 dc.

Rnd 7: Ch 3, dc in next dc and in each dc around working (2 dc, ch 1, 2 dc) in each corner dc; join with slip st to first dc, finish off: 108 dc.

ASSEMBLY

With **wrong** sides together and White, and working through **both** loops, whipstitch Squares together *(Fig. 30a, page 139)*. Form 5 vertical strips of 7 Squares each, then whipstitch strips together, securing seam at each joining.

EDGING

Rnd 1: With **right** side facing, join Variegated with sc in any dc *(see Joining With Sc, page 136)*; sc in next dc and in each dc and each joining around working 3 sc in each corner ch-1 sp; join with slip st to first sc.

Rnd 2: Ch 1, sc in same st and in each sc around working 3 sc in each corner sc; join with slip st to first sc, finish off.

Rnd 3: With **right** side facing, join White with sc in any corner sc; sc in same st and in each sc across to next corner sc, ★ 3 sc in corner sc, sc in each sc across to next corner sc; repeat from ★ around, sc in same st as first sc; join with slip st to first sc.

Rnd 4: Ch 1, sc in same st, ch 7, ★ † skip next 2 sc, sc in next sc, ch 7, (skip next 3 sc, sc in next sc, ch 7) across to within 2 sc of next corner sc, skip next 2 sc †, (sc, ch 7) twice in corner sc; repeat from ★ 2 times **more**, then repeat from † to † once, sc in same st as first sc, ch 3, tr in first sc to form last loop.

Rnd 5: Work (beginning tr Cluster, ch 4, dc Cluster) in same sp, sc in next loop, ★ work (dc Cluster, ch 4, tr Cluster, ch 4, dc Cluster) in next loop, sc in next loop; repeat from ★ around, work dc Cluster in same loop as beginning tr Cluster, ch 4; join with slip st to top of beginning tr Cluster.

Rnd 6: Slip st in first ch-4 sp, ch 1, (3 sc, work Picot, 3 sc) in same sp, sc in next sc, (3 sc, work Picot) twice in next ch-4 sp, ★ (3 sc, work Picot, 3 sc) in next ch-4 sp, sc in next sc, (3 sc, work Picot) twice in next ch-4 sp; repeat from ★ around; join with slip st to first sc, finish off.

GRANDPA'S BUDDY AFGHAN

Tickle Grandpa's little buddy with a cozy blanket sized just for him! This unique charmer is worked in small squares, which are whipstitched together. A pleasing combination of blue and white sport weight yarn makes this afghan a classic.

Finished Size: 36" x 47"

MATERIALS

Sport Weight Yarn:
　　Blue - 17 ounces, (480 grams, 1,805 yards)
　　White - 8 ounces, (230 grams, 850 yards)
　　Crochet hook, size E (3.50 mm) **or** size needed for gauge
　　Yarn needle

GAUGE SWATCH: 3³/₄" square
Work same as Square.

STITCH GUIDE

LONG SINGLE CROCHET (abbreviated Long sc)
Working **around** previous rnd, insert hook in beginning ring, YO and pull up a loop **even** with loop on hook, YO and draw through both loops on hook *(Fig. 9, page 134)*.

CLUSTER
YO, insert hook in same sp as last Cluster made, YO and pull up a loop, YO and draw through 2 loops on hook, YO, insert hook in next ch-3 sp, YO and pull up a loop, YO and draw through 2 loops on hook, YO and draw through all 3 loops on hook *(Figs. 11a & b, page 134)*.

FRONT POST DOUBLE CROCHET (abbreviated FPdc)
YO, insert hook from **front** to **back** around posts of Cluster one rnd **below** next dc *(Fig. 16, page 135)*, YO and pull up a loop, (YO and draw through 2 loops on hook) twice. Skip dc behind FPdc.

SQUARE (Make 108)

With Blue, ch 4; join with slip st to form a ring.
Rnd 1 (Right side): Ch 3 **(counts as first dc, now and throughout)**, 15 dc in ring; join with slip st to first dc, finish off: 16 dc.
Note: Loop a short piece of yarn around any stitch to mark Rnd 1 as **right** side.
Rnd 2: With **right** side facing, join White with sc in any dc *(see Joining With Sc, page 136)*; ch 3, work Long sc, ch 3, skip dc behind Long sc, ★ sc in next dc, ch 3, work Long sc, ch 3, skip dc behind Long sc; repeat from ★ around; join with slip st to first sc, finish off: 16 ch-3 sps.
Rnd 3: With **right** side facing, join Blue with slip st in any ch-3 sp; [ch 2, dc in next ch-3 sp **(counts as first Cluster)**], (ch 1, work Cluster) 3 times, ★ ch 5, work Cluster, (ch 1, work

Cluster) 3 times; repeat from ★ around working last Cluster in same sp as first Cluster, ch 5; skip beginning ch-2 and join with slip st to first dc, finish off: 16 Clusters and 4 ch-5 sps.
Rnd 4: With **right** side facing, join White with slip st in any corner ch-5 sp; ch 3, (2 dc, ch 4, 3 dc) in same sp, dc in next Cluster, (dc in next ch-1 sp and in next Cluster) 3 times, ★ (3 dc, ch 4, 3 dc) in next corner ch-5 sp, dc in next Cluster, (dc in next ch-1 sp and in next Cluster) 3 times; repeat from ★ around; join with slip st to first dc, finish off: 52 dc and 4 ch-4 sps.
Rnd 5: With **right** side facing, join Blue with sc in any corner ch-4 sp; (sc, ch 2, 2 sc) in same sp, sc in next 3 dc, work FPdc, (sc in next dc, work FPdc) 3 times, sc in next 3 dc, ★ (2 sc, ch 2, 2 sc) in next corner ch-4 sp, sc in next 3 dc, work FPdc, (sc in next dc, work FPdc) 3 times, sc in next 3 dc; repeat from ★ around; join with slip st to first sc: 68 sts and 4 ch-2 sps.
Rnd 6: Ch 1, sc in same st and in each st around working 3 sc in each corner ch-2 sp; join with slip st to first sc, finish off: 80 sc.

ASSEMBLY

With **wrong** sides together and Blue, and working through **inside** loops only, whipstitch Squares together *(Fig. 30b, page 139)*. Form 9 vertical strips of 12 Squares each, then whipstitch strips together, securing seam at each joining.

EDGING

Rnd 1: With **right** side facing and working in Back Loops Only *(Fig. 21, page 136)*, join Blue with slip st in first sc to left of any corner sc; ch 1, work 19 sc across each Square working sc in each joining and 3 sc in each corner sc; join with slip st to first sc.
Rnd 2: Ch 3, dc in both loops of next sc and in each sc around working 3 dc in each corner sc; join with slip st to first dc, finish off.
Rnd 3: With **right** side facing, join White with sc in any corner dc; ch 2, sc in same st, ch 2, skip next dc, sc in next dc, ch 2, (skip next 2 dc, sc in next dc, ch 2) across to next corner 3-dc group, skip next dc, ★ (sc, ch 2) twice in next dc, skip next dc, sc in next dc, ch 2, (skip next 2 dc, sc in next dc, ch 2) across to next corner 3-dc group, skip next dc; repeat from ★ around; join with slip st to first sc, finish off.
Rnd 4: With **right** side facing, join Blue with slip st in any corner ch-2 sp; ch 3, 4 dc in same sp, 3 dc in next ch-2 sp and in each ch-2 sp around working 5 dc in each corner ch-2 sp; join with slip st to first dc, finish off.

GRANDMA'S SWEETHEART COVER-UP

Rock Grandma's girl off to dreamland cradled in this sweetheart cover-up. Embellished with cushy heart motifs, the flirty throw makes a wonderful welcome-home surprise for Mom and baby.

Finished Size: 33" x 43"

MATERIALS

Sport Weight Yarn:
   White - 11 ounces, (310 grams, 1,170 yards)
   Pink - 8 ounces, (230 grams, 850 yards)
Crochet hook, size F (3.75 mm) **or** size needed for gauge
Yarn needle

GAUGE: Each Motif = 3³/4"w x 4"h

Gauge Swatch: 2¹/4"w x 2¹/2"h
Work same as Motif through Rnd 4.

STITCH GUIDE

2-DC CLUSTER
★ YO, insert hook in beginning ring, YO and pull up a loop, YO and draw through 2 loops on hook; repeat from ★ once **more**, YO and draw through all 3 loops on hook *(Figs. 10a & b, page 134)*.

3-DC CLUSTER
★ YO, insert hook in beginning ring, YO and pull up a loop, YO and draw through 2 loops on hook; repeat from ★ 2 times **more**, YO and draw through all 4 loops on hook.

2-TR CLUSTER
★ YO twice, insert hook in beginning ring, YO and pull up a loop, (YO and draw through 2 loops on hook) twice; repeat from ★ once **more**, YO and draw through all 3 loops on hook.

2-DTR CLUSTER
★ YO 3 times, insert hook in beginning ring, YO and pull up a loop, (YO and draw through 2 loops on hook) 3 times; repeat from ★ once **more**, YO and draw through all 3 loops on hook.

CLUSTER (uses 3 sts)
YO, insert hook in same st as last st worked, YO and pull up a loop, YO and draw through 2 loops on hook, YO, skip next sc, insert hook in next sc, YO and pull up a loop, YO and draw through 2 loops on hook, YO and draw through all 3 loops on hook *(Figs. 11a & b, page 134)*.

MOTIF (Make 80)

With Pink, ch 6; join with slip st to form a ring.

Rnd 1 (Right side): Ch 2, in ring work [2-dc Cluster, ch 1, 3-dc Cluster, ch 1, (2-tr Cluster, ch 1) twice, (2-dtr Cluster, ch 1) twice, (2-tr Cluster, ch 1) twice, 3-dc Cluster, ch 1, 2-dc Cluster, ch 2, slip st].

Rnd 2: 2 Sc in first ch-2 sp, 2 sc in next Cluster and in next ch-1 sp, (sc in next Cluster and in next ch-1 sp) 3 times, sc in next Cluster, (sc, ch 2, sc) in next ch-1 sp, sc in next Cluster, (sc in next ch-1 sp and in next Cluster) 3 times, 2 sc in next ch-1 sp, 2 sc in next Cluster and in last ch-2 sp; do **not** join: 28 sc.

Rnd 3: Working in Back Loops Only *(Fig. 21, page 136)*, 2 sc in each of next 2 sc, sc in next sc, 2 sc in next sc, sc in each sc around to next ch-2, 2 sc in next ch, ch 2, 2 sc in next ch, sc in next 10 sc, 2 sc in next sc, sc in next sc, 2 sc in each of next 2 sc; do **not** join: 38 sc.

Rnd 4 (Ruffle): Working in free loops of Rnd 2 *(Fig. 22a, page 136)*, slip st in next sc, (ch 3, slip st in next sc) 6 times, (ch 3, skip next sc, slip st in next sc) 3 times, ch 3, skip next sc, slip st in next ch, ch 3, slip st in next ch, (ch 3, skip next sc, slip st in next sc) 4 times, (ch 3, slip st in next sc) around working last slip st in same st as first slip st; finish off.

Rnd 5: With **right** side facing and working behind ruffle, join White with sc in ch-2 sp on Rnd 3 at point of heart *(see Joining With Sc, page 136)*; ch 3, skip next 3 sc, sc in next sc, ch 5, skip next sc, sc in next sc, ch 3, skip next sc, sc in next sc, (ch 2, skip next sc, sc in next sc) twice, ch 3, skip next sc, sc in next sc, ch 2, skip next 2 sc, sc in next sc, ch 2, skip next 4 sc, sc in next sc, ch 2, skip next 2 sc, sc in next sc, ch 3, skip next sc, sc in next sc, (ch 2, skip next sc, sc in next sc) twice, ch 3, skip next sc, sc in next sc, ch 5, skip next sc, sc in next sc, ch 1, skip last 3 sc, hdc in first sc to form last sp: 15 sps.

Rnd 6: Ch 1, sc in same sp, ch 2, sc in next sc, ch 2, sc in next ch-3 sp, ch 3, (sc, ch 4) twice in next ch-5 sp, [(sc in next sp, ch 3) 3 times, (sc, ch 3) twice in next sp] twice, sc in next sp, (ch 3, sc in next sp) twice, (ch 4, sc) twice in next ch-5 sp, ch 3; join with slip st to first sc.

Rnd 7: Slip st in first ch-2 sp, ch 1, 2 sc in same sp and in each of next 2 sps, (2 sc, ch 2, 2 sc) in next sp, ★ 2 sc in each of next 4 sps, (2 sc, ch 2, 2 sc) in next sp; repeat from ★ 2 times **more**, 2 sc in last sp; join with slip st to first sc: 48 sc and 4 ch-2 sps.

Rnd 8: Ch 2, ★ hdc in next sc and in each sc across to next corner ch-2 sp, (hdc, ch 2, hdc) in corner ch-2 sp; repeat from ★ 3 times **more**, hdc in last 4 sc; join with slip st to top of beginning ch-2, finish off.

ASSEMBLY

With **wrong** sides together and White, and working through **inside** loops only, whipstitch Motifs together *(Fig. 30b, page 139)*. Form 8 vertical strips of 10 Motifs each, then whipstitch strips together, securing seam at each joining.

EDGING

Rnd 1: With **right** side facing, and working in Back Loops Only, join Pink with sc in any corner ch-2 sp; 2 sc in same sp, ★ † sc in next 14 hdc, (sc in next ch, sc in joining and in next ch, sc in next 14 hdc) across to next corner ch-2 sp †, 3 sc in corner ch-2 sp; repeat from ★ 2 times **more**, then repeat from † to † once; join with slip st to first sc, finish off: 612 sc.

Rnd 2: With **right** side facing and working in both loops, join White with sc in any corner sc; ch 3, skip next sc, (sc in next sc, ch 3, skip next sc) around; join with slip st to first sc: 306 ch-3 sps.

Rnd 3: Slip st in first ch-3 sp, ch 1, 2 sc in same sp and in each ch-3 sp across to next corner sc, ch 3, ★ 2 sc in next ch-3 sp and in each ch-3 sp across to next corner sc, ch 3; repeat from ★ around; join with slip st to first sc: 612 sc and 4 ch-3 sps.

Rnd 4: Slip st in next sc, ch 4, ★ † (work Cluster, ch 1) across to next corner ch-3 sp, dc in same st as last Cluster just worked, (2 dc, ch 2, 2 dc) in corner ch-3 sp, skip next sc †, dc in next sc, ch 1; repeat from ★ 2 times **more**, then repeat from † to † once; join with slip st to third ch of beginning ch-4.

Rnd 5: Ch 1, sc in same st and in each st and each ch-1 sp around working 3 sc in each corner ch-2 sp; join with slip st to first sc, finish off.

fashion corner

You're going to love the trendy designs in our fashion corner! For the style-conscious teen, our argyle pullover and Western vest are sure to please, and a little girl will adore the festive holiday sweater. You can keep youngsters warm with our colorful caps, and let your toddler stay cool by the pool in a cute bikini and cover-up set. Crocheting individuality into your family's wardrobe is easy with these smart selections!

ARGYLE PULLOVER

Greet the cold-weather season wearing this pretty argyle pullover! A classic addition to your wardrobe, the mock turtleneck features alternating diamonds in black, teal, and royal. The raspberry stripes are added after the front is finished. Instructions are given for sizes small, medium, and large.

Size:	Small	Medium	Large
Finished Chest			
Measurement:	36"	40"	44"

MATERIALS
Sport Weight Yarn:
   Black - 13 ounces, (370 grams, 1,340 yards)
   Teal - 3 ounces, (90 grams, 310 yards)
   Royal - 3 ounces, (90 grams, 310 yards)
   Raspberry - 30 yards
Crochet hooks, sizes F (3.75 mm) **and** H (5.00 mm) **or**
   sizes needed for gauge
10 bobbins
Yarn needle
2 - 1/2" buttons

GAUGE: With large size hook (size H), 16 sc and 16 rows = 4"
   With small size hook (size F), 12 sc and 12 rows = 2"

Gauge Swatch: 4" square
With large size hook, ch 17 **loosely**.
Row 1: Sc in second ch from hook and in each ch across: 16 sc.
Rows 2-16: Ch 1, turn; sc in each sc across.
Finish off.

STITCH GUIDE

DECREASE (uses next 2 sc)
Pull up a loop in next 2 sc, YO and draw through all 3 loops on hook **(counts as one sc)**.

SLEEVE (Make 2)
RIBBING
With small size hook and Black, ch 16 **loosely**.
Row 1: Sc in second ch from hook and in each ch across: 15 sc.
Row 2: Ch 1, turn; sc in Back Loop Only of each sc across *(Fig. 21, page 136)*.
Repeat Row 2 until 18{19-20} ribs [36{38-40} rows] are complete; do **not** finish off.

BODY

Change to large size hook.

Row 1 (Right side)**:** Ch 1, sc in end of each row across: 36{38-40} sc.

Note: Loop a short piece of yarn around any stitch to mark Row 1 as **right** side.

Row 2: Ch 1, turn; sc in each sc across.

Row 3 (Increase row)**:** Ch 1, turn; 2 sc in first sc, sc in each sc across to last sc, 2 sc in last sc: 38{40-42} sc.

Increase every other row, 2{7-12} times **more**, then increase every fourth row, 11{9-7} times: 64{72-80} sc.

Repeat Row 2 until Sleeve measures 17{17$\frac{1}{2}$-18}" from bottom edge; finish off.

BACK
RIBBING

With small size hook and Black, ch 13 **loosely**.

Row 1: Sc in second ch from hook and in each ch across: 12 sc.

Row 2: Ch 1, turn; sc in Back Loop Only of each sc across.

Repeat Row 2 until 36{40-44} ribs [72{80-88} rows] are complete; do **not** finish off.

BODY

Change to large size hook.

Row 1: Ch 1, 2 sc in end of first row, sc in end of each row across: 73{81-89} sc.

Row 2 (Right side)**:** Ch 1, turn; sc in each sc across.

Note: Mark Row 2 as **right** side.

Repeat Row 2 until Back measures 23$\frac{1}{2}${24$\frac{1}{2}$-25$\frac{1}{2}$}" from bottom edge, ending by working a **right** side row; do **not** finish off.

LEFT NECK AND SHOULDER SHAPING

Row 1: Ch 1, turn; sc in first 23{26-30} sc, decrease, leave remaining sc unworked: 24{27-31} sc.

Row 2: Ch 1, turn; sc in each sc across.

Row 3: Turn; slip st in first 9{10-11} sc, ch 1, sc in same st and in each sc across: 16{18-21} sc.

Row 4: Ch 1, turn; sc in first 8{9-11} sc, leave remaining 8{9-10} sc unworked; finish off: 8{9-11} sc.

RIGHT NECK AND SHOULDER SHAPING

Row 1: With **wrong** side facing, skip 23{25-25} sc from Left Neck and join Black with slip st in next sc; ch 1, decrease, sc in each sc across: 24{27-31} sc.

Row 2: Ch 1, turn; sc in each sc across.

Row 3: Ch 1, turn; sc in first 16{18-21} sc, leave remaining 8{9-10} sc unworked: 16{18-21} sc.

Row 4: Turn; slip st in first 9{10-11} sc, ch 1, sc in same st and in each sc across; finish off: 8{9-11} sc.

FRONT
RIBBING

Work same as Back.

Note #1: Wind yarn on bobbins and work each section with separate yarn. When changing color within the row *(Fig. 28a, page 138)*, keep unused color on **wrong** side; do **not** cut yarn until color is no longer needed.

Note #2: Each square on the Chart represents one single crochet and each row of squares represents one row of stitches. Raspberry lines indicate slip st chains that are worked later.

BODY

Change to large size hook.

Row 1: Ch 1, 2 sc in end of first row, sc in end of each row across: 73{81-89} sc.

Row 2 (Right side)**:** Ch 1, turn; sc in first 10{14-18} sc changing to Teal in last sc worked, sc in next sc changing to Black, ★ sc in next 12 sc changing to Royal in last sc worked, sc in next sc changing to Black, sc in next 12 sc changing to Teal in last sc worked, sc in next sc changing to Black; repeat from ★ once **more**, sc in last 10{14-18} sc.

Note: Mark Row 2 as **right** side.

Beginning with Row 3, follow Chart Rows 2-53 until Front measures 21$\frac{1}{2}${22$\frac{1}{2}$-23$\frac{1}{2}$}" from bottom edge, ending by working a **right** side row; do **not** finish off.

RIGHT NECK AND SHOULDER SHAPING

Note: Continue to follow Chart throughout.

Row 1: Ch 1, turn; sc in first 25{28-32} sc, decrease, leave remaining sc unworked: 26{29-33} sc.

Row 2: Ch 1, turn; decrease, sc in each sc across: 25{28-32} sc.

Row 3: Ch 1, turn; sc in each sc across to last 2 sc, decrease: 24{27-31} sc.

Rows 4-10: Ch 1, turn; sc in each sc across.

Row 11: Turn; slip st in first 9{10-11} sc, ch 1, sc in same st and in each sc across: 16{18-21} sc.

Row 12: Ch 1, turn; sc in first 8{9-11} sc, leave remaining 8{9-10} sc unworked; finish off: 8{9-11} sc.

LEFT NECK AND SHOULDER SHAPING

Note: Continue to follow Chart throughout.

Row 1: With **wrong** side facing, skip 19{21-21} sc from Right Neck and join yarn with slip st in next sc; ch 1, decrease, sc in each sc across: 26{29-33} sc.

Row 2: Ch 1, turn; sc in each sc across to last 2 sc, decrease: 25{28-32} sc.

Row 3: Ch 1, turn; decrease, sc in each sc across: 24{27-31} sc.

Rows 4-10: Ch 1, turn; sc in each sc across.

Row 11: Ch 1, turn; sc in first 16{18-21} sc, leave remaining {9-10} sc unworked: 16{18-21} sc.
Row 12: Turn; slip st in first 9{10-11} sc, ch 1, sc in same st and in each sc across; finish off: 8{9-11} sc.

FINISHING
SLIP ST CHAINS

With **right** side of Front facing, large size hook, and working diagonally upward to the right, hold Raspberry at back of work, insert hook from **front** to **back** in sp between sts as indicated on Chart, YO and pull up a 1/2" loop, ★ insert hook in st 2 rows above next st, YO and draw through loop on hook pulling loop up 1/2"; repeat from ★ across; finish off.

Work in same manner, beginning in sps between sts as indicated across bottom edge, and then beginning in sps between sts along left edge.

Working diagonally upward to the left, work remaining chains in same manner.

With **wrong** sides together and Black, and working through both loops, whipstitch shoulder seams *(Fig. 30a, page 139)*.

Whipstitch Sleeves to pullover, matching center of Sleeve to shoulder seam and beginning 8{9-10}" down from shoulder seam.
Whipstitch underarm and side in one continuous seam.

NECK RIBBING
Foundation Rnd: With **right** side facing and small size hook, join Black with slip st at center Back; ch 1, sc in each st and in end of each row around; join with slip st to first sc: 74{78-78} sc. Ch 16 **loosely**.
Row 1: Sc in second ch from hook and in each ch across, with **right** side facing, sc in first 2 sc on Foundation Rnd: 17 sc.
Row 2: Turn; skip first 2 sc, sc in Back Loop Only of each sc across: 15 sc.
Row 3: Ch 1, turn; sc in Back Loop Only of each sc across, sc in next 2 sc on Foundation Rnd: 17 sc.
Repeat Rows 2 and 3 around, ending by working Row 2.
Buttonhole Row: Ch 1, turn; sc in Back Loop Only of first 2 sc, ch 3 (buttonhole), skip next 3 sc, sc in Back Loop Only of next 3 sc, ch 3 (buttonhole), skip next 3 sc, sc in Back Loop Only of each sc across, slip st in last sc on Foundation Rnd; finish off.

Sew buttons to Neck Ribbing opposite buttonholes.

CHART

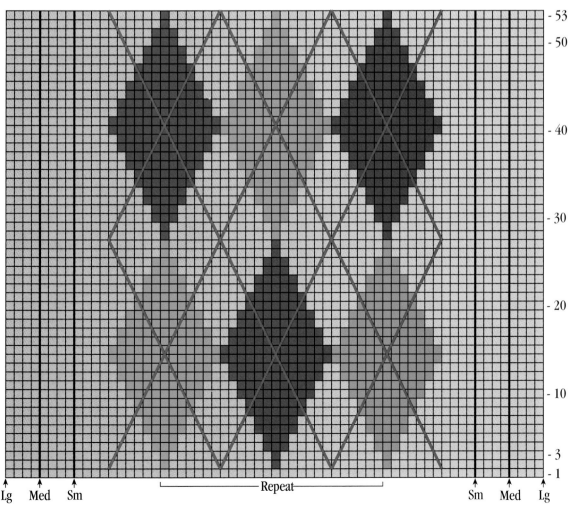

These easy-to-stitch toppers are "snow" cute! Fashioned in popular watch cap and stocking cap styles, they'll keep youngsters' heads warm when they're out enjoying frosty fun.

Finished Size: 6 to 12 years

MATERIALS
Worsted Weight Yarn:
   Watch Cap
      3 ounces, (90 grams, 190 yards)
   Stocking Cap
      Yellow - 1 ounce, (30 grams, 65 yards)
      Blue - 3 ounces, (90 grams, 190 yards)
   Crochet hook, size I (5.50 mm) **or** size needed for gauge
   Yarn needle

GAUGE: 7 dc and 4 rows = 2"

Gauge Swatch: 3" in diameter
Work same as Rnds 1 and 2 of Watch Cap.

STITCH GUIDE

> **FRONT POST DOUBLE CROCHET** *(abbreviated FPdc)*
> YO, insert hook from **front** to **back** around post of st indicated *(Fig. 15, page 135)*, YO and pull up a loop **even** with loop on hook, (YO and draw through 2 loops on hook) twice.
>
> **FRONT POST TREBLE CROCHET** *(abbreviated FPtr)*
> YO twice, insert hook from **front** to **back** around post of st indicated, YO and pull up a loop **even** with loop on hook, (YO and draw through 2 loops on hook) 3 times. Skip st behind FPtr.
>
> **REVERSE SINGLE CROCHET** *(abbreviated reverse sc)*
> Working from **left** to **right**, insert hook in st to right of hook, YO and draw through, under and to left of loop on hook (2 loops on hook), YO and draw through both loops on hook *(Figs. 14a-d, page 135)*.

WATCH CAP
CROWN
Ch 6; join with slip st to form a ring.
Rnd 1 (Right side): Ch 3 **(counts as first dc, now and throughout)**, 17 dc in ring; join with slip st to first dc: 18 dc.
Note: Loop a short piece of yarn around any stitch to mark Rnd 1 as **right** side.
Rnd 2: Ch 3, work FPdc around same st, dc in next dc, work FPdc around same st, ★ dc in next 2 dc, work FPdc around same st, dc in next dc, work FPdc around same st; repeat from ★ around to last dc, dc in last dc; join with slip st to first dc: 30 sts.

Rnd 3: Ch 3, work FPdc around next FPdc, skip st behind FPdc **(now and throughout)**, dc in next dc, work FPdc around next FPdc, 2 dc in next dc, ★ (dc in next dc, work FPdc around next FPdc) twice, 2 dc in next dc; repeat from ★ around; join with slip st to first dc: 36 sts.
Rnd 4: Ch 3, (work FPdc around next FPdc, dc in next dc) twice, 2 dc in next dc, ★ dc in next dc, (work FPdc around next FPdc, dc in next dc) twice, 2 dc in next dc; repeat from ★ around; join with slip st to first dc: 42 sts.
Rnd 5: Ch 3, work FPdc around next FPdc, dc in next dc, work FPdc around next FPdc, 2 dc in next dc, dc in next 2 dc, ★ 2 dc in next dc, work FPdc around next FPdc, dc in next dc, work FPdc around next FPdc, 2 dc in next dc, dc in next 2 dc; repeat from ★ around, dc in same st as first dc; join with slip st to first dc: 54 sts.
Rnd 6: Ch 3, work FPdc around next FPdc, dc in next dc, work FPdc around next FPdc, dc in next 2 dc, 2 dc in next dc, ★ dc in next 3 dc, work FPdc around next FPdc, dc in next dc, work FPdc around next FPdc, dc in next 2 dc, 2 dc in next dc; repeat from ★ around to last 2 dc, dc in last 2 dc; join with slip st to first dc: 60 sts.
Rnds 7-17: Ch 3, work FPdc around next FPdc, dc in next dc, work FPdc around next FPdc, ★ dc in next 7 dc, work FPdc around next FPdc, dc in next dc, work FPdc around next FPdc; repeat from ★ around to last 6 dc, dc in last 6 dc; join with slip st to first dc; do **not** finish off.

CUFF
Rnd 1: Ch 3, **turn**; working in Back Loops Only *(Fig. 21, page 136)*, dc in next dc and in each st around; join with slip st to first dc.
Rnds 2 and 3: Ch 3, working in both loops, dc in next 6 dc, work FPdc around next st, dc in next dc, work FPdc around next st, ★ dc in next 7 dc, work FPdc around next st, dc in next dc, work FPdc around next st; repeat from ★ around; join with slip st to first dc.
Rnd 4: Ch 1, work reverse sc in each st around; join with slip st to first st, finish off.
Trim: With **right** side facing, Cuff turned up, and top of Cap towards you, join yarn with slip st in free loop of any st on Rnd 17 of Crown *(Fig. 22a, page 136)*; slip st **loosely** in each st around; join with slip st to first slip st, finish off.

Make a Pom-pom *(Figs. 31a & b, page 139)* and sew to Crown of Cap.

STOCKING CAP
STOCKING AND CROWN

Rnd 1 (Right side): With Blue, ch 2, 8 sc in second ch from hook; join with slip st to first sc.

Note: Loop a short piece of yarn around any stitch to mark Rnd 1 as **right** side.

Rnd 2: Ch 3 **(counts as first dc, now and throughout)**, dc in next sc, (dc in next sc, 2 dc in next sc) around; join with slip st to first dc: 12 dc.

Rnd 3: Ch 3, dc in next dc and in each dc around; join with slip st to first dc.

Rnd 4: Ch 3, dc in next dc, 2 dc in next dc, (dc in next 2 dc, dc in next dc) around; join with slip st to first dc: 16 dc.

Rnd 5: Ch 3, dc in next dc and in each dc around; join with slip st to first dc.

Rnd 6: Ch 3, dc in next 2 dc, 2 dc in next dc, (dc in next 3 dc, dc in next dc) around; join with slip st to first dc: 20 dc.

Rnd 7: Ch 3, dc in next dc and in each dc around; join with slip st to first dc changing to Yellow *(Fig. 28b, page 138)*.

Rnd 8: Repeat Rnd 6: 25 dc.

Rnds 9 and 10: Ch 3, dc in next dc and in each dc around; join with slip st to first dc.

Rnd 11: Ch 3, dc in next 3 dc, 2 dc in next dc, (dc in next 4 dc, 2 dc in next dc) around; join with slip st to first dc: 30 dc.

Rnds 12 and 13: Ch 3, dc in next dc and in each dc around; join with slip st to first dc changing to Blue at end of Rnd 13.

Rnds 14-19: Ch 3, dc in next dc and in each dc around; join with slip st to first dc changing to Yellow at end of Rnd 19.

Rnds 20-25: Ch 3, dc in next dc and in each dc around; join with slip st to first dc changing to Blue at end of Rnd 25.

Rnd 26: Ch 3, dc in same st and in next 4 dc, (2 dc in next dc, dc in next 4 dc) around; join with slip st to first dc: 36 dc.

Rnd 27: Ch 3, dc in same st, dc in next 5 dc, (2 dc in next dc, dc in next 5 dc) around; join with slip st to first dc: 42 dc.

Rnd 28: Ch 3, dc in next dc, work FPtr around dc on rnd **below** next dc, (dc in next 2 dc, work FPtr around dc on rnd **below** next dc) around; join with slip st to first dc.
Rnd 29: Ch 3, 2 dc in next dc, (dc in next 2 sts, 2 dc in next dc) around to last FPtr, dc in last FPtr; join with slip st to first dc: 56 dc.
Rnd 30: Ch 3, dc in next 2 dc, work FPtr around FPtr on rnd **below** next dc, ★ dc in next 3 dc, work FPtr around FPtr on rnd **below** next dc; repeat from ★ around; join with slip st to first dc.
Rnd 31: Ch 3, dc in next dc and in each st around; join with slip st to first dc.
Rnds 32-41: Repeat Rnds 30 and 31, 5 times.
Rnd 42: Ch 3, dc in next 2 dc, work FPtr around FPtr on rnd **below** next dc, ★ dc in next 3 dc, work FPtr around FPtr on rnd **below** next dc; repeat from ★ around; join with slip st to first dc changing to Yellow.

CUFF
Rnd 1: Ch 3, **turn**; dc in Back Loop Only of next st and in each st around *(Fig. 21, page 136)*; join with slip st to first dc.
Rnd 2: Ch 3, dc in both loops of next dc and in each dc around; join with slip st to first dc.
Rnd 3: Ch 3, work FPtr around dc on rnd **below** next dc, ★ dc in next 3 dc, work FPtr around dc on rnd **below** next dc; repeat from ★ around to last 2 dc, dc in last 2 dc; join with slip st to first dc.
Rnd 4: Ch 2, sc in second ch from hook, skip next st, ★ slip st in next st, ch 2, sc in second ch from hook, skip next st; repeat from ★ around; join with slip st to first slip st, finish off.
Trim: With **right** side facing, Cuff turned up, and top of Cap towards you, join Yellow with slip st in free loop of any st on Rnd 42 of Crown *(Fig. 22a, page 136)*; slip st **loosely** in each st around; join with slip st to first slip st, finish off.

With Blue, make a Pom-pom *(Figs. 31a & b, page 139)* and sew to end of Stocking.

$\mathcal{Q}uick$ HOLIDAY HAPPINESS SWEATER

Sprinkled with French-knot "confetti," a purchased sweater for a little girl features a year of holiday motifs crocheted with colorful thread! The motifs include Valentine hearts, a shamrock, an Easter bunny, an American flag, a jack-o'-lantern, and Santa. As a finishing touch, "I Love Holidays" is embroidered across the front.

MATERIALS
Bedspread Weight Cotton Thread (size 10):
Large Heart
  Red - 7 yards
  White - 4 yards
Small Heart
  Red - 4 yards **each**
Shamrock
  Green - 5 yards
  White - 2 yards
Bunny
  White - 13 yards
  Orange - 1 yard
  Green, Pink, Red and Black - small amount of each
Flag
  Red - 10 yards
  White - 8 yards
  Blue - 5 yards
Pumpkin
  Orange - 8 yards
  Green - 1 yard
Santa
  Red - 4 yards
  White - 5 yards
  Pink - 3 yards
Steel crochet hook, size 6 (1.80 mm)
Purchased sweater
Transfer paper or pen
Tapestry needle
Felt: Pink for Bunny and Black for Pumpkin
Glue
4 - 5 mm wiggle eyes
7 mm jingle bell

Note: Gauge is not important. Motifs can be larger or smaller without changing the overall effect.

STITCH GUIDE

PICOT
Ch 2, slip st in side of st just worked *(Fig. 27, page 138)*.
DECREASE (uses next 2 sts)
★ YO, insert hook in **next** st, YO and pull up a loop, YO and draw through 2 loops on hook; repeat from ★ once **more**, YO and draw through all 3 loops on hook **(counts as one dc)**.

LARGE HEART

Rnd 1 (Right side)**:** With Red, ch 4, 13 dc in fourth ch from hook; join with slip st to top of beginning ch: 14 sts.
Note: Loop a short piece of thread around any stitch to mark Rnd 1 as **right** side.
Rnd 2: Ch 3 **(counts as first dc, now and throughout)**, dc in same st, 2 dc in next dc and in each dc around; join with slip st to first dc: 28 dc.
Rnd 3: Ch 2, dc in same st and in next dc, (dc, tr) in next dc, tr in next dc, 2 tr in next dc, tr in next dc, (tr, dc) in next dc, dc in next dc, (dc, hdc) in next dc, hdc in next 3 dc, sc in next dc, 2 sc in each of next 2 dc, sc in next dc, hdc in next 3 dc, (hdc, dc) in next dc, dc in next dc, (dc, tr) in next dc, tr in next dc, 2 tr in next dc, tr in next dc, (tr, dc) in next dc, dc in next dc, (dc, ch 2, slip st) in last dc; do **not** join.
Rnd 4: Ch 1, sc in first 2 chs, hdc in next dc, 2 dc in next dc, tr in next dc, 2 tr in next tr, tr in next tr, 2 dc in each of next 2 tr, dc in next tr, 2 hdc in next tr, hdc in next dc, 2 hdc in next dc, hdc in next 3 sts, dc in next hdc, 2 hdc in next hdc, dc in next 2 sc, (dc, 2 tr) in next sc, (2 tr, dc) in next sc, dc in next 2 sc, 2 hdc in next hdc, dc in next hdc, hdc in next 3 sts, 2 hdc in next dc, hdc in next dc, 2 hdc in next tr, dc in next tr, 2 dc in each of next 2 tr, tr in next tr, 2 tr in next tr, tr in next dc, 2 dc in next dc, hdc in next dc, sc in last 2 chs; join with slip st to first sc changing to White *(Fig. 28b, page 138)*: 60 sts.
Rnd 5: Ch 1, sc in same st and in next sc, work Picot, (sc in next 3 sts, work Picot) around to last sc, sc in last sc; join with slip st to first sc, finish off.

SMALL HEART (Make 10)

Row 1 (Right side)**:** With Red, ch 4 **loosely**, sc in second ch from hook and in each ch across: 3 sc.
Note: Mark Row 1 as **right** side.
Row 2: Ch 1, turn; 2 sc in first sc, sc in next sc, 2 sc in last sc: 5 sc.
Row 3: Ch 1, turn; sc in each sc across.
Rows 4-6: Ch 1, turn; 2 sc in first sc, sc in each sc across to last sc, 2 sc in last sc: 11 sc.
Row 7: Ch 1, turn; sc in first sc, ★ hdc in next sc, 2 dc in each of next 2 sc, hdc in next sc, sc in next sc; repeat from ★ once **more**: 15 sts.

Edging: Ch 1, do **not** turn; sc evenly around to first sc on Row 7, sc in first sc, † hdc in next st, 2 dc in each of next 3 dc, hdc in next st, sc in next st †, slip st in next sc, sc in next hdc, repeat from † to † once; join with slip st to first sc, finish off.

SHAMROCK

Rnd 1: With Green, ch 4, 14 dc in fourth ch from hook; join with slip st to top of beginning ch: 15 sts.
Note: Mark Rnd 1 as **right** side.
Rnd 2: Ch 1, ★ (sc, hdc) in next dc, (dc, 4 tr) in next dc, (4 tr, dc) in next dc, (hdc, sc) in next dc, slip st in next dc; repeat from ★ around working last slip st in same st as joining.
Stem: Ch 7 **loosely**; hdc in third ch from hook and in next ch, sc in next 3 chs, slip st in same st as joining, finish off.
Trim: With **right** side facing and working in sps between sts, hold White at back of work, insert hook from **front** to **back** between first 2 sts on Rnd 2, YO and pull up a loop, ★ insert hook in next sp, YO and draw through loop on hook; repeat from ★ around to last sc; finish off.

BUNNY
HEAD

Rnd 1 (Right side)**:** With White, ch 4, 13 dc in fourth ch from hook; join with slip st to top of beginning ch: 14 sts.
Note: Mark Rnd 1 as **right** side.
Rnd 2: Ch 3 **(counts as first dc, now and throughout)**, dc in same st, 2 dc in each of next 5 dc, 2 hdc in each of next 2 dc, 2 dc in each of last 6 dc; join with slip st to first dc: 28 sts.
Rnd 3: Ch 1, sc in same st and in next dc, † ch 12 **loosely**; sc in second ch from hook and in next ch, hdc in next 2 chs, dc in next 2 chs, tr in next 3 chs, dc in next ch, hdc in last ch, sc in next st (ear) †, (2 sc in next st, sc in next st) 12 times, repeat from † to † once; join with slip st to first sc, finish off.

BODY

Rnd 1 (Right side)**:** With White, ch 4, 13 dc in fourth ch from hook; join with slip st to top of beginning ch: 14 sts.
Note: Mark Rnd 1 as **right** side.
Rnd 2: Ch 3, dc in same st, 2 dc in next dc and in each dc around; join with slip st to first dc: 28 dc.
Rnd 3: Ch 3, 2 dc in next dc, (dc in next dc, 2 dc in next dc) around; join with slip st to first dc: 42 dc.
Rnd 4: Ch 3, dc in next dc, 2 dc in next dc, (dc in next 2 dc, 2 dc in next dc) around; join with slip st to first dc, finish off: 56 dc.

CARROT

With Orange, ch 9 **loosely**; dc in fourth ch from hook, hdc in next 2 chs, sc in next 2 chs, slip st in last ch; finish off leaving a long end for sewing.

FINISHING

Sew Head to Body.

Using pattern, page 142, cut inner ears from pink felt and glue to ears.

With Red, add Straight St for mouth *(Fig. 34, page 141)*.

Holding 2 strands of Black together, tie knot around st above mouth for nose and whiskers. Glue wiggle eyes to Head.

Using 2 strands of Green, each 2" long, add fringe to top of Carrot *(Figs. 33a & b, page 139)*. Sew Carrot to Body.

Tie two, 2" strands of Pink in a bow; glue to joining of Body and Head.

FLAG

With Red, ch 26 **loosely**.

Row 1 (Right side)**:** Hdc in third ch from hook **(2 skipped chs count as first hdc)** and in each ch across changing to White in last hdc worked *(Fig. 28a, page 138)*: 25 hdc.

Note: Mark Row 1 as **right** side.

Row 2: Ch 2 **(counts as first hdc, now and throughout)**, turn; hdc in next hdc and in each hdc across changing to Red in last hdc worked.

Row 3: Ch 2, turn; hdc in next hdc and in each hdc across changing to White in last hdc worked.

Rows 4-6: Repeat Rows 2 and 3, once, then repeat Row 2 once **more**.

Row 7: Ch 2, turn; hdc in next 13 hdc changing to Blue in last hdc worked, hdc in last 11 hdc.

Row 8: Ch 2, turn; hdc in next 10 hdc changing to White in last hdc worked, hdc in each hdc across changing to Red in last hdc worked.

Rows 9-13: Repeat Rows 7 and 8 twice, then repeat Row 7 once **more**.

Finish off.

PUMPKIN

Rnd 1: With Orange, ch 4, 13 dc in fourth ch from hook; join with slip st to top of beginning ch: 14 sts.

Note: Mark Rnd 1 as **right** side.

Rnd 2: Ch 3 **(counts as first dc, now and throughout)**, dc in same st, 2 dc in next dc and in each dc around; join with slip st to first dc: 28 dc.

Rnd 3: Ch 3, dc in same st and in next dc, (2 dc in next dc, dc in next dc) around; join with slip st to first dc: 42 dc.

Rnd 4: Ch 1, sc in same st, hdc in next dc, 2 dc in next dc, (dc in next 2 dc, 2 dc in next dc) 5 times, hdc in next 2 dc, 2 sc in next dc, hdc in next 2 dc, 2 dc in next dc, (dc in next 2 dc, 2 dc in next dc) 5 times, hdc in next dc, sc in next dc changing to Green *(Fig. 28a, page 138)*, cut Orange, slip st in last dc, ch 5 **loosely**; hdc in second ch from hook, sc in next 3 chs, slip st in same st as slip st; finish off.

Using pattern, page 142, cut mouth, nose, and eyes from black felt and glue to Pumpkin.

SANTA

FACE

Rnd 1 (Right side)**:** With Pink, ch 4, 6 dc in fourth ch from hook changing to White in last dc worked *(Fig. 28a, page 138)*, cut Pink, 7 dc in same st; join with slip st to top of beginning ch changing to Pink, cut White: 14 sts.

Note: Mark Rnd 1 as **right** side.

Rnd 2: Ch 3 **(counts as first dc, now and throughout)**, dc in same st, 2 dc in each of next 6 dc, dc in next dc changing to White, cut Pink, dc in same st, 2 dc in each of last 6 dc; join with slip st to first dc: 28 dc.

Rnd 3: Ch 2, 2 hdc in next dc, (hdc in next dc, 2 hdc in next dc) 7 times, (ch 1, hdc in next dc) 12 times; join with slip st to top of beginning ch-2, do **not** finish off: 12 ch-1 sps.

BEARD

Row 1: Ch 4, **turn**; sc in next ch-1 sp, (ch 4, sc in next ch-1 sp) 10 times, ch 2, hdc in last ch-1 sp to form last sp, leave remaining 23 hdc unworked: 12 sps.

Row 2: Ch 4, turn; sc in next ch-4 sp, (ch 4, sc in next ch-4 sp) 10 times; finish off: 11 ch-4 sps.

HAT

Row 1: With **right** side facing and working on Rnd 3 of Face, skip 4 hdc from Beard and join Red with slip st in next hdc; ch 3, decrease, dc in next 9 hdc, decrease, dc in next hdc, leave remaining 4 hdc unworked: 13 dc.

Rows 2 and 3: Ch 3, turn; decrease, dc in next dc and in each dc across to last 3 dc, decrease, dc in last dc: 9 dc.

Row 4: Ch 3, turn; decrease 4 times: 5 dc.

Row 5: Ch 3, turn; ★ YO, insert hook in **next** dc, YO and pull up a loop, YO and draw through 2 loops on hook; repeat from ★ 3 times **more**, YO and draw through all 5 loops on hook, ch 1 **tightly**; finish off.

NOSE

With Red, ch 3, 4 dc in third ch from hook, drop loop from hook, insert hook in top of beginning ch, hook dropped loop and draw through, ch 1 **tightly**; finish off leaving a long end for sewing.

With **right** side facing, sew Nose to center of Face.

Glue wiggle eyes to Face.

Sew jingle bell to end of Hat.

FINISHING

Using photo as a guide for placement, transfer "I Love Holidays" pattern, page 142, onto purchased sweater.

Using Outline St *(Figs. 38a & b, page 141)* and White, embroider words.

Sew Motifs to sweater, placing 2 Small Hearts on each of the sleeves.

Using White, work French knots scattered across sweater *(Fig. 36, page 141)*.

TODDLER BIKINI AND COVER-UP

Life's a beach for girls who just want to have fun, so dress your little mermaid in this darling bikini and hooded cover-up for splashy pool-side play. Designed in three toddler sizes, the cute ensemble has convenient ties on the bikini top and bottom for a comfortable fit.

Size:	1T	2T	3T
Finished Chest			
Measurement:	21"	22"	23"

Size Note: Instructions are written for size 1T with sizes 2T and 3T in braces { }. Instructions will be easier to read if you circle all the numbers pertaining to your size. If only one number is given, it applies to all sizes.

MATERIALS

Sport Weight Yarn:
    White - 4¹/₂{5¹/₂-6} ounces,
      [130{160-170} grams, 385{470-515} yards]
    Red - 1³/₄{2-2¹/₄} ounces,
      [50{60-65} grams, 150{170-195} yards]
Crochet hook, size D (3.25 mm) **or** size needed for gauge
11 - 6 mm beads
Tapestry needle

GAUGE: In pattern for Bikini,
    12 sts = 2" and 4 rows = 1¹/₂"
    In pattern for Cover-up, 5 sps and 5 rows = 2"

Gauge Swatch: 2" square
Ch 20 **loosely**.
Work same as Cover-up Body, page 107, for 5 rows: 5 sps.
Finish off.

STITCH GUIDE

> **FRONT POST DOUBLE CROCHET** *(abbreviated FPdc)*
> YO, insert hook from **front** to **back** around post of st indicated *(Fig. 15, page 135)*, YO and pull up a loop **even** with loop on hook, (YO and draw through 2 loops on hook) twice. Skip st behind FPdc.
>
> **BACK POST DOUBLE CROCHET** *(abbreviated BPdc)*
> YO, insert hook from **back** to **front** around post of st indicated, YO and pull up a loop **even** with loop on hook, (YO and draw through 2 loops on hook) twice. Skip st in front of BPdc.

BIKINI TOP

With Red, ch 48{52-56} **loosely**.
Row 1 (Right side)**:** Sc in second ch from hook and in each ch across: 47{51-55} sc.
Note: Loop a short piece of yarn around any stitch to mark Row 1 as **right** side.

Row 2: Ch 3 **(counts as first dc, now and throughout)**, turn; dc in next sc and in each sc across changing to White in last dc worked *(Fig. 28a, page 138)*.
Row 3: Ch 3, turn; work FPdc around next dc, (dc in next 3 dc, work FPdc around next dc) across to last dc, dc in last dc: 12{13-14} FPdc.
Row 4: Ch 3, turn; dc in next st and in each st across changing to Red in last dc worked.
Row 5: Ch 3, turn; work FPdc around next dc, (dc in next 3 dc, work FPdc around next dc) across to last dc, dc in last dc changing to White.
Row 6: Ch 3, turn; work BPdc around next st, (dc in next 3 dc, work BPdc around next st) across to last dc, dc in last dc.
Row 7: Ch 3, turn; dc in next st and in each st across changing to Red in last dc worked.
Row 8: Ch 3, turn; work BPdc around next dc, (dc in next 3 dc, work BPdc around next dc) across to last dc, dc in last dc.
Row 9: Ch 1, turn; sc in first 6{8-10} sts, ch 3, sc in each st across to last 6{8-10} sts, ch 3, sc in each st across; do **not** finish off.

FIRST SIDE

Row 1: Ch 4, skip first row, dc in end of next row, (ch 1, dc in end of next row) 7 times: 8 sps.
Row 2: Ch 3, turn; skip next dc, dc in next dc, (ch 1, dc in next dc) 4 times, skip next dc and next ch, dc in next ch: 7 dc.
Row 3: Turn; skip first dc, slip st in next dc, ch 3, (skip next dc, dc in next dc) twice.
Tie: Turn; skip first dc, slip st in next dc, chain a 16" length; finish off.
Slip bead on Tie; knot end.

SECOND SIDE

Row 1: With **right** side facing, join Red with slip st in end of first row, ch 4; dc in end of next row, (ch 1, dc in end of next row) 7 times: 8 sps.
Complete same as First Side.

NECK TIE

With Red, chain a 40" length; finish off.
Pull each end of Neck Tie from **back** to **front** through ch-3 sps on Row 9.
Slip one bead on each end of Neck Tie; knot ends.

FINISHING

With Red and tapestry needle, weave yarn through sts in center of Top on **wrong** side from bottom edge to top edge. Insert needle through Row 9 to **right** side and slip bead on yarn. Insert needle through beginning ch; weave through sts on **wrong** side. Pull ends tightly to gather Top to 1¼" width at center; secure ends.

BIKINI BOTTOM

BACK

With White, ch 11{15-19} **loosely**.

Row 1 (Right side): Dc in fourth ch from hook and in each ch across: 9{13-17} sts.

Note: Mark Row 1 as **right** side.

Row 2: Ch 3, turn; dc in next dc and in each st across.

Rows 3 thru 4{6-8}: Repeat Row 2, 2{4-6} times.

Rows 5{7-9} thru 9{11-13}: Ch 3, turn; 2 dc in next dc, dc in each dc across to last 2 dc, 2 dc in next dc, dc in last dc: 19{23-27} dc.

Row 10{12-14}: Ch 3, turn; 2 dc in next dc, dc in each dc across to last 2 dc, 2 dc in next dc, dc in last dc changing to Red: 21{25-29} dc.

Row 11{13-15}: Ch 3, turn; dc in next dc, work FPdc around next dc, (dc in next 3 dc, work FPdc around next dc) across to last 2 dc, dc in last 2 dc changing to White in last dc worked.

Row 12{14-16}: Ch 3, turn; dc in next dc, work BPdc around next st, (dc in next 3 dc, work BPdc around next st) across to last 2 dc, dc in last 2 dc.

Row 13{15-17}: Ch 3, turn; 2 dc in next dc, dc in each st across to last 2 dc, 2 dc in next dc, dc in last dc changing to Red: 23{27-31} dc.

Row 14{16-18}: Ch 3, turn; dc in next 2 dc, (work BPdc around next dc, dc in next 3 dc) across changing to White in last dc worked.

Row 15{17-19}: Ch 3, turn; dc in next 2 dc, (work FPdc around next st, dc in next 3 dc) across.

Last 3 Rows: Ch 3, turn; 2 dc in next dc, dc in each st across to last 2 dc, 2 dc in next dc, dc in last dc: 29{33-37} dc. Finish off.

FRONT

Row 1: With **right** side facing and working in free loops of beginning ch *(Fig. 22b, page 136)*, join White with slip st in first ch; ch 3, dc in next ch and in each ch across: 9{13-17} dc

Row 2: Ch 3, turn; 2 dc in next dc, dc in each dc across to last 2 dc, 2 dc in next dc, dc in last dc changing to Red: 11{15-19} dc

Row 3: Ch 3, turn; 2 dc in next dc, dc in next dc, work FPdc around next dc, (dc in next 3 dc, work FPdc around next dc) 1{2-3} times, dc in next dc, 2 dc in next dc, dc in last dc changing to White: 13{17-21} sts.

Row 4: Ch 3, turn; 2 dc in next dc, dc in next 2 dc, work BPdc around next st, (dc in next 3 dc, work BPdc around next st) 1{2-3} times, dc in next 2 dc, 2 dc in next dc, dc in last dc: 15{19-23} sts.

Row 5: Ch 3, turn; 2 dc in next dc, dc in each st across to last 2 dc, 2 dc in next dc, dc in last dc changing to Red: 17{21-25} dc

Row 6: Ch 3, turn; dc in next dc, work BPdc around next dc, (dc in next 3 dc, work BPdc around next dc) across to last 2 dc, dc in last 2 dc changing to White in last dc worked.

Row 7: Ch 3, turn; 2 dc in next dc, dc in each st across to last 2 dc, 2 dc in next dc, dc in last dc: 19{23-27} dc.

Rows 8-10: Repeat Row 7, 3 times; at end of Row 10, change to Red in last dc worked: 25{29-33} dc.

EDGING

Rnd 1: Ch 3, turn; dc in next dc, work FPdc around next dc, (dc in next 3 dc, work FPdc around next dc) 5{6-7} times, dc in next dc, 3 dc in last dc; 2 dc in end of each row across; 3 dc in first dc, dc in next dc, work FPdc around next dc, (dc in next 3 dc, work FPdc around next dc) 6{7-8} times, dc in next dc, 3 dc in last dc; 2 dc in end of each row across; 2 dc in same st as first dc; join with slip st to first dc: 174{190-206} sts.

Rnd 2: Ch 1, sc in each st around working (sc, ch 3, sc) in each corner dc; join with slip st to first sc, finish off.

TIE (Make 2)

With Red, chain an 18" length; finish off.

Pull each end of each Tie through ch-3 sps at corners on Front and Back.

Slip one bead on each end of Ties; knot ends.

COVER-UP

BODY

With White, ch 155{164-170} **loosely**.

Row 1 (Right side): Dc in eighth ch from hook **(counts as first dc plus ch 2)**, (ch 2, skip next 2 chs, dc in next ch) across: 50{53-55} sps.

Note: Mark Row 1 as **right** side.

Row 2: Ch 5 **(counts as first dc plus ch 2, now and throughout)**, turn; dc in next dc, (ch 2, dc in next dc) across. Repeat Row 2 until Body measures 6$\frac{1}{2}${7$\frac{1}{2}$-8$\frac{1}{2}$}" from beginning ch, ending by working a **wrong** side row; do **not** finish off.

RIGHT FRONT

Row 1: Ch 5, turn; dc in next dc, (ch 2, dc in next dc) 11{12-12} times, leave remaining sts unworked: 12{13-13} sps.

Row 2: Ch 5, turn; dc in next dc, (ch 2, dc in next dc) across. Repeat Row 2 until Right Front measures 10{12-13}" from beginning ch, ending by working a **wrong** side row; do **not** finish off.

Place marker around last dc of last row for Hood placement.

NECK SHAPING

Row 1: Turn; slip st in first 7 sts, ch 5, dc in next dc, (ch 2, dc in next dc) across: 10{11-11} sps.

Row 2: Ch 5, turn; dc in next dc, (ch 2, dc in next dc) 7{8-8} times, leave remaining 2 dc unworked: 8{9-9} sps.

Row 3: Turn; slip st in first 7{10-10} sts, ch 5, dc in next dc, (ch 2, dc in next dc) across; finish off: 6 sps.

BACK

Row 1: With **right** side facing, join White with slip st in first unworked dc on last row of Body; ch 5, dc in next dc, (ch 2, dc in next dc) 23{24-26} times, leave remaining 13{14-14} dc unworked: 24{25-27} sps.

Row 2: Ch 5, turn; dc in next dc, (ch 2, dc in next dc) across. Repeat Row 2 until Back measures same as Front. Finish off.

LEFT FRONT

Row 1: With **right** side facing, join White with slip st in first unworked dc on last row of Body; ch 5, dc in next dc, (ch 2, dc in next dc) across: 12{13-13} sps.

Row 2: Ch 5, turn; dc in next dc, (ch 2, dc in next dc) across. Repeat Row 2 until Left Front measures same as Right Front to Neck Shaping, ending by working a **wrong** side row; do **not** finish off.

NECK SHAPING

Row 1: Ch 5, turn; dc in next dc, (ch 2, dc in next dc) 9{10-10} times, leave remaining 2 dc unworked: 10{11-11} sps.

Row 2: Turn; slip st in first 7 sts, ch 5, dc in next dc, (ch 2, dc in next dc) across: 8{9-9} sps.

Row 3: Ch 5, turn; dc in next dc, (ch 2, dc in next dc) 5 times, leave remaining 2{3-3} dc unworked; finish off: 6 sps.

With **wrong** sides together and White, and working through **both** loops, whipstitch shoulder seams *(Fig. 30a, page 139)*.

HOOD

Row 1: With **right** side facing, join White with slip st in marked dc on Right Front; ch 5, (dc in next dc, ch 2, dc in st at base of first dc of next row, ch 2, dc in top of same dc, ch 2) twice, (dc in next dc, ch 2) 1{2-2} times, dc in st at base of first dc of next row, ch 2, dc in joining, (ch 2, dc in next dc) across to next joining, ch 2, dc in joining, ch 2, dc in base of first dc of next row, (ch 2, dc in next dc) 2{3-3} times, [ch 2, dc in st at base of last dc worked into, (ch 2, dc in next dc) twice] 2 times: 30{33-35} sps.

Row 2: Ch 5, turn; dc in next dc, (ch 2, dc in next dc) across. Repeat Row 2 until Hood measures 12{13-13$\frac{1}{2}$}" from marker; finish off.

With **wrong** side together and White, and working through **both** loops, whipstitch seam at top of Hood.

EDGING

Rnd 1: With **right** side facing, join Red with slip st in bottom corner sp on Right Front; ch 3, 4 dc in same sp, 2 dc in end of each row across to next corner sp, 5 dc in corner sp; 2 dc in each sp across bottom edge; join with slip st to first dc.

Rnd 2: Ch 1, sc in each dc around; join with slip st to first sc, finish off.

TIE

With **right** side facing, join Red with slip st in sc on Edging even with shoulder seam, chain a 12" length; finish off.
Slip bead on Tie; knot end.
Repeat for second side.

ARMHOLE EDGING

Rnd 1: With **right** side facing, join Red with slip st in first skipped ch-2 sp on Body; ch 3, dc in same sp, 2 dc in end of each row around; join with slip st to first dc.

Rnd 2: Ch 1, sc in each dc around; join with slip st to first sc, finish off.
Repeat for second armhole.

COLORFUL WESTERN VEST

*D*on *this Western-style vest to add cowgirl chic to a plain shirt and jeans! The concho-trimmed cover-up is crocheted using a variety of single crochet stitches. A color-sequence chart is provided for your convenience.*

Size:	Small	Medium	Large
Finished Chest			
Measurement:	36¹/₂"	41"	45"

Size Note: Instructions are written for size Small with sizes Medium and Large in braces { }. Instructions will be easier to read if you circle all the numbers pertaining to your size. If only one number is given, it applies to all sizes.

MATERIALS
Sport Weight Yarn:
Black - 3¹/₂{3³/₄-4} ounces,
[90{105-110} grams, 335{385-410} yards]
Red, Gold, and Teal - 1¹/₄{1¹/₂-1¹/₂} ounces,
[35{40-40} grams, 130{155-155} yards] **each**
White and Maroon - 1{1¹/₄-1¹/₄} ounces,
[30{35-35} grams, 105{130-130} yards] **each**
Purple and Turquoise - ¹/₂{³/₄-³/₄} ounce,
[15{20-20} grams, 50{75-75} yards] **each**
Crochet hook, size G (4.00 mm) **or** size needed for gauge
Yarn needle
4 conchos

STITCH GUIDE

DECREASE (uses next 2 sc)
Pull up a loop in next 2 sc, YO and draw through all 3 loops on hook **(counts as one sc)**.
ADD ON SC
Insert hook in base of last sc worked *(Fig. 24a, page 136)*, YO and pull up a loop, YO and draw through one loop on hook, YO and draw through both loops on hook.
LONG SINGLE CROCHET *(abbreviated Long sc)*
Working **around** previous sts, insert hook in sc 2 rows **below** next sc **or** in second sc **below** sc at end of next row, YO and pull up a loop **even** with loop on hook, YO and draw through both loops on hook *(Fig. 9, page 134)*.
REVERSE SINGLE CROCHET *(abbreviated reverse sc)*
Working from **left** to **right**, insert hook in stitch to right of hook, YO and draw through, under and to left of loop on hook, YO and draw through both loops on hook *(Figs. 14a-d, page 135)*.

GAUGE: 18 sc and 22 rows = 4"

Gauge Swatch: 4" square
Ch 19 **loosely.**
Row 1: Sc in second ch from hook and in each ch across: 18 sc.
Rows 2-22: Ch 1, turn; sc in each sc across.
Finish off.

CHANGING COLORS
When changing colors at the end of the row *(Fig. 28a, page 138)*, cut old yarn. When changing color within the row, keep unused color on **wrong** side, holding it with normal tension; do **not** cut yarn until color is no longer needed.

FOLLOWING CHART
Left Front is worked following a color chart, page 111. The written instructions are provided to assist you in following the chart. The following are hints for reading the chart: Each square on the chart represents one single crochet and each row of squares represents one row of stitches. Read **right** side rows from **right** to **left**; read **wrong** side rows from **left** to **right**. Each size is outlined by a different color on the chart. Edges shared by more than one size are outlined in black; sizes are indicated on the chart at the bottom edge next to each outline.

LEFT FRONT
BODY
Row 1 (Right side): With Black, ch 2, 3 sc in second ch from hook.
Note: Loop a short piece of yarn around any stitch to mark Row 1 as **right** side.
Row 2: Ch 1, turn; sc in each sc across, add on 2 sc: 5 sc.
Row 3: Ch 1, turn; 2 sc in first sc, sc in each sc across to last sc, 2 sc in last sc: 7 sc.
Rows 4 thru 20{22-22}: Repeat Rows 2 and 3, 8{9-9} times, then repeat Row 2 once **more**: 41{45-45} sc.
Size Small Only - Row 21: Ch 1, turn; sc in each sc across to last sc, 2 sc in last sc: 42 sc.
Sizes Medium and Large Only - Row 23: Ch 1, turn; 2 sc in first sc, sc in each sc across: 46 sc.
Size Large Only
Row 24: Ch 1, turn; sc in each sc across, add on 2 sc: 48 sc.
Row 25: Ch 1, turn; 2 sc in first sc, sc in each sc across: 49 sc.
Row 26: Ch 1, turn; sc in each sc across to last sc, 2 sc in last sc: 50 sc.
All Sizes - Rows 22{24-27} thru 67: Ch 1, turn; sc in each sc across.

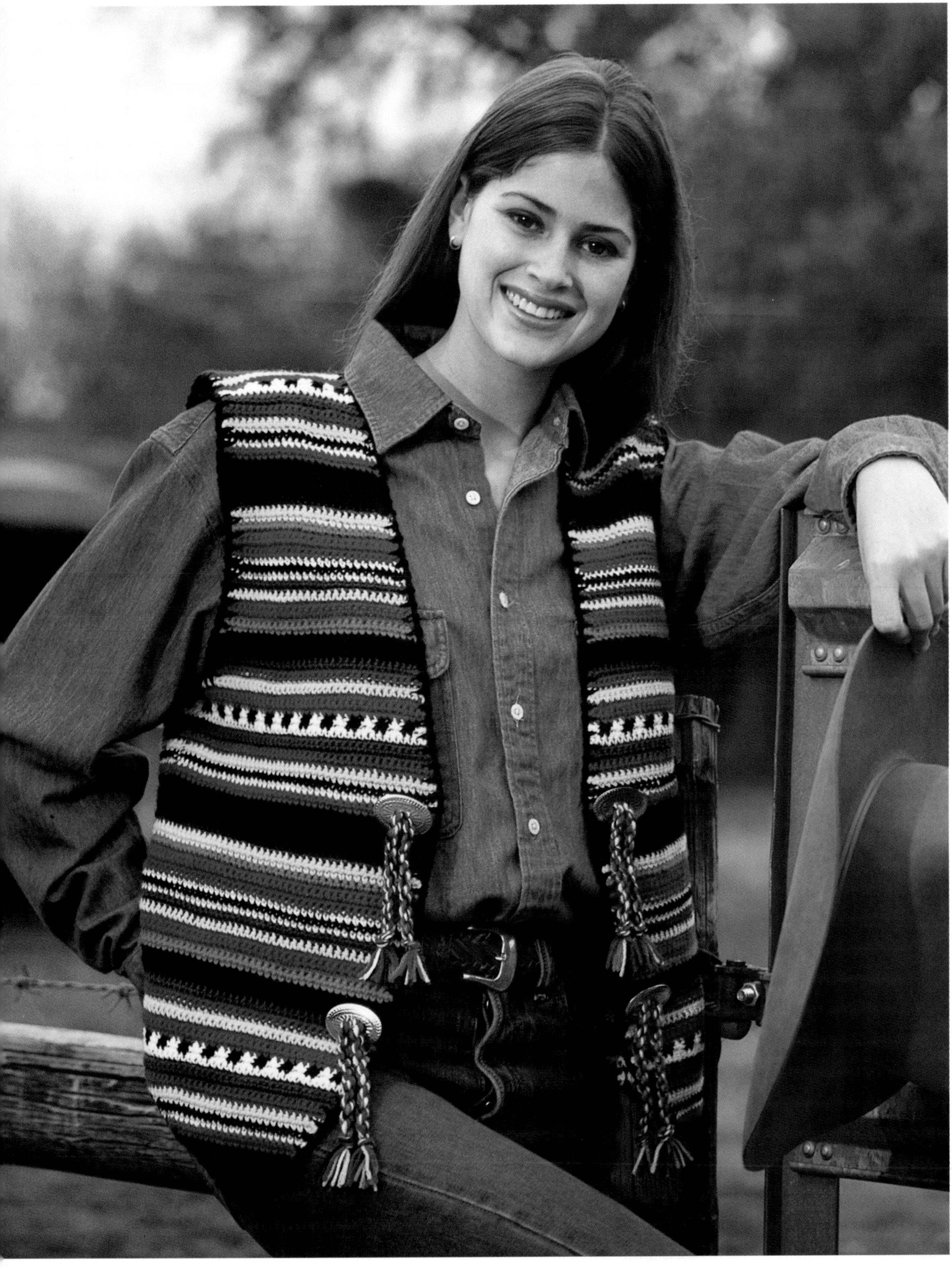

NECK AND ARMHOLE SHAPING

Row 68 (Decrease row): Ch 1, turn; decrease, sc in each sc across: 41{45-49} sc.

Rows 69-71: Ch 1, turn; sc in each sc across.

Rows 72 thru 76{80-84}: Repeat Rows 68-71, 1{2-3} times, then repeat Row 68 once **more**; sizes Small and Large only, finish off at end of last row: 39{42-45} sc.

Sizes Small and Large Only - Row 77{85}: With **right** side facing, skip first 5 sc and join next color with slip st in next sc; ch 1, sc in same st and in each sc across: 34{40} sc.

Size Medium Only - Row 81: Turn; slip st in first 6 sc, ch 1, sc in same st and in each sc across: 37 sc.

All Sizes

Row 78{82-86}: Ch 1, turn; sc in each sc across.

Rows 79{83-87} thru 81{85-89}: Ch 1, turn; decrease, sc in each sc across: 31{34-37} sc.

Rows 82{86-90} thru 85{89-93}: Repeat Rows 78{82-86} thru 81{85-89} once: 28{31-34} sc.

Row 86{90-94}: Ch 1, turn; sc in each sc across.

Rows 87{91-95} and 88{92-96}: Ch 1, turn; decrease, sc in each sc across: 26{29-32} sc.

Continue to decrease one stitch at neck edge, every fourth row, 8 times **more**, then work even for 5{11-13} rows: 18{21-24} sc. Finish off.

RIGHT FRONT
BODY

Note: Work in same color sequence as Left Front.

Row 1 (Right side): With Black, ch 2, 3 sc in second ch from hook.

Note: Mark Row 1 as **right** side.

Row 2: Ch 3, turn; sc in second ch from hook and in next ch, sc in each sc across: 5 sc.

Row 3: Ch 1, turn; 2 sc in first sc, sc in each sc across to last sc, 2 sc in last sc: 7 sc.

Rows 4 thru 20{22-22}: Repeat Rows 2 and 3, 8{9-9} times, then repeat Row 2 once **more**: 41{45-45} sc.

Size Small Only - Row 21: Ch 1, turn; 2 sc in first sc, sc in each sc across: 42 sc.

Sizes Medium and Large Only - Row 23: Ch 1, turn; sc in each sc across to last sc, 2 sc in last sc: 46 sc.

Size Large Only

Row 24: Ch 3, turn; sc in second ch from hook and in next ch, sc in each sc across: 48 sc.

Row 25: Ch 1, turn; sc in each sc across to last sc, 2 sc in last sc: 49 sc.

Row 26: Ch 1, turn; 2 sc in first sc, sc in each sc across: 50 sc.

All Sizes - Rows 22{24-27} thru 67: Ch 1, turn; sc in each sc across.

NECK AND ARMHOLE SHAPING

Row 68 (Decrease row): Ch 1, turn; sc in each sc across to last 2 sc, decrease: 41{45-49} sc.

Rows 69-71: Ch 1, turn; sc in each sc across.

Rows 72 thru 76{80-84}: Repeat Rows 68-71, 1{2-3} times, then repeat Row 68 once **more**.

Row 77{81-85}: Ch 1, turn; sc in each sc across to last 5 sc, leave remaining sc unworked: 34{37-40} sc.

Row 78{82-86}: Ch 1, turn; sc in each sc across.

Rows 79{83-87} thru 81{85-89}: Ch 1, turn; sc in each sc across to last 2 sc, decrease: 31{34-37} sc.

Rows 82{86-90} thru 85{89-93}: Repeat Rows 78{82-86} thru 81{85-89} once: 28{31-34} sc.

Row 86{90-94}: Ch 1, turn; sc in each sc across.

Rows 87{91-95} and 88{92-96}: Ch 1, turn; sc in each sc across to last 2 sc, decrease: 26{29-32} sc.

Continue to decrease one stitch at neck edge, every fourth row, 8 times **more**, then work even for 5{11-13} rows: 18{21-24} sc. Finish off.

BACK
BODY

With Teal{Black-Red}, ch 83{93-103} **loosely**.

Note: Work in same color sequence as Fronts, beginning with Row 20{23-26} of Chart.

Row 1: Sc in second ch from hook and in each ch across: 82{92-102} sc.

Row 2: Ch 1, turn; sc in each sc across.

Note: Mark Row 2{1-2} as **right** side.

Rows 3 thru 57{58-59}: Ch 1, turn; sc in each sc across; sizes Small and Large only, finish off at end of last row.

ARMHOLE SHAPING

Sizes Small and Large Only - Row 58{60}: With **right** side facing, skip first 5 sc and join Red{Black} with slip st in next sc; ch 1, sc in same st and in each sc across to last 5 sc, leave remaining sc unworked: 72{92} sc.

Size Medium Only - Row 59: Turn; slip st in first 6 sc, ch 1, sc in same st and in each sc across to last 5 sc, leave remaining sc unworked: 82 sc.

All Sizes

Row 59{60-61}: Ch 1, turn; sc in each sc across.

Row 60{61-62}: Ch 1, turn; decrease, sc in each sc across to last 2 sc, decrease: 70{80-90} sc.

Rows 61{62-63} thru 68{69-70}: Repeat last 2 rows, 4 times: 62{72-82} sc.

Rows 69{70-71} thru 106{113-116}: Ch 1, turn; sc in each sc across.

Finish off.

FINISHING

ASSEMBLY

With **wrong** sides together and working through
both loops, whipstitch shoulder seams (*Fig. 30a,
page 139*).
With **wrong** sides together and matching rows,
whipstitch side seams.

FRONT AND BACK EDGING

Rnd 1: With **right** side facing, join Black with slip st in
any sc at center of Back neck edge; ch 1, (work Long sc,
ch 1) evenly around; join with slip st to first Long sc.
Rnd 2: Ch 1, work reverse sc in each ch-1 sp around;
join with slip st to first st, finish off.

ARMHOLE EDGING

Rnd 1: With **right** side facing, join Black with slip st in
any sc at underarm; ch 1, (work Long sc, ch 1) evenly
around; join with slip st to first Long sc.
Rnd 2: Ch 1, work reverse sc in each ch-1 sp around;
join with slip st to first st, finish off.
Repeat for second Armhole.

VEST TIE (Make 4)

To make twisted cord, cut one 36" strand of each color.
Holding all strands together, fasten one end to a
stationary object or have another person hold it; twist
until tight. Fold in half and let it twist itself; knot both
ends and cut the loops on the folded end. Trim the ends
evenly.
Pull ends of twisted cord through openings in concho
from **back** to **front**.

With White, ch 30; finish off.
Pull ends of chain through openings in concho from
front to **back** below twisted cord.

Using photo as a guide for placement and with **wrong**
side of concho and **right** side of Vest together, draw ends
of chain through Vest to **wrong** side. Tie ends in a bow
to secure and to allow removal for cleaning.
Repeat for remaining Ties.

LEFT FRONT CHART

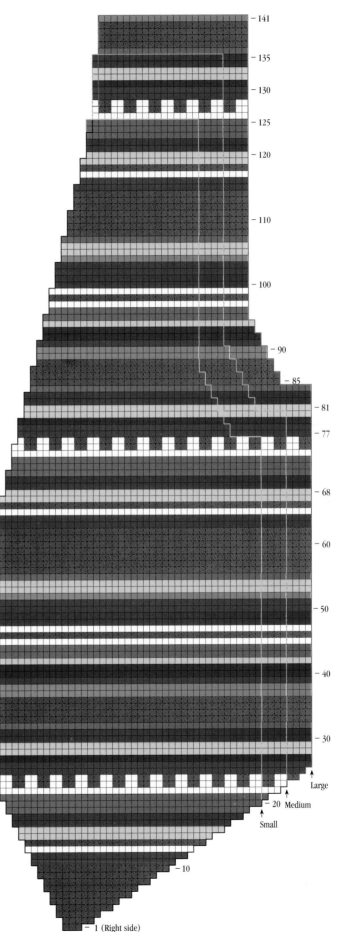

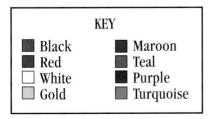

KEY	
■ Black	■ Maroon
■ Red	■ Teal
□ White	■ Purple
■ Gold	■ Turquoise

hooked on holidays

Dressing up our homes for the holidays — whether with grand decorations or simple little touches — is part of what makes these occasions so much fun! To encourage you to observe special days all year long, this assortment features an Easter bonnet, an all-American pillow, a lacy Christmas stocking, and more. Crochet these charming designs to keep or to give to someone you love — after all, celebrations are more enjoyable when you share a part of yourself.

VALENTINE'S DAY

A valentine who's as sweet as sugar will adore this romantic cover-up, which showcases a favorite childhood verse. Embellished with three-dimensional roses, violets, and leaves, the wrap makes a heartwarming token of affection.

ROMANTIC COVER-UP

Finished Size: 48" x 66"

MATERIALS
Worsted Weight Yarn:
   Ecru - 41 ounces, (1,160 grams, 2,810 yards)
   Red - 6 ounces, (170 grams, 375 yards)
   Green - 5 ounces, (140 grams, 345 yards)
   Purple - 5 ounces, (140 grams, 345 yards)
Crochet hooks, sizes G (4.00 mm) **and** I (5.50 mm) **or**
   sizes needed for gauge
Yarn needle

GAUGE: With large size hook (size I), in pattern,
      7 Cross Sts = 5" and 10 rows = 3½"

Gauge Swatch: 5½"w x 3½"h
With Ecru and large size hook, ch 24 **loosely**.
Work same as Rows 1-10 of Body, page 114.
Finish off.

STITCH GUIDE

CROSS ST
Skip next 2 sc, dc in next sc, ch 1, working **around** last dc made, dc in first skipped sc *(Fig. 1)*.

Fig. 1

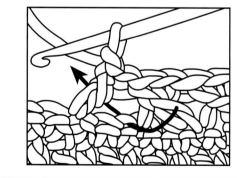

BODY

With Ecru and large size hook, ch 102 **loosely**.

Row 1 (Right side): Sc in second ch from hook and in each ch across: 101 sc.

Note: Loop a short piece of yarn around any stitch to mark Row 1 as **right** side and bottom.

Row 2: Ch 3 **(counts as first dc, now and throughout)**, turn; work Cross St across to last sc, dc in last sc: 33 Cross Sts.

Row 3: Ch 1, turn; sc in each dc and in each ch-1 sp across. Repeat Rows 2 and 3 for pattern until afghan measures 42", ending by working Row 3, do **not** finish off.

EDGING

Rnd 1: Ch 1, 2 sc in same st, work 143 sc evenly spaced across end of rows; working in free loops of beginning ch *(Fig. 22b, page 136)*, 3 sc in first ch, work 81 sc evenly spaced across to last ch, 3 sc in last ch; work 143 sc evenly spaced across end of rows; 3 sc in first st, work 81 sc evenly spaced across last row, sc in same st as first sc; join with slip st to first sc: 460 sc.

Rnd 2: Ch 1, 3 sc in same st, sc in each sc around working 3 sc in each corner sc; join with slip st to first sc, finish off: 468 sc.

Rnd 3: With **right** side facing, join Green with slip st in any corner sc; ch 3, dc in same st, dc in next sc and in each sc across to next corner sc, ★ (2 dc, ch 1, 2 dc) in corner sc, dc in next sc and in each sc across to next corner sc; repeat from ★ around, 2 dc in same st as first dc, ch 1; join with slip st to first dc, finish off: 480 dc.

Rnd 4: With **right** side facing, join Ecru with slip st in any corner ch-1 sp; ch 4 **(counts as first dc plus ch 1, now and throughout)**, 2 dc in same sp, dc in each dc across to next corner ch-1 sp, ★ (2 dc, ch 1, 2 dc) in corner ch-1 sp, dc in each dc across to next corner ch-1 sp; repeat from ★ around, dc in same sp as first dc; join with slip st to first dc: 496 dc.

Rnds 5 and 6: Slip st in first ch-1 sp, ch 4, 2 dc in same sp, dc in each dc across to next corner ch-1 sp, ★ (2 dc, ch 1, 2 dc) in corner ch-1 sp, dc in each dc across to next corner ch-1 sp; repeat from ★ around, dc in same sp as first dc; join with slip st to first dc: 528 dc.

Rnd 7: Slip st in first ch-1 sp, ch 1, 2 sc in same sp, sc in each dc across to next corner ch-1 sp, ★ 3 sc in corner ch-1 sp, sc in each dc across to next corner ch-1 sp; repeat from ★ around, sc in same sp as first sc; join with slip st to first sc: 540 sc.

Rnds 8-13: Ch 1, 2 sc in same st, sc in each sc around working 3 sc in each corner sc, sc in same st as first sc; join with slip st to first sc: 588 sc.

Rnd 14: Ch 4, 2 dc in same st, dc in next sc and in each sc across to next corner sc, ★ (2 dc, ch 1, 2 dc) in corner sc, dc in next sc and in each sc across to next corner sc; repeat from ★ around, dc in same st as first dc; join with slip st to first dc: 600 dc.

Rnds 15 and 16: Repeat Rnd 5, twice; at end of Rnd 16, finish off: 632 dc.

Rnd 17: With **right** side facing, join Green with slip st in any corner ch-1 sp; ch 4, 2 dc in same sp, dc in each dc across to next corner ch-1 sp, ★ (2 dc, ch 1, 2 dc) in corner ch-1 sp, dc in each dc across to next corner ch-1 sp; repeat from ★ around, dc in same sp as first dc; join with slip st to first dc, finish off: 648 dc.

Rnd 18: With **right** side facing, join Ecru with slip st in any corner ch-1 sp; ch 4, 2 dc in same sp, dc in each dc across to next corner ch-1 sp, ★ (2 dc, ch 1, 2 dc) in corner ch-1 sp, dc in each dc across to next corner ch-1 sp; repeat from ★ around, dc in same sp as first dc; join with slip st to first dc: 664 dc.

Rnds 19-27: Repeat Rnd 5, 9 times; at end of Rnd 27, finish off: 808 dc.

Rnd 28: Repeat Rnd 17: 824 dc.

Rnd 29: With **right** side facing, join Ecru with slip st in any corner ch-1 sp; ch 1, (3 sc in corner ch-1 sp, sc in each dc across to next corner ch-1 sp) around; join with slip st to first sc: 836 sc.

Rnd 30: Ch 1, sc in same st, ch 3, sc in side of sc just worked *(Fig. 27, page 138)*, skip next sc, ★ sc in next sc, ch 3, sc in side of sc just worked, skip next sc; repeat from ★ around; join with slip st to first sc, finish off: 418 sc.

ROSE (Make 20)

With Red and small size hook, ch 4; join with slip st to form a ring.

Rnd 1 (Wrong side): Ch 1, (sc in ring, ch 3) 4 times; join with slip st to first sc: 4 ch-3 sps.

Rnd 2: Ch 1, (sc, 5 dc, sc) in each ch-3 sp around; join with slip st to first sc: 4 petals.

Rnd 3: Ch 1, working in **front** of petals, sc around post of first sc on Rnd 1 *(Fig. 15, page 135)*, ch 3, (sc around post of next sc on Rnd 1, ch 3) 3 times; join with slip st to first sc: 4 ch-3 sps.

Rnd 4: Ch 1, (sc, 5 tr, sc) in each ch-3 sp around; join with slip st to first sc: 4 petals.

Rnd 5: Ch 1, working in **front** of petals, sc around post of first sc on Rnd 3, ch 3, sc around post of next sc on Rnd 3, ch 3, sc in base of center tr on next petal, ch 3, (sc around post of next sc on Rnd 3, ch 3) twice, sc in base of center tr on next petal, ch 3; join with slip st to first sc: 6 ch-3 sps.

Rnd 6: Ch 1, (sc, 7 tr, sc) in each ch-3 sp around; join with slip st to first sc, finish off: 6 petals.

Sew edges of first petal together to form center bud.

ROSE LEAF (Make 20)

With Green and small size hook, ch 8 **loosely**.

Rnd 1 (Right side): Dc in fourth ch from hook, hdc in next 2 chs, sc in next ch, 3 sc in last ch; working in free loops of beginning ch, sc in next ch, hdc in next 2 chs, (dc, ch 3, slip st) in next ch; do **not** join.

Rnd 2: (Ch 1, slip st in next st) around; finish off leaving a long end for sewing.

VIOLET (Make 20)

With Purple and small size hook, ch 4; join with slip st to form a ring.

Rnd 1: (Ch 2, 3 dc, ch 2, slip st) 3 times in ring (bottom petals made), work (ch 3, 4 tr, ch 3, slip st) twice in ring (top petals made); finish off leaving a long end for sewing.

VIOLET LEAF (Make 20)

With Green and small size hook, ch 9 **loosely**.

Rnd 1: 4 Tr in fourth ch from hook, 2 tr in next ch, dc in next ch, hdc in next ch, sc in next ch, work 3 slip sts in last ch; working in free loops of beginning ch, sc in next ch, hdc in next ch, dc in next ch, 2 tr in next ch, work (4 tr, ch 3, slip st) in next ch; finish off leaving a long end for sewing.

FINISHING

With a single strand of Purple and following Charts, add cross-stitched words on Rnds 7-13 of Edging **(Fig. 37, page 141)**. Using double strands of Red, cross stitch hearts.

Using photo as a guide for placement, sew Roses, Violets, and Leaves to Edging.

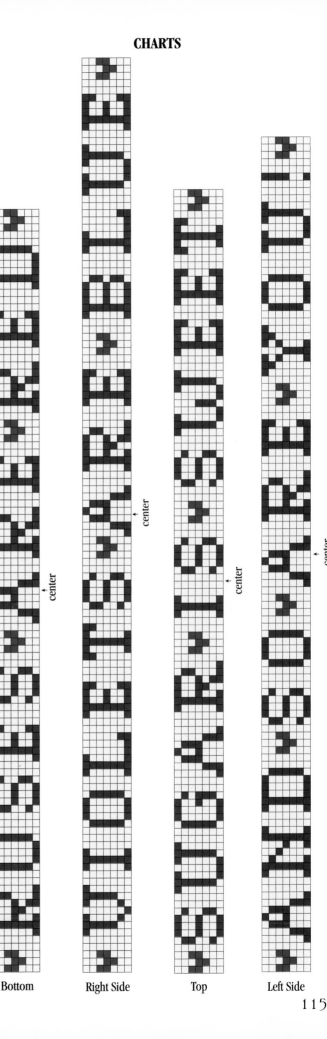

CHARTS

Bottom   Right Side   Top   Left Side

115

With all the pretty frills upon it, you'll want to show off this Easter bonnet as soon as spring arrives! Crocheted with delicate thread, the lacy wall decoration is stiffened and then accented with satin ribbon and tiny flowers.

EASTER BONNET

Finished Size: 18¹/₂" in diameter

MATERIALS

Bedspread Weight Cotton Thread (size 10), 350 yards
Steel crochet hook, size 5 (1.90 mm) **or** size needed for gauge
Starching materials: Commercial fabric stiffener, blocking board, plastic wrap, resealable plastic bag, terry towel, paper towels, and stainless steel pins
Glue gun
Flowers
Ribbon: 1 yard of ⁵/₈" wide pink, 1 yard of 2¹/₈" wide pink, 1¹/₄ yards of ¹/₁₆" wide pink, and 24" length of ¹/₄" wide ecru

GAUGE SWATCH: 2¹/₄" in diameter
Work same as Hat through Rnd 2.

STITCH GUIDE

SHELL
(2 Dc, ch 2, 2 dc) in st or sp indicated.
PICOT
Ch 3, slip st in side of st just worked *(Fig. 27, page 138)*.
KNOT ST
Ch 1, ★ pull up loop on hook ³/₈", YO and draw through loop on hook, insert hook in loop just made *(Fig. 1)*, YO and draw through same loop, YO and draw through both loops on hook; repeat from ★ once **more**.

Fig. 1

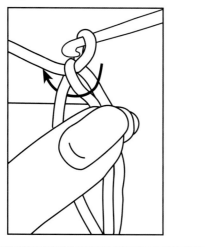

Ch 5; join with slip st to form a ring.
Rnd 1 (Right side)**:** Ch 3 **(counts as first dc, now and throughout)**, 23 dc in ring; join with slip st to first dc: 24 dc.
Rnd 2: Ch 6, (tr in Back Loop Only of next dc, ch 2) around *(Fig. 21, page 136)*; join with slip st to fourth ch of beginning ch-6: 24 ch-2 sps.
Rnd 3: Ch 3, working in both loops, (dc, ch 2, 2 dc) in same st, sc in next tr, (work Shell in next tr, sc in next tr) around; join with slip st to first dc: 12 Shells.
Rnd 4: Slip st in next dc and in next ch-2 sp, ch 1, sc in same sp work Picot, ★ ch 7, sc in next Shell (ch-2 sp), work Picot; repeat from ★ around, ch 4, dc in first sc to form last loop: 12 loops.
Rnd 5: Ch 3, dc in same loop, ch 3, skip next Picot and next ch, dc in next 2 chs, ch 3, skip next ch, ★ dc in next 2 chs, ch 3, skip next Picot and next ch, dc in next 2 chs, ch 3, skip next ch repeat from ★ around; join with slip st to first dc: 24 ch-3 sps.
Rnd 6: Ch 3, dc in same st, ch 2, 2 dc in next dc, sc in next ch-3 sp, ★ 2 dc in next dc, ch 2, 2 dc in next dc, sc in next ch-3 sp; repeat from ★ around; join with slip st to first dc: 24 sc.
Rnd 7: Slip st in next dc and in next ch-2 sp, ch 3, (dc, ch 2, 2 dc) in same sp, ch 1, (work Shell in next ch-2 sp, ch 1) around; join with slip st to first dc: 24 Shells.
Rnds 8-13: Slip st in next dc and in next ch-2 sp, ch 3, (dc, ch 2, 2 dc) in same sp, ch 2, (work Shell in next Shell, ch 2) around; join with slip st to first dc.
Rnd 14: Slip st in next dc and in next ch-2 sp, ch 3, (dc, ch 2, 2 dc) in same sp, ch 2, sc in next ch-2 sp, ch 2, ★ work Shell in next Shell, ch 2, sc in next ch-2 sp, ch 2; repeat from ★ around; join with slip st to first dc.
Rnd 15: Ch 3, dc in same st and in next dc, 5 dc in next ch-2 sp dc in next dc, 2 dc in next dc, ★ skip next 2 ch-2 sps, 2 dc in next dc, dc in next dc, 5 dc in next ch-2 sp, dc in next dc, 2 dc in next dc; repeat from ★ around; join with slip st to first dc.
Rnd 16: Slip st in next 3 dc, ch 7, working in Back Loops Only dtr in next dc, (ch 2, dtr in next dc) 3 times, ★ skip next 6 dc, dtr in next dc, (ch 2, dtr in next dc) 4 times; repeat from ★ around; join with slip st to fifth ch of beginning ch-7.
Rnd 17: Ch 3, working in both loops, (dc, ch 2, 2 dc) in same st, ch 1, sc in next dtr, ch 1, work Shell in next dtr, ch 1, sc in next dtr, ch 1, skip next dtr, ★ (work Shell in next dtr, ch 1, sc in next dtr, ch 1) twice, skip next dtr; repeat from ★ around; join with slip st to first dc: 48 Shells.

Rnd 18: Slip st in next dc and in next ch-2 sp, ch 1, sc in same sp, ch 6, (sc in next Shell, work Picot, ch 6) around; join with slip st to first sc, ch 3, slip st in same st: 48 loops.

Rnd 19: Slip st in first 2 chs, ch 1, sc in same loop, work Knot St, sc in next loop, (ch 7, sc in next loop, work Knot St, sc in next loop) around, ch 3, tr in first sc to form last loop: 24 Knot Sts.

Rnd 20: Ch 3, (dc, ch 2, 2 dc) in same sp, ch 5, sc in next Knot St (center st), work Picot, ch 5, ★ work Shell in center ch of next loop, ch 5, sc in next Knot St, work Picot, ch 5; repeat from ★ around; join with slip st to first dc.

Rnd 21: Ch 3, dc in same st and in next dc, ★ † 5 dc in next ch-2 sp, dc in next dc, 2 dc in next dc, sc in next ch-5-sp, 5 dc in next Picot, sc in next ch-5 sp †, 2 dc in next dc, dc in next dc; repeat from ★ around to last ch-2 sp, then repeat from † to † once; join with slip st to first dc.

Rnd 22: Slip st in next 2 dc, ch 7, working in Back Loops Only, dtr in next dc, (ch 2, dtr in next dc) 5 times, ★ skip next 11 sts, dtr in next dc, (ch 2, dtr in next dc) 6 times; repeat from ★ around; join with slip st to fifth ch of beginning ch-7.

Rnd 23: Ch 3, working in both loops, dc in each ch and in each dtr around; join with slip st to first dc: 456 dc.

Rnd 24: Ch 3, dc in same st, ch 3, skip next 2 dc, (2 dc in Back Loop Only of next dc, ch 3, skip next 2 dc) around; join with slip st to first dc: 152 ch-3 sps.

Rnd 25: Ch 2, working in both loops, dc in next dc and in each ch and each dc around; skip beginning ch-2 and join with slip st to first dc: 759 dc.

Rnd 26: Ch 1, sc in same st, ch 3, skip next 2 dc, (sc in Back Loop Only of next dc, ch 3, skip next 2 dc) around; join with slip st to first sc, finish off: 253 ch-3 sps.

FINISHING

See Starching and Blocking, page 140.
Weave 5/8" wide ribbon through Rnd 16 and glue ends together. Tie 2 1/8" wide ribbon in a bow and glue to Hat. Cut remaining pink ribbon in 3 equal pieces and tie each in a bow. Tie ecru ribbon in a double bow.
Glue flowers and bows to large bow as desired.

INDEPENDENCE DAY

A symbol of the ingenuity and perseverance of American pioneers, the Log Cabin quilt block has long been a favorite among needlecrafters. We chose a patriotic color scheme to fashion this spirited pillow.

AMERICAN LOG CABIN PILLOW

Finished Size: 14" square

MATERIALS

Worsted Weight Yarn:

Navy - 1¼ ounces, (35 grams, 80 yards)

Blue - 1 ounce, (30 grams, 65 yards)

Ecru - 1 ounce, (30 grams, 65 yards)

Beige - 1 ounce, (30 grams, 65 yards)

Gray - 1 ounce, (30 grams, 65 yards)

Maroon - 1 ounce, (30 grams, 65 yards)

Red - 7 yards

Crochet hook, size K (6.50 mm) **or** size needed for gauge

Yarn needle

14" purchased pillow form **or** ½ yard 44/45" wide fabric and polyester fiberfill

GAUGE: 12 sc and 16 rows = 4"

Gauge Swatch: 1⅝" x 1½"
Work same as Square through Row 6.

SQUARE (Make 2)

With Red, ch 6 **loosely**.

Row 1 (Right side): Sc in second ch from hook and in each ch across: 5 sc.

Note: Loop a short piece of yarn around any stitch to mark Row 1 as **right** side.

Rows 2-6: Ch 1, turn; sc in each sc across, changing to Ecru in last sc worked on Row 6 *(Figs. 28a & b, page 138)*.

Rows 7-11: Ch 1, turn; sc in each sc across.

Row 12: Ch 1, working in end of rows, sc in first 2 rows, skip next row, sc in next 5 rows, skip next row, sc in last 2 rows: 9 sc.

Rows 13-16: Ch 1, turn; sc in each sc across, changing to Blue in last sc worked on Row 16.

Row 17: Ch 1, working in end of rows, sc in first 2 rows, skip next row, sc in next 2 rows, sc in free loop of next 5 chs *(Fig. 22b, page 136)*: 9 sc.

Rows 18-21: Ch 1, turn; sc in each sc across.

Row 22: Ch 1, working in end of rows, sc in first 2 rows, skip next row, sc in next 5 rows, (skip next row, sc in next 3 rows) twice: 13 sc.

Rows 23-26: Ch 1, turn; sc in each sc across, changing to Beige in last sc worked on Row 26.

Row 27: Ch 1, working in end of rows, sc in first 2 rows, skip next row, sc in next 2 rows, sc in next 5 sc, sc in next 2 rows, skip next row, sc in last 2 rows: 13 sc.

Rows 28-31: Ch 1, turn; sc in each sc across.

Row 32: Ch 1, working in end of rows, sc in first 2 rows, skip next row, sc in next 2 rows, sc in next 9 sc, sc in next 2 rows, skip next row, sc in last 2 rows: 17 sc.

Rows 33-36: Ch 1, turn; sc in each sc across, changing to Maroon in last sc worked on Row 36.

Row 37: Repeat Row 32.

Rows 38-41: Ch 1, turn; sc in each sc across.

Row 42: Ch 1, working in end of rows, sc in first 2 rows, skip next row, sc in next 2 rows, sc in next 13 sc, sc in next 2 rows, skip next row, sc in last 2 rows: 21 sc.

Rows 43-46: Ch 1, turn; sc in each sc across, changing to Gray in last sc worked on Row 46.

Row 47: Repeat Row 42.

Rows 48-51: Ch 1, turn; sc in each sc across.

Row 52: Ch 1, working in end of rows, sc in first 2 rows, skip next row, sc in next 2 rows, sc in next 17 sc, sc in next 2 rows, skip next row, sc in last 2 rows: 25 sc.

Rows 53-56: Ch 1, turn; sc in each sc across, changing to Navy in last sc worked on Row 56.

Row 57: Repeat Row 52.

Rows 58-61: Ch 1, turn; sc in each sc across.

Row 62: Ch 1, working in end of rows, sc in first 2 rows, skip next row, sc in next 2 rows, sc in next 21 sc, sc in next 2 rows, skip next row, sc in last 2 rows: 29 sc.

Rows 63-66: Ch 1, turn; sc in each sc across, changing to Ecru in last sc worked on Row 66; do **not** finish off.

EDGING

Rnd 1: Ch 1, work 3 sc evenly spaced across end of rows and sc in each sc around working 3 sc in each corner sc; join with slip st to first sc changing to Beige: 120 sc.

Note: Work in the following color sequence: 1 rnd each Beige, Gray, Blue, Maroon, Navy.

Rnds 2-5: Ch 1, sc in each sc around working 3 sc in each corner sc; join with slip st to first sc changing to next color.

Rnd 6: Ch 1, sc in each sc around working 3 sc in each corner sc; join with slip st to first sc, finish off.

FINISHING

Make pillow form if desired, page 138.

ASSEMBLY

With **wrong** sides together and Navy, and working through **inside** loops only, whipstitch Squares together inserting pillow form before closing *(Fig. 30b, page 139)*.

*H*olding a pretty little surprise that he's picked just for you, our pumpkin patch pal is ready to brighten your Halloween celebration! The cute fellow is stitched with worsted weight yarn and then stuffed with fiberfill for huggable softness.

PUMPKIN PATCH PAL

Finished Size: 23" tall

MATERIALS
Worsted Weight Yarn:
    Blue - 6 ounces, (170 grams, 380 yards)
    Yellow - 4 ounces, (110 grams, 255 yards)
    Black - 4 ounces, (110 grams, 255 yards)
    Red - 2 ounces, (60 grams, 125 yards)
    White - 2 ounces, (60 grams, 125 yards)
    Orange - 1¼ ounces, (35 grams, 80 yards)
Crochet hook, size G (4.00 mm) **or** size needed for gauge
2 - ⅝" black buttons (eyes)
2 - ⅝" gray buttons (pants)
2 - Sunflowers: 3" and 4" in diameter
Bandanna
Brown felt - 1" x 2" piece
Craft glue
Tapestry needle
Polyester fiberfill

Note: Entire project is worked holding 2 strands of yarn together.

GAUGE: 7 sc and 7 rows = 2"

Gauge Swatch: 4" square
Ch 15 **loosely**.
Row 1: Sc in second ch from hook and in each ch across: 14 sc.
Rows 2-14: Ch 1, turn; sc in each sc across.
Finish off.

STITCH GUIDE

> **DECREASE** (uses next 2 sts)
> Pull up a loop in next 2 sc, YO and draw through all 3 loops on hook (**counts as one sc**).

HEAD (Make 2)
With Yellow, ch 4; join with slip st to form a ring.
Rnd 1 (Right side): 8 Sc in ring; do **not** join, place marker *(see Markers, page 136)*.
Note: Loop a short piece of yarn around any stitch to mark Rnd 1 as **right** side.

Rnd 2: (Sc in next sc, 2 sc in next sc) around: 12 sc.
Rnd 3: 2 Sc in each sc around: 24 sc.
Rnd 4: (Sc in next sc, 2 sc in next sc) around: 36 sc.
Rnd 5: Sc in each sc around.
Rnd 6: (Sc in next 2 sc, 2 sc in next sc) around: 48 sc.
Rnds 7-9: Sc in each sc around; at end of Rnd 9, slip st in next sc, finish off.
With **wrong** sides together and working through **inside** loops only, whipstitch both sides of Head together leaving 10 sts on each piece unworked for neck *(Fig. 30b, page 139)*.

NECK
Rnd 1: With **right** side facing, join Yellow with slip st to any unworked st on Head; ch 1, sc in each sc around; join with slip st to first sc: 20 sc.
Rnd 2: Ch 1, sc in each sc around; join with slip st to first sc, finish off.

BODY
With Blue, ch 18 **loosely**.
Rnd 1 (Right side): 2 Sc in second ch from hook, sc in next 15 chs, 4 sc in last ch; working in free loops of beginning ch *(Fig. 22b, page 136)*, sc in next 15 chs, 2 sc in next ch; join with slip st to first sc: 38 sc.
Note: Mark Rnd 1 as **right** side.
Rnd 2: Ch 1, 2 sc in same st, sc in next 17 sc, 2 sc in each of next 2 sc, sc in next 17 sc, 2 sc in last sc; join with slip st to first sc: 42 sc.
Rnd 3: Ch 1, 2 sc in same st and in next sc, sc in next 17 sc, 2 sc in each of next 4 sc, sc in next 17 sc, 2 sc in each of last 2 sc; join with slip st to first sc: 50 sc.
Rnd 4: Ch 1, 2 sc in same st, sc in next sc, 2 sc in next sc, sc in next 20 sc, (2 sc in next sc, sc in next sc) twice, 2 sc in next sc, sc in next 20 sc, 2 sc in each of last 2 sc; join with slip st to first sc: 56 sc.
Rnd 5: Ch 1, sc in Back Loop Only of each sc around *(Fig. 21, page 136)*; join with slip st to first sc.
Rnds 6-14: Ch 1, sc in both loops of each sc around; join with slip st to first sc.
Rnd 15: Ch 1, sc in same st and in next 4 sc, decrease, (sc in next 5 sc, decrease) around; join with slip st to first sc, finish off: 48 sc.

FRONT BIB

Row 1: With **right** side facing and working in Front Loops Only, skip first 9 sc and join Blue with slip st in next sc; ch 1, sc in same st and in next 11 sc: 12 sc.

Rows 2-8: Ch 1, turn; sc in both loops of each sc across. Finish off.

BACK BIB

Row 1: With **right** side facing and working in Front Loops Only, skip 14 sc from Front Bib and join Blue with slip st in next sc on Body; ch 1, sc in same st and in next 7 sc: 8 sc.

Rows 2-4: Ch 1, turn; sc in both loops of each sc across; do **not** finish off.

RIGHT STRAP

Row 1: Ch 1, turn; sc in first 3 sc, leave remaining 5 sc unworked: 3 sc.

Rows 2-21: Ch 1, turn; sc in each sc across. Finish off leaving a long end for sewing.

LEFT STRAP

Row 1: With **right** side facing, skip 2 sc from Right Strap and join Blue with slip st in next sc on Row 4 of Back Bib; ch 1, sc in same st and in last 2 sc: 3 sc.

Rows 2-21: Ch 1, turn; sc in each sc across. Finish off leaving a long end for sewing.

SHIRT

Rnd 1: With **right** side facing and working in Back Loops Only of unworked sc of Body and in free loops of sts behind Bibs, join Red with slip st in first sc on Rnd 15; ch 3 **(counts as first dc, now and throughout)**, dc in next sc changing to White *(Fig. 28a, page 138)*, do **not** cut yarn, dc in next 2 sc changing to Red in last dc worked, (dc in next 2 sc changing colors in last dc worked) around to last 2 sc, dc in last 2 sc; join with slip st to first dc: 48 dc.

Rnd 2: Ch 3, working in Back Loops Only, dc in next dc changing to Red, (dc in next 2 dc changing colors in last dc worked) around to last 2 dc, dc in last 2 dc; join with slip st to first dc.

Rnd 3: Ch 3, working in Back Loops Only, dc in next dc changing to White, (dc in next 2 dc changing colors in last dc worked) around to last 2 dc, dc in last 2 dc; join with slip st to first dc.

Rnds 4-6: Repeat Rnds 2 and 3 once, then repeat Rnd 2 once **more**.

Finish off; cut White.

With **wrong** sides together, flatten Shirt across Rnd 6. Working through **inside** loops only, whipstitch shoulder seams, working across 7 dc on each side and leaving 20 center sts unworked for neck opening.

Stuff Body firmly with polyester fiberfill.

ARM (Make 2)

With Yellow, ch 4; join with slip st to form a ring.

Rnd 1 (Right side): Ch 1, 6 sc in ring; join with slip st to first sc.
Note: Mark Rnd 1 as **right** side.

Rnd 2: Ch 1, 2 sc in each sc around; join with slip st to first sc: 12 sc.

Rnd 3: Ch 1, sc in same st, 2 sc in next sc, (sc in next sc, 2 sc in next sc) around; join with slip st to first sc: 18 sc.

Rnds 4-8: Ch 1, sc in each sc around; join with slip st to first sc. Finish off.

Rnd 9: With **right** side facing and working in Back Loops Only, join Red with slip st in first sc; ch 3, dc in same st changing to White, dc in next 2 sc changing to Red in last dc worked, (dc in next 2 sc changing colors in last dc worked) around to last sc, 2 dc in last sc; join with slip st to first dc: 20 dc.

Rnd 10: Ch 3, working in Back Loops Only, dc in next dc changing to Red, (dc in next 2 dc changing colors in last dc worked) around to last 2 dc, dc in last 2 dc; join with slip st to first dc.

Rnd 11: Ch 3, working in Back Loops Only, dc in next dc changing to White, (dc in next 2 dc changing colors in last dc worked) around to last 2 dc, dc in last 2 dc; join with slip st to first dc.

Rnds 12-16: Repeat Rnds 10 and 11 twice, then repeat Rnd 10 once **more**.

Finish off; cut White.

Stuff Arm with polyester fiberfill.

Flatten Arm across Rnd 16 with joining at fold; working through **inside** loops only, whipstitch seam.

Sew Arms to Rnds 2-6 on each side of Shirt.

LEG (Make 2)
BOOT

With Black, ch 11 **loosely**.

Rnd 1 (Right side): Sc in second ch from hook and in each ch across to last ch, 3 sc in last ch; working in free loops of beginning ch, sc in next 8 chs, 3 sc in next ch; join with slip st to first sc: 23 sc.
Note: Mark Rnd 1 as **right** side.

Rnd 2: Ch 1, sc in same st and in next 9 sc, 2 sc in next sc, sc in next 11 sc, 3 sc in last sc, sc in same st as first sc; join with slip st to first sc: 27 sc.

Rnd 3: Ch 1, sc in same st and in next 10 sc, 2 sc in next sc, sc in next 13 sc, 2 sc in each of last 2 sc; join with slip st to first sc 30 sc.

Rnd 4: Ch 1, sc in Back Loop Only of each sc around; join with slip st to first sc.

Rnds 5-6: Ch 1, sc in both loops of each sc around; join with slip st to first sc, do **not** finish off.

INSTEP

Row 1: Ch 1, turn; sc in next 7 sts, leave remaining sts unworked.

Rows 2-4: Ch 1, turn; sc in each sc across.

Finish off.

With **wrong** sides together, sew each side of Instep to 3 sts on Rnd 6 of Boot.

SIDES

Rnd 1: With **right** side facing, skip 8 sc from Instep and join Black with slip st in next sc; ch 1, sc in same st and in each sc around; join with slip st to first sc: 24 sc.

Rnds 2-4: Ch 1, sc in each sc around; join with slip st to first sc.

Rnd 5: Ch 1, sc in each sc around; join with slip st to first sc changing to Yellow.

STRAW

Rnds 1-3: Ch 1, sc in Back Loop Only of each sc around; join with slip st to first sc.

Finish off.

PANT LEG

Rnd 1: With **right** side facing and working in Back Loops Only, join Blue with slip st in first sc; slip st in each sc around; join with slip st to first st.

Rnd 2: Ch 1, working in Back Loops Only, sc in same st and in next 4 sts, 2 sc in next st, (sc in next 5 sts, 2 sc in next st) around; join with slip st to first sc: 28 sc.

Rnds 3-16: Ch 1, sc in both loops of each sc around; join with slip st to first sc.

Finish off.

Stuff Leg with polyester fiberfill.

Flatten Leg across Rnd 16; working through **inside** loops only, whipstitch seam.

Working across front of Body, sew Legs to free loops of Rnd 4.

HAT

With Black, ch 4; join with slip st to form a ring.

Rnd 1 (Right side): Ch 1, 8 sc in ring; join with slip st to first sc.

Note: Mark Rnd 1 as **right** side.

Rnd 2: Ch 1, sc in same st, 2 sc in next sc, (sc in next sc, 2 sc in next sc) around; join with slip st to first sc: 12 sc.

Rnd 3: Ch 1, 2 sc in each sc around; join with slip st to first sc: 24 sc.

Rnd 4: Ch 1, sc in same st, 2 sc in next sc, (sc in next sc, 2 sc in next sc) around; join with slip st to first sc: 36 sc.

Rnd 5: Ch 1, sc in each sc around; join with slip st to first sc.

Rnd 6: Ch 1, sc in same st and in next sc, 2 sc in next sc, (sc in next 2 sc, 2 sc in next sc) around; join with slip st to Back Loop Only of first sc: 48 sc.

Rnd 7: Ch 1, sc in Back Loop Only of each sc around; join with slip st to first sc.

Rnds 8-10: Ch 1, sc in both loops of each sc around; join with slip st to first sc.

Rnd 11: Ch 1, working in Front Loops Only, sc in same st and in next sc, 2 sc in next sc, (sc in next 2 sc, 2 sc in next sc) around; join with slip st to first sc: 64 sc.

Rnd 12: Ch 1, sc in both loops of each sc around; join with slip st to first sc.

Rnd 13: Ch 1, sc in same st, 2 sc in next sc, (sc in next sc, 2 sc in next sc) around; join with slip st to first sc: 96 sc.

Rnd 14: Ch 1, sc in each sc around; join with slip st to first sc, finish off.

PUMPKIN

With Orange, ch 4; join with slip st to form a ring.

Rnd 1 (Right side): Ch 1, 6 sc in ring; join with slip st to first sc.

Rnd 2: Ch 1, sc in same st, 2 sc in next sc, (sc in next sc, 2 sc in next sc) twice; join with slip st to first sc: 9 sc.

Rnds 3 and 4: Ch 1, 2 sc in each sc around; join with slip st to first sc: 36 sc.

Rnds 5-12: Ch 1, sc in each sc around; join with slip st to first sc.

Rnd 13: Ch 1, sc in same st, decrease, (sc in next sc, decrease) around; join with slip st to first sc: 24 sc.

Stuff Pumpkin with polyester fiberfill.

Rnds 14-16: Ch 1, decrease around; join with slip st to first sc: 3 sc.

Finish off, leaving a 30" end.

Thread needle with end; wrap long end around side of Pumpkin and pull yarn through beginning ring to top of Pumpkin.

Continue in same manner creating 5 sections; secure end. Sew Pumpkin to hand.

FINISHING

Sew buttons to Head for eyes.

With Black add Straight St for mouth *(Fig. 34, page 141)*.

Cut nose from felt using pattern and glue to Head.

Stuff Head lightly with polyester fiberfill.

Working through **inside** loops only and matching seams, whipstitch unworked sts on Neck to unworked sts on Shirt.

Add fringe using 3 strands of Yellow, each 7" long *(Figs. 33a & b, page 139)* to free loop of 8 sc along each side of Head, to top center 4 sc, in each sc on Rnd 8 of each Arm, and in each sc on Rnd 2 of Straw on each Leg.

Sew Straps to Front Bib; sew buttons to Straps.

Sew Hat to Head, curling brim up.

Attach large sunflower to top of Hat above brim and small sunflower to side of Bib.

Cut 2 opposite corners off bandanna, leaving a 4" wide strip. Tie strip around Neck.

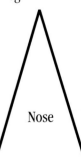

Nose

THANKSGIVING

Nestle our Thanksgiving turkey in an arrangement of autumn leaves, corn, and squash for a unique holiday centerpiece. Worked primarily with single crochets while holding two strands of yarn, he's quick to stitch and simply stuffed with fiberfill for a nice, plump finish.

TURKEY CENTERPIECE

Finished Size: 7" tall

MATERIALS

Worsted Weight Yarn:
Brown - 5 ounces, (140 grams, 330 yards)
Red - ³/₄ ounce, (20 grams, 50 yards)
Gold - ³/₄ ounce, (20 grams, 50 yards)
Orange - ¹/₂ ounce, (15 grams, 35 yards)
Crochet hooks, sizes H (5.00 mm) **and** K (6.50 mm) **or** sizes needed for gauge
2 - 12 mm gold animal eyes
Yarn needle
Polyester fiberfill
Craft glue

Note: Turkey is worked holding 2 strands of yarn together unless otherwise specified.

GAUGE: With large hook (size K), 7 sc and 7 rnds = 3"
With small hook (size H), 4 sc = 1"

Gauge Swatch: 3" square
With large hook (size K), ch 8 **loosely**.
Row 1: Sc in second ch from hook and in each ch across: 7 sc.
Rows 2-7: Ch 1, turn; sc in each sc across.
Finish off.

STITCH GUIDE

CLUSTER
★ YO, insert hook in st indicated, YO and pull up a loop, YO and draw through 2 loops on hook; repeat from ★ 2 times **more**, YO and draw through all 4 loops on hook *(Figs. 10a & b, page 134)*.
DECREASE (uses next 2 sc)
Pull up a loop in next 2 sc, YO and draw through all 3 loops on hook **(counts as one sc)**.

BODY

With large size hook and Brown, ch 3 **loosely**; being careful not to twist ch, join with slip st to form a ring.
Rnd 1 (Right side): 2 Sc in each ch around; do **not** join, place marker *(see Markers, page 136)*: 6 sc.
Rnd 2: 2 Sc in each sc around: 12 sc.

Rnd 3: (Sc in next sc, 2 sc in next sc) around: 18 sc.
Rnd 4: (Sc in next 2 sc, 2 sc in next sc) around: 24 sc.
Rnd 5: (Sc in next 3 sc, 2 sc in next sc) around: 30 sc.
Rnd 6: (Sc in next 4 sc, 2 sc in next sc) around: 36 sc.
Rnd 7: (Sc in next 5 sc, 2 sc in next sc) around: 42 sc.
Rnds 8-18: Sc in each sc around.
Rnd 19: (Sc in next 5 sc, decrease) around: 36 sc.
Rnd 20: (Sc in next 4 sc, decrease) around: 30 sc.
Rnd 21: (Sc in next 3 sc, decrease) around: 24 sc.
Rnd 22: (Sc in next 2 sc, decrease) around: 18 sc.
Rnd 23: (Sc in next sc, decrease) around: 12 sc.
Stuff Body lightly with polyester fiberfill.
Rnd 24: Decrease around: 6 sc.
Rnd 25: (Skip next sc, slip st in next sc) around; finish off: 3 sts.

HEAD AND NECK

With large size hook and Brown, ch 3 **loosely**; being careful not to twist ch, join with slip st to form a ring.
Rnd 1 (Right side): 2 Sc in each ch around; do **not** join, place marker: 6 sc.
Rnd 2: 2 Sc in each sc around: 12 sc.
Rnd 3: (Sc in next sc, 2 sc in next sc) around: 18 sc.
Rnds 4-8: Sc in each sc around.
Rnd 9: Decrease 4 times, sc in each sc around: 14 sc.
Rnds 10-14: Sc in each sc around.
Rnds 15-18: Hdc in next 7 sts, slip st in next 7 sts.
Rnd 19: 2 Hdc in next hdc, (hdc in next hdc, 2 hdc in next hdc) 3 times, sc in next 7 sts: 18 sts.
Rnd 20: (Sc in next 2 sts, 2 sc in next st) around; slip st in next sc, finish off leaving a long end for sewing: 24 sc.
Stuff Head and Neck lightly with polyester fiberfill.
Using photo as a guide for placement, sew last rnd of Neck to Body; tack back of Neck to Body.

TAIL FEATHER (Make 9)

With large size hook and Gold, ch 3 **loosely**; being careful not to twist ch, join with slip st to form a ring.
Rnd 1 (Right side): 2 Sc in each ch around; do **not** join, place marker: 6 sc.
Rnd 2: (Sc in next 2 sc, 2 sc in next sc) twice: 8 sc.
Rnd 3: Sc in each sc around, changing to Orange in last sc worked *(Fig. 28a, page 138)*.
Rnds 4-6: Sc in each sc around, changing to Red in last sc worked on Rnd 6.

Rnds 7 and 8: Sc in each sc around.

Rnd 9: (Sc in next 2 sc, decrease) twice changing to Brown in last decrease worked: 6 sc.

Rnd 10: Sc in each sc around; slip st in next sc, finish off leaving a long end for sewing.

Stuff Tail Feather lightly with polyester fiberfill.

Sew one Tail Feather to Rnd 19 of Body, lining it up with back of Head.

Sew 4 Feathers to Rnd 19 on each side of center Feather.

With 2 strands of Orange and working through sts on Rnd 5 between Feathers, secure yarn to first Feather. Insert needle through center of each Feather, joining them together. Insert needle back through each Feather one rnd below, leaving one stitch in between. Secure yarn.

WING (Make 2)

Note: Work in Back Loops Only throughout (Fig. 21, page 136).
With large size hook and Brown, ch 11 **loosely**.

Row 1: Sc in second ch from hook and in next 4 chs, slip st in last 5 chs: 10 sts.

Row 2: Ch 1, turn; slip st in first 5 sts, sc in next 4 sc, 2 sc in last sc: 11 sts.

Row 3: Ch 1, turn; 2 sc in first sc and in next 5 sc, slip st in last 5 sts: 12 sts.

Row 4: Ch 1, turn; slip st in first 5 sts, sc in next 6 sc, 2 sc in last sc: 13 sts.

Continued on page 131.

CHRISTMAS

An elegant addition to the Yuletide mantel, this handmade stocking features a lacy cuff kissed with golden thread. Whether used as a decoration or to hold Santa's goodies, it's sure to become a favorite Christmas keepsake.

Quick ELEGANT STOCKING

Finished Size: 7" top width x 16½" long

MATERIALS
Bedspread Weight Cotton Thread (size 10),
   100 yards
Gold Metallic Braid (size 8), 8 yards
Steel crochet hook, size 7 (1.65 mm) **or** size needed for gauge
Tapestry needle
Sewing needle and thread to match Edging
Stocking fabric - 2 pieces 12" x 18"
Lining fabric - 2 pieces 12" x 18"
Tracing paper
Straight pins
Fabric marking pencil
5" length of ⅜" wide ribbon

GAUGE: 9 dc and 4 rows = 1"

Gauge Swatch: 2"w x 1"h
With thread, ch 23 **loosely**.
Work same as Edging through Row 4: 6 sps.
Finish off.

STITCH GUIDE

> **POPCORN**
> 5 Dc in ch indicated, drop loop from hook, insert hook in first dc of 5-dc group, hook dropped loop and draw through *(Fig. 12b, page 134)*.

EDGING
With thread, ch 152 **loosely**.
Row 1 (Right side)**:** Dc in eighth ch from hook, (ch 2, skip next 2 chs, dc in next ch) across: 49 sps.
Note: Loop a short piece of thread around any stitch to mark Row 1 as **right** side.
Row 2: Ch 3 **(counts as first dc)**, turn; (2 dc in next ch-2 sp, dc in next dc) across to last sp, 2 dc in last sp, dc in next ch: 148 dc.

Row 3: Ch 5 **(counts as first dc plus ch 2, now and throughout)**, turn; skip next 2 dc, dc in next dc, (ch 2, skip next 2 dc, dc in next dc) across: 49 sps.
Rows 4 and 5: Ch 5, turn; dc in next dc, (ch 2, dc in next dc) across.
Row 6: Ch 5, turn; dc in next dc, ch 2, dc in next dc, ch 5, dc in next dc, ★ (ch 2, dc in next dc) 3 times, ch 5, dc in next dc; repeat from ★ across to last 2 dc, (ch 2, dc in next dc) twice.
Row 7: Ch 5, turn; dc in next dc, ★ ch 5, skip next ch-2 sp, work Popcorn in center ch of next ch-5, ch 5, skip next dc, dc in next dc, ch 2, dc in next dc; repeat from ★ across: 12 Popcorns.
Row 8: Ch 6 **(counts as first tr plus ch 2, now and throughout)**, turn; tr in next dc, ★ ch 4, dc in top of next Popcorn, ch 4, tr in next dc, ch 2, tr in next dc; repeat from ★ across.
Row 9: Ch 6, turn; tr in next tr, ★ ch 2, (3 tr, ch 3, 3 tr) in next dc, (ch 2, tr in next tr) twice; repeat from ★ across.
Row 10: Ch 6, turn; tr in next tr, ★ ch 2, skip next ch-2 sp, (3 tr, ch 3, 3 tr) in next ch-3 sp, (ch 2, skip next ch-2 sp, tr in next tr) twice; repeat from ★ across.
Row 11: Ch 6, turn; ★ tr in next 4 tr, (3 tr, ch 3, 3 tr) in next ch-3 sp, tr in next 4 tr, ch 2; repeat from ★ across to last tr, tr in last tr.
Row 12: Ch 4, turn; skip next tr, tr in next 6 tr, (3 tr, ch 3, 3 tr) in next ch-3 sp, tr in next 6 tr, ★ skip next 2 tr, tr in next 6 tr, (3 tr, ch 3, 3 tr) in next ch-3 sp, tr in next 6 tr; repeat from ★ across to last 2 tr, skip next tr, tr in last tr; finish off.
Row 13: With **right** side facing and working in Back Loops Only *(Fig. 21, page 136)*, join Gold with slip st in first tr; ch 1, sc in each tr across working 2 sc in each ch-3 sp; finish off.

STOCKING
Matching arrows to form one pattern, trace outline of stocking pattern, page 143, onto tracing paper; cut out pattern.
Center pattern on **wrong** side of one piece of fabric and use a fabric marking pencil to draw around pattern. Do **not** cut out shape. With **right** sides together, pin fabric pieces together. Sew directly on pencil line, leaving top edge open.
Cut out Stocking leaving a ¼" seam allowance along seam and ¾" across top.

Clip seam allowance at curves. Turn Stocking right side out. Repeat for lining; do **not** turn right side out.
Press top edge of Stocking and lining 3/4" to **wrong** side.
With **wrong** sides together, insert lining into Stocking; pin pieces together.

For hanger, fold ribbon in half matching ends. Place ends of ribbon between lining and Stocking at right seam line with 2" of hanger extending above Stocking; pin in place.
Securing hanger, sew lining to Stocking.

FINISHING
Sew short edges of Edging together. Pin Edging to Stocking along top edge, easing to fit. Sew in place.

HOLY NIGHT ANGEL

Finished Size: 11" high

MATERIALS

Bedspread Weight Cotton Thread (size 10), 280 yards
Steel crochet hook, size 6 (1.80 mm) **or** size needed for gauge
Starching materials: Commercial fabric stiffener, blocking
  board, 8" plastic foam cone, plastic drinking straws,
  plastic wrap, small bowl, terry towel, paper towels, and
  stainless steel pins
Polyester fiberfill
1 yard length of strung flat 7 mm pearls
16" length of 1" wide gathered lace
Curly doll hair
Metallic Gold spray paint
18" length of 3/8" wide gold ribbon
18" length of 1/8" wide gold braid
2" plastic Harp
Glue gun

GAUGE: 8 sc and 8 rows = 1"

Gauge Swatch: 2"w x 1"h
Ch 17 **loosely.**
Row 1: Sc in second ch from hook and in each ch across: 16 sc.
Rows 2-8: Ch 1, turn; sc in each sc across.
Finish off.

STITCH GUIDE

> **SC DECREASE** (uses next 2 sc)
> Pull up a loop in next 2 sc, YO and draw through all 3 loops
> on hook **(counts as one sc).**
> **HDC DECREASE** (uses next 2 hdc)
> (YO, insert hook in **next** hdc, YO and pull up a loop) twice,
> YO and draw through all 5 loops on hook **(counts as one
> hdc).**
> **V-ST**
> (Dc, ch 1, dc) in st or sp indicated.

HEAD

Ch 5; join with slip st to form a ring.
Rnd 1 (Right side): Ch 1, 10 sc in ring; do **not** join, place
marker *(see Markers, page 136)*.
Rnd 2: Sc in each sc around.
Rnd 3: 2 Sc in each sc around: 20 sc.
Rnd 4: Sc in each sc around.
Rnd 5: (Sc in next 4 sc, 2 sc in next sc) around: 24 sc.
Rnds 6-10: Sc in each sc around.
Rnd 11: (Sc in next 4 sc, sc decrease) around: 20 sc.
Rnd 12: Sc in each sc around.
Rnd 13: (Sc in next 8 sc, sc decrease) twice: 18 sc.

Rnd 14: Sc in each sc around.
Rnd 15: Sc in next 2 sc, (sc decrease, sc in next 2 sc) around:
14 sc.
Rnd 16: Sc in next 2 sc, (sc decrease, sc in next sc) around: 10 sc.
Rnd 17: Sc in each sc around; remove marker, slip st in next
sc, do **not** finish off.

DRESS

Rnd 1: Ch 3 **(counts as first dc, now and throughout)**, dc
in same st, 2 dc in next sc and in each sc around; join with
slip st to first dc: 20 dc.
Rnd 2: Ch 4 **(counts as first dc plus ch 1, now and
throughout)**, dc in same st, work V-St in next dc and in each
dc around; join with slip st to first dc: 20 V-Sts.
Rnd 3: Slip st in first ch-1 sp, ch 4, dc in same sp, work V-St in
next V-St (ch-1 sp) and in each V-St around; join with slip st to
first dc.
Rnd 4: Ch 4, dc in same st, work V-St in next dc and in each dc
around; join with slip st to first dc: 40 V-Sts.
Rnd 5: Slip st in first ch-1 sp, ch 4, dc in same sp, work V-St in
next 3 V-Sts, † place marker around dc just worked, work V-St in
next 14 V-Sts, skip 14 V-Sts just worked and slip st in marked dc
(armhole) †, work V-St in next 6 V-Sts, repeat from † to † once,
work V-St in last 2 V-Sts; join with slip st to first dc: 12 V-Sts.
Rnd 6: Slip st in first ch-1 sp, ch 4, dc in same sp, work V-St in
next 3 V-Sts, work V-St in next slip st, work V-St in next 6 V-Sts,
work V-St in next slip st, work V-St in last 2 V-Sts; join with
slip st to first dc: 14 V-Sts.
Rnd 7: Repeat Rnd 3.
Rnd 8: Slip st in first ch-1 sp, ch 4, dc in same sp, (work
2 V-Sts in next V-St, work V-St in next V-St) 3 times, (dc, ch 5,
dc) in next V-St, (work V-St in next V-St, work 2 V-Sts in next
V-St) 3 times; join with slip st to first dc: 20 sps.
Rnd 9: Slip st in first ch-1 sp, ch 4, dc in same sp, work V-St in
next 9 V-Sts, work 2 V-Sts in next ch-5 sp, work V-St in each V-St
around; join with slip st to first dc: 21 V-Sts.
Rnd 10: Repeat Rnd 3.
Rnd 11: Slip st in first ch-1 sp, ch 4, dc in same sp, work V-St in
next 5 V-Sts, work 2 V-Sts in next V-St, (work V-St in next 6 V-Sts,
work 2 V-Sts in next V-St) twice; join with slip st to first dc: 24 V-Sts.
Rnds 12 and 13: Repeat Rnd 3, twice.
Rnd 14: Slip st in first ch-1 sp, ch 4, dc in same sp, work V-St in
next 2 V-Sts, work 2 V-Sts in next V-St, (work V-St in next 3 V-Sts,
work 2 V-Sts in next V-St) around; join with slip st to first dc:
30 V-Sts.
Rnds 15 and 16: Repeat Rnd 3, twice.
Rnd 17: Slip st in first ch-1 sp, ch 4, dc in same sp, work V-St in
next 4 V-Sts, work 2 V-Sts in next V-St, (work V-St in next 5 V-Sts,
work 2 V-Sts in next V-St) around; join with slip st to first dc:
35 V-Sts.
Rnds 18-20: Repeat Rnd 3, 3 times.

Display this golden-haired angel as a reminder of the heavenly messengers who brought the good news of the Christ Child's birth on that Holy Night long ago.

Rnd 21: Slip st in first ch-1 sp, ch 4, dc in same sp, work V-St in next 5 V-Sts, work 2 V-Sts in next V-St, (work V-St in next 6 V-Sts, work 2 V-Sts in next V-St) around; join with slip st to first dc: 0 V-Sts.

Rnds 22-24: Repeat Rnd 3, 3 times.

Rnd 25: Slip st in first ch-1 sp, ch 4, dc in same sp, work V-St in next 6 V-Sts, work 2 V-Sts in next V-St, (work V-St in next 7 V-Sts, work 2 V-Sts in next V-St) around; join with slip st to first dc: 45 V-Sts.

Rnds 26-28: Repeat Rnd 3, 3 times.

Rnd 29: Slip st in first ch-1 sp, ch 4, dc in same sp, work V-St in next 7 V-Sts, work 2 V-Sts in next V-St, (work V-St in next 8 V-Sts, work 2 V-Sts in next V-St) around; join with slip st to first dc: 50 V-Sts.

Rnds 30 and 31: Repeat Rnd 3, twice.

Rnd 32: Slip st in first ch-1 sp, ch 4, dc in same sp, (dc, ch 5, dc) in next V-St, ★ work V-St in next V-St, (dc, ch 5, dc) in next V-St; repeat from ★ around; join with slip st to first dc: 25 V-Sts.

Rnd 33: Slip st in first ch-1 sp, ch 1, sc in same sp, (4 dc, ch 2, 4 dc) in next ch-5 sp, ★ sc in next V-St, (4 dc, ch 2, 4 dc) in next ch-5 sp; repeat from ★ around; join with slip st to first sc: 25 scallops.

Rnd 34: Ch 1, sc in first sc, ★ † ch 3, skip next 2 dc, sc in sp **before** next dc *(Fig. 23, page 136)*, ch 3, (sc, ch 3, sc) in next ch-2 sp, ch 3, skip next 2 dc, sc in sp **before** next dc, ch 3 †, sc in next sc; repeat from ★ around to last scallop, then repeat from † to † once; join with slip st to first sc, finish off.

SLEEVE

Rnd 1: With **right** side facing, join thread with slip st in first skipped V-St on armhole; ch 6, dc in same sp, (dc, ch 3, dc) in next V-St and in each V-St around; join with slip st to third ch of beginning ch-6: 14 ch-3 sps.

Rnd 2: Slip st in first ch-3 sp, ch 1, sc in same sp, (3 dc, ch 1, 3 dc) in next ch-3 sp, ★ sc in next ch-3 sp, (3 dc, ch 1, 3 dc) in next ch-3 sp; repeat from ★ around; join with slip st to first sc.

Rnd 3: Ch 1, sc in same st, ch 3, skip next dc, sc in next dc, ch 3, (sc, ch 3, sc) in next ch-1 sp, ch 3, skip next dc, sc in next dc, ch 3, ★ sc in next sc, ch 3, skip next dc, sc in next dc, ch 3, (sc, ch 3, sc) in next ch-1 sp, ch 3, skip next dc, sc in next dc, ch 3; repeat from ★ around; join with slip st to first sc, finish off.
Repeat for second Sleeve.

ARM

Ch 22 **loosely**; being careful not to twist ch, join with slip st to form a ring.

Rnd 1: Ch 2 **(counts as first hdc, now and throughout)**, hdc in next ch and in each ch around; join with slip st to first hdc: 22 hdc.

Rnds 2-4: Ch 2, hdc in next hdc and in each hdc around; join with slip st to first hdc.

Rnd 5: Ch 2, hdc in next hdc, (hdc decrease, hdc in next 3 hdc) around; join with slip st to first hdc: 18 hdc.

Rnd 6: Ch 2, hdc in next hdc and in each hdc around; join with slip st to first hdc.

Rnd 7: Ch 2, hdc in next 3 hdc, hdc decrease, (hdc in next 4 hdc, hdc decrease) twice; join with slip st to first hdc: 15 hdc.

Rnd 8: Ch 2, hdc in next hdc and in each hdc around; join with slip st to first hdc.

Rnd 9: Ch 2, hdc in next 2 hdc, hdc decrease, (hdc in next 3 hdc, hdc decrease) twice; join with slip st to first hdc: 12 hdc.

Rnd 10: Ch 2, hdc in next 3 hdc, hdc decrease, hdc in next 4 hdc, hdc decrease; join with slip st to first hdc: 10 hdc.

Rnds 11-19: Ch 2, hdc in next hdc and in each hdc around; join with slip st to first hdc.
Finish off.
Repeat for second Arm; do **not** finish off.

Ring: Ch 10 **loosely**, skip next 4 hdc, slip st in next hdc, turn; sc in back ridge of each ch *(Fig. 2a, page 133)*, slip st in same st as joining; finish off.

WING (Make 2)
Ch 8 **loosely**.

Row 1 (Right side)**:** Sc in second ch from hook and in each ch across: 7 sc.

Note: Loop a short piece of thread around any stitch to mark Row 1 as **right** side.

Row 2: Ch 3, turn; dc in next sc and in each sc across.

Row 3: Ch 3, turn; work V-St in same st and in each dc across, dc in same st as last V-St worked: 7 V-Sts.

Row 4: Ch 3, turn; work V-St in each V-St across, dc in last dc.

Row 5: Ch 3, turn; work V-St in first V-St, (work 2 V-Sts in next V-St, work V-St in next V-St) across, dc in last dc: 10 V-Sts.

Row 6: Ch 3, turn; work V-St in each V-St across, dc in last dc.

Row 7: Ch 3, turn; work V-St in first 2 V-Sts, (work 2 V-Sts in each of next 2 V-Sts, work V-St in next 2 V-Sts) twice, dc in last dc: 14 V-Sts.

Row 8: Ch 3, turn; work V-St in each V-St across, dc in last dc.

Row 9: Ch 3, turn; (work 2 V-Sts in next V-St, work V-St in next 2 V-Sts) twice, work 2 V-Sts in each of next 2 V-Sts, (work V-St in next 2 V-Sts, work 2 V-Sts in next V-St) twice, dc in last dc: 20 V-Sts.

Row 10: Ch 3, turn; work V-St in each V-St across, dc in last dc.

Edging: Ch 1, turn; sc in first 2 dc and in next ch-1 sp, ch 3, (sc, ch 3) twice in each of next 18 V-Sts, sc in next ch-1 sp and in last 2 dc; ch 3, sc in end of first row, ch 3, (sc in end of next row, ch 3) 7 times, skip last 2 rows; working in free loops of beginning ch *(Fig. 22b, page 136)*, sc in each ch across; ch 3, skip first 2 rows, (sc in end of next row, ch 3) across; join with slip st to first sc, finish off.

HALO

Ch 30 **loosely**; being careful not to twist ch, join with slip st to form a ring.

Rnd 1: Ch 1, sc in each ch around; join with slip st to first sc: 30 sc.

Rnd 2: Ch 1, sc in first sc, (ch 3, skip next sc, sc in next sc) around to last sc, ch 1, skip last sc, hdc in first sc to form last sp: 15 sps.

Rnd 3: Ch 1, sc in same sp, ch 3, (sc in next ch-3 sp, ch 3) around; join with slip st to first sc, finish off.

FINISHING

See Starching and Blocking, page 140.
Spray paint doll hair with metallic gold paint; let dry.
Glue lace to wrong side of Wings along last row. Glue a 7½" length of pearls to right side of each Wing along top of Row 10.
Glue remaining length of pearls to Dress along Rnd 31.
Insert Arms in armhole and glue in place.
Glue first Arm to Ring of second Arm.
Glue doll hair to Head, styling as desired.
Glue Halo to top of Head.
Glue Wings to back of Dress with pieces touching along beginning ch.
Glue harp to front of Angel with bottom edge sitting on Ring.
Tie a bow using gold braid and ribbon; glue bow to front of harp covering Ring.

TURKEY CENTERPIECE

Continued from page 125.

Row 5: Ch 1, turn; 2 sc in first sc and in next 7 sc, slip st in last sts: 14 sts.
Row 6: Ch 1, turn; slip st in first 5 sts, sc in next 8 sc, 2 sc in last sc: 15 sts.
Row 7: Ch 1, turn; sc in first 10 sc, slip st in last 5 sts.
Row 8: Ch 1, turn; slip st in first 5 sts, sc in each sc across.
Row 9: Ch 1, turn; sc in first 10 sc, slip st in last 5 sts.
Row 10: Ch 1, turn; slip st in first 5 sts, sc in next 8 sc, decrease: 14 sts.
Row 11: Ch 1, turn; decrease, sc in next 7 sc, slip st in last sts; finish off leaving a long end for sewing: 13 sts.
Using photo as a guide for placement, sew Wings to each side of Body, with Row 1 at bottom edge and smaller edge of Wings placed toward the Head. Tack center top of each Wing to Body.

FOOT (Make 2)

With large size hook and Gold, ch 8 **loosely**; working in back ridge of chs **(Fig. 2a, page 133)**, slip st in second ch from hook and in next 2 chs, (ch 4, slip st in second ch from hook and in next 2 chs) twice, slip st in remaining 4 chs of beginning ch-8; finish off.

LEG (Make 2)

With large size hook, Brown, and leaving a long end for sewing, ch 4 **loosely**; being careful not to twist ch, join with slip st to form a ring.
Rnd 1 (Right side): Sc in each ch around; do **not** join, place marker: 4 sc.
Rnds 2 and 3: (Sc in next sc, 2 sc in next sc) around: 9 sc.

Rnd 4: (Sc in next 2 sc, 2 sc in next sc) around; slip st in next sc, finish off leaving a long end for sewing: 12 sc.
Sew Rnd 1 of Leg to top of Foot.
Stuff Leg firmly with polyester fiberfill.
Sew Legs to Rnds 11-13 of Body, placing them 2 inches apart.

FACE

With large size hook and Brown, ch 3 **loosely**; being careful not to twist ch, join with slip st to form a ring.
Rnd 1 (Right side): Ch 1, 2 sc in each ch around; join with slip st to first sc: 6 sc.
Rnd 2: Ch 1, 2 sc in each sc around; join with slip st to first sc, finish off leaving a long end for sewing: 12 sc.
Sew Face to front of Head over Rnds 5-8, stuffing lightly with polyester fiberfill before closing.

BEAK

Rnd 1 (Right side): With small size hook and one strand of Gold, ch 2, 4 sc in second ch from hook; do **not** join, place marker.
Rnd 2: (Sc in next sc, 2 sc in next sc) twice: 6 sc.
Rnd 3: (Sc in next 2 sc, 2 sc in next sc) twice: 8 sc.
Rnd 4: (Sc in next 3 sc, 2 sc in next sc) twice; slip st in next sc, finish off leaving a long end for sewing: 10 sc.
Stuff Beak lightly with polyester fiberfill.
Sew Beak below beginning ring of Face.

WATTLE

With small size hook and one strand of Red, ch 13 **loosely**.
Rnd 1 (Right side): Work Cluster in third ch from hook, ch 1, (slip st in next ch pushing Cluster to right side, work Cluster in next ch, ch 1) across, (slip st, work Cluster) in same ch, ch 1; working in free loops of beginning ch **(Fig. 22b, page 136)**, (slip st in next ch, work Cluster in next ch, ch 1) across, slip st in side of Cluster just worked and in next 4 sts: 12 Clusters.
Rnd 2: (Work Cluster in next slip st, ch 1, skip next st, slip st in next st) 11 times; finish off leaving a long end for sewing: 11 Clusters.

COMB

With small size hook and one strand of Red, ch 22 **loosely**; working in back ridge of chs, work Cluster in third ch from hook, ch 1, (slip st in next ch, work Cluster in next ch, ch 1) 3 times, slip st in next 7 chs, sc in next 5 chs, slip st in last ch; finish off.

FINISHING

Sew Wattle to Head and Neck under Beak.
Sew beginning end of Comb from top of Head to top of Face; allow remaining sts to hang down along side of Beak.
Glue eyes to Face.

general instructions

basic information

ABBREVIATIONS

Crochet instructions are written in a special language consisting of abbreviations, punctuation marks, and other terms and symbols. This method of writing saves time and space and is actually easy to read once you understand the crochet "shorthand".

BPdc	Back Post double crochet(s)
BPtr	Back Post treble crochet(s)
ch(s)	chain(s)
dc	double crochet(s)
dtr	double treble crochet(s)
Ex sc	Extended single crochet(s)
FPdc	Front Post double crochet(s)
FPtr	Front Post treble crochet(s)
hdc	half double crochet(s)
mm	millimeters
Rnd(s)	Round(s)
sc	single crochet(s)
sp(s)	space(s)
st(s)	stitch(es)
tr	treble crochet(s)
YO	yarn over

SYMBOLS

★ — work instructions following ★ as many **more** times as indicated in addition to the first time.

† to † — work all instructions from first † to second † **as many** times as specified.

( ) or [ ] — work enclosed instructions **as many** times as specified by the number immediately following **or** work all enclosed instructions in the stitch or space indicated **or** contains explanatory remarks.

GAUGE

Gauge is the number of stitches and rows or rounds per inch and is used to determine the finished size of a project. All crochet patterns will specify the gauge that you must match to ensure proper size and to be sure you have enough yarn to complete the project.

Hook sizes given in instructions are merely guides. Because everyone crochets differently — loosely, tightly, or somewhere in between — the finished size can vary even when crocheters use the very same pattern, yarn, and hook.

Before beginning any crocheted item, it is absolutely necessary for you to crochet a gauge swatch in the pattern stitch indicated with the weight of yarn or thread and hook size suggested. Lay your swatch on a hard, smooth, flat surface, then measure it. If your swatch is smaller than specified or you have too many stitches per inch, try again with a larger size hook; if your swatch is larger or you don't have enough stitches per inch, try again with a smaller size hook. Keep trying until you find the size that will give you the specified gauge. DO NOT HESITATE TO CHANGE HOOK SIZE TO OBTAIN CORRECT GAUGE. On garment and afghans, once proper gauge is obtained, measure width of piece approximately every 3" to be sure gauge remains consistent.

basic stitch guide

CHAIN

When beginning a first row of crochet in a chain, always skip the first chain from the hook and work into the second chain from hook (for single crochet), third chain from hook (for half double crochet), or fourth chain from hook (for double crochet), etc. *(Fig. 1)*.

Fig. 1

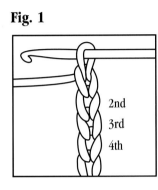

WORKING INTO THE CHAIN

Method 1: Insert hook into back ridge of each chain indicated *(Fig. 2a)*.
Method 2: Insert hook under top two strands of each chain *(Fig. 2b)*.

Fig. 2a   **Fig. 2b**

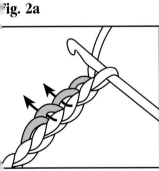
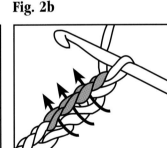

SLIP STITCH *(abbreviated slip st)*

This stitch is used to attach new yarn, to join work, or to move the yarn across a group of stitches without adding height. Insert hook in stitch or space indicated, YO and draw through stitch **and** loop on hook *(Fig. 3)*.

Fig. 3

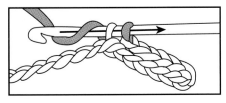

SINGLE CROCHET *(abbreviated sc)*

Insert hook in stitch or space indicated, YO and pull up a loop, YO and draw through both loops on hook *(Fig. 4)*.

Fig. 4

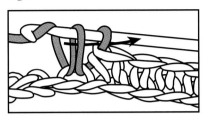

HALF DOUBLE CROCHET *(abbreviated hdc)*

YO, insert hook in stitch or space indicated, YO and pull up a loop, YO and draw through all 3 loops on hook *(Fig. 5)*.

Fig. 5

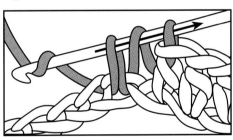

DOUBLE CROCHET *(abbreviated dc)*

YO, insert hook in stitch or space indicated, YO and pull up a loop, YO and draw through 2 loops on hook *(Fig. 6a)*, YO and draw through remaining 2 loops on hook *(Fig. 6b)*.

Fig. 6a   **Fig. 6b**

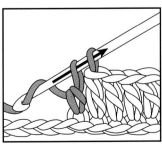

TREBLE CROCHET (abbreviated tr)

YO twice, insert hook in stitch or space indicated, YO and pull up a loop (*Fig. 7a*), (YO and draw through 2 loops on hook) 3 times (*Fig. 7b*).

Fig. 7a

Fig. 7b

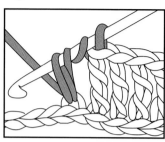

DOUBLE TREBLE CROCHET
(abbreviated dtr)

YO three times, insert hook in stitch or space indicated, YO and pull up a loop (*Fig. 8a*), (YO and draw through 2 loops on hook) 4 times (*Fig. 8b*).

Fig. 8a

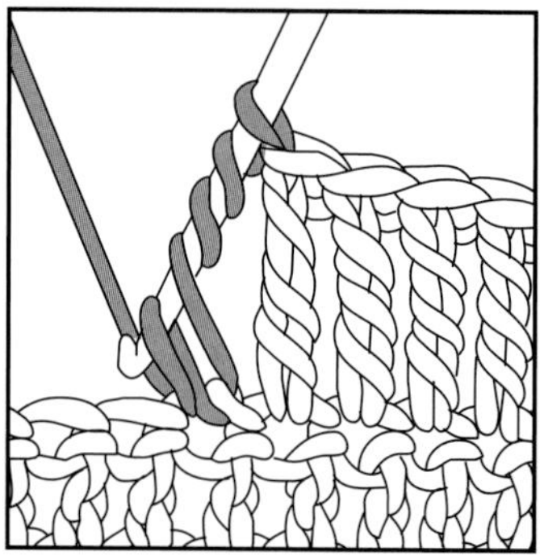

Fig. 8b

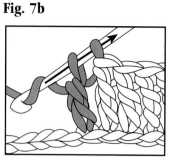

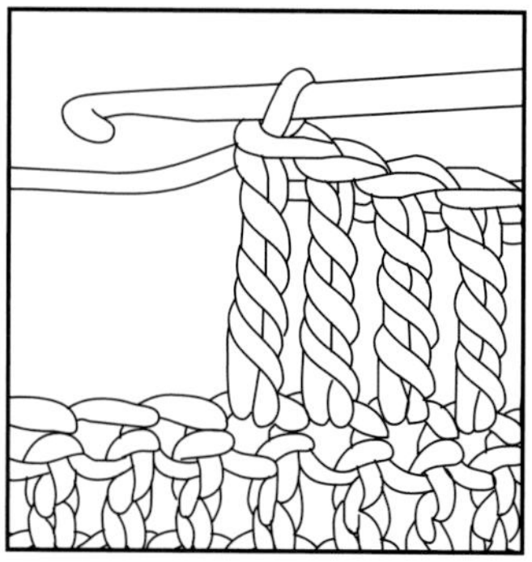

LONG SINGLE CROCHET
(abbreviated Long sc)

Insert hook in stitch indicated (*Fig. 9*), YO and pull up a loop **even** with loop on hook, YO and draw through both loops on hook (**counts as one sc**).

Fig. 9

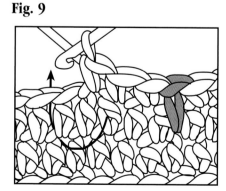

CLUSTER

A Cluster can be worked all in the same stitch or space (*Figs. 10a & b*), **or** across several stitches (*Figs. 11a & b*).

Fig. 10a

Fig. 10b

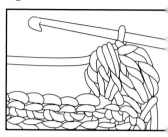
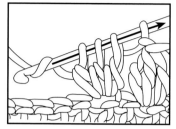

Fig. 11a

Fig. 11b

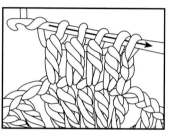
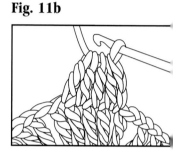

POPCORN

Work specified number of dc in stitch or space indicated, drop loop from hook, insert hook in first dc of dc group, hook dropped loop and draw through (*Figs. 12a &b*).

Fig. 12a

Fig. 12b

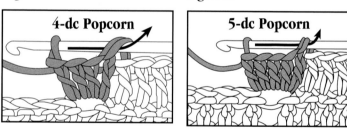

4-dc Popcorn

5-dc Popcorn

PUFF STITCH

(YO, insert hook in stitch or space indicated, YO and pull up a loop even with loop on hook) 4 times (*Fig. 13*), YO and draw through all 9 loops on hook.

Fig. 13

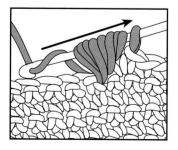

REVERSE SINGLE CROCHET
(abbreviated reverse sc)

Working from **left** to **right**, insert hook in stitch to right of hook *(Fig. 14a)*, YO and draw through, under and to left of loop on hook (2 loops on hook) *(Fig. 14b)*, YO and draw through both loops on hook *(Fig. 14c)* (**reverse sc made, Fig. 14d**).

Fig. 14a

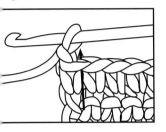

Fig. 14b

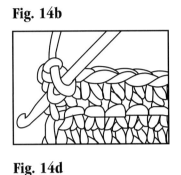

Fig. 14c

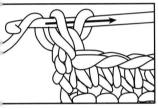

Fig. 14d

POST STITCH

Work around post of stitch indicated, inserting hook in direction of arrow *(Fig. 15)*.

Fig. 15

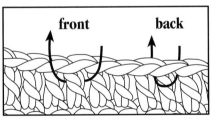

FRONT POST DOUBLE CROCHET
(abbreviated FPdc)

YO, insert hook from **front** to **back** around post of stitch indicated *(Fig. 15)*, YO and pull up a loop *(Fig. 16)*, (YO and draw through 2 loops on hook) twice.

Fig. 16

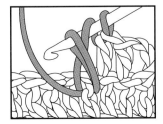

BACK POST DOUBLE CROCHET
(abbreviated BPdc)

YO, insert hook from **back** to **front** around post of stitch indicated *(Fig. 15)*, YO and pull up a loop *(Fig. 17)*, (YO and draw through 2 loops on hook) twice.

Fig. 17

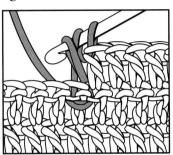

FRONT POST TREBLE CROCHET
(abbreviated FPtr)

YO twice, insert hook from **front** to **back** around post of stitch indicated *(Fig. 15)*, YO and pull up a loop *(Fig. 18)*, (YO and draw through 2 loops on hook) 3 times.

Fig. 18

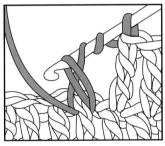

BACK POST TREBLE CROCHET
(abbreviated BPtr)

YO twice, insert hook from **back** to **front** around post of stitch indicated *(Fig. 15)*, YO and pull up a loop *(Fig. 19)*, (YO and draw through 2 loops on hook) 3 times.

Fig. 19

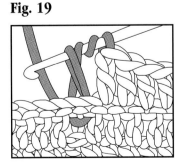

135

HOW TO DETERMINE THE RIGHT SIDE

Many designs are made with the **front** of the stitch as the **right** side. Notice that the **fronts** of the stitches are smooth *(Fig. 20a)* and the **backs** of the stitches are bumpy *(Fig. 20b)*. For easy identification, it may be helpful to loop a short piece of yarn, thread, or fabric around any stitch to mark **right** side.

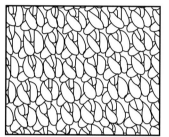

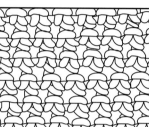

JOINING WITH SC

When instructed to join with sc, begin with a slip knot on hook. Insert hook in stitch or space indicated, YO and pull up a loop, YO and draw through both loops on hook.

MARKERS

Markers are used to help distinguish the beginning of each round being worked. Place a 2" scrap piece of yarn or fabric before the first stitch of each round, moving marker after each round is complete. Remove when no longer needed.

BACK OR FRONT LOOP ONLY

Work only in loop(s) indicated by arrow *(Fig. 21)*.

Fig. 21

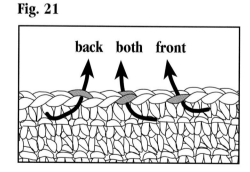

FREE LOOP

After working in Back or Front Loops Only on a row or round, there will be a ridge of unused loops. These are called the free loops. Later, when instructed to work in the free loops of the same row or round, work in these loops *(Fig. 22a)*. When instructed to work in a free loop of a beginning chain, work in loop indicated by arrow *(Fig. 22b)*.

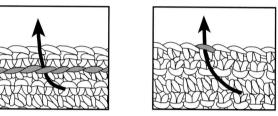

WORKING BETWEEN STITCHES

When instructed to work in spaces **between** stitches or in space **before** a stitch, insert hook in space indicated by arrow *(Fig. 23)*.

Fig. 23

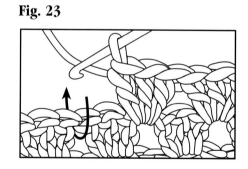

ADDING ON STITCHES

Work as specified in instructions, inserting hook in base of last stitch worked *(Figs. 24a & b)*.

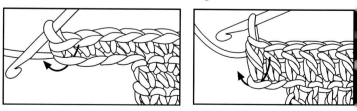

PREPARING FABRIC STRIPS

Fabrics selected should be high quality, 100% cotton, such as those sold for piecing quilts. Yardage given is based on fabrics 44/45" wide.

If the fabric is not pre-shrunk, it should be gently machine washed and dried. Straighten your fabric by pulling it across the bias. It may be necessary to lightly press the fabric.

To avoid joining strips often, we recommend that your strips be two yards or longer.

TEARING STRIPS

Tear off selvages, then tear fabric into the width of strips specified for pattern.

CUTTING STRIPS

1. Fold the fabric in half, short end to short end, as many times as possible, while still being able to cut through all thicknesses *(Fig. 25a)*.

Fig. 25a

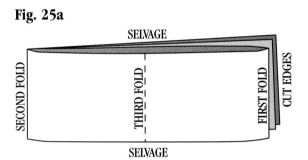

2. Cut off selvages, then cut fabric into 1" wide strips *(Fig. 25b)*. For quick results, a rotary cutter and mat may be used to cut several layers of fabric at one time.

Fig. 25b

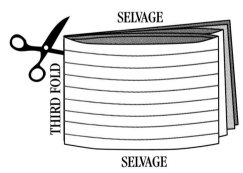

JOINING FABRIC STRIPS

The following is a technique for joining fabric strips without sewing strips together, which eliminates knots or ends to weave in later.

1. To join a new strip of fabric to working strip, cut a 1/2" slit about 1/2" from ends of both fabric strips *(Fig. 26a)*.

Fig. 26a

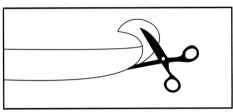

2. With **right** sides up, place end of new strip over end of working strip and match slits *(Fig. 26b)*.

Fig. 26b

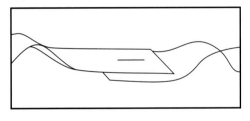

3. Pull free end of new strip through both slits from bottom to top *(Fig. 26c)*.

Fig. 26c

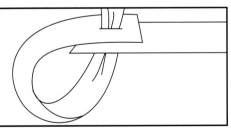

4. Pull new strip firmly to form a small knot *(Fig. 26d)*. Right sides of both strips should be facing up. Continue working with new strip.

Fig. 26d

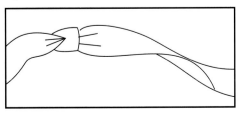

WORKING IN SIDE OF STITCH

When instructed to work in side of stitch just worked, insert hook as indicated by arrow *(Fig. 27)*.

Fig. 27

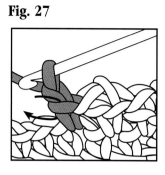

CHANGING COLORS

Work the last stitch to within one step of completion, hook new yarn *(Fig. 28a)* and draw through loops on hook. Cut old yarn and work over both ends unless otherwise specified.

When working in rounds, drop old yarn and join with slip stitch to first stitch using new yarn *(Fig. 28b)*.

Fig. 28a   **Fig. 28b**

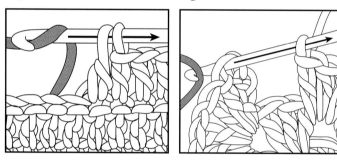

NO-SEW JOINING

Hold Squares, Motifs, or Strips with **wrong** sides together. Work slip stitch or sc into space as indicated *(Fig. 29)*.

Fig. 29

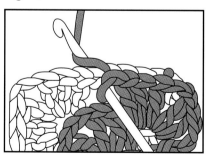

MAKING PILLOW FORM

Using crocheted piece for pattern and adding 1/4" seam allowance, cut two pieces of fabric.

With **right** sides together, sew seam leaving a 2" opening for turning.

Turn form right side out; stuff firmly and sew opening closed.

WASHING AND BLOCKING

Blocking "sets" a crocheted item and smooths the stitches to give your work a professional appearance. Before blocking, check the yarn label for any special instructions because many acrylics and some blends may be damaged during blocking.

Thread projects should be washed before blocking. Using a mild detergent and warm water, gently squeeze suds through the piece, being careful not to rub, twist, or wring. Rinse several times in cool, clear water. Roll piece in a clean terry towel and gently press out the excess moisture. Lay piece on a flat surface and shape to proper size; where needed, pin in place using stainless steel pins. Allow to dry **completely**. Doilies can be spray starched for extra crispness.

On fragile **acrylics** that can be blocked, pin the item to the correct size on a towel-covered board and cover the item with dampened bath towels. When the towels are dry, the item is blocked.

If the item is **hand washable**, carefully launder it using a mild soap or detergent. Rinse it without wringing or twisting. Remove any excess moisture by rolling it in a succession of dry towels. If you prefer, you may put it in the final spin cycle of your washer — but do not use water. Lay the item on a large towel on a flat surface away from direct sunlight. Gently smooth and pat the item to the desired size and shape, comparing the measurements to the pattern instructions as necessary. When the item is completely dry, it is blocked.

Steaming is an excellent method of blocking crocheted items, especially those made with **wool or wool blends**. Turn the item wrong side out and pin it to the correct size on a board covered with towels. Hold a steam iron or steamer just above the item and steam it thoroughly. Never let the weight of the iron touch your item because it will flatten the stitches. Leave the garment pinned until it is completely dry.

WHIPSTITCH

With **wrong** sides together and beginning in corner stitch, sew through both pieces once to secure the beginning of the seam, leaving an ample yarn end to weave in later. Insert needle from **front** to **back** through **both** loops of **each** piece *(Fig. 30a)* or through **inside** loops *(Fig. 30b)*. Bring needle around and insert it from **front** to **back** through the next loops of **both** pieces. Continue in this manner across to corner, keeping the sewing yarn fairly loose.

Fig. 30a   **Fig. 30b**

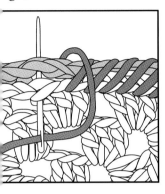 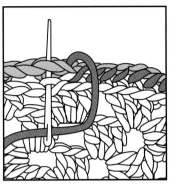

POM-POM

Cut a piece of cardboard 4" square. Wind the yarn around the cardboard until it is approximately ¹/₂" thick in the middle *(Fig. 31a)*; cut yarn end.
Carefully slip the yarn off the cardboard and firmly tie an 18" length of yarn around the middle *(Fig. 31b)*. Leave the yarn ends long enough to attach the pom-pom.
Cut the loops on both ends and trim the pom-pom into a smooth ball.

Fig. 31a   **Fig. 31b**

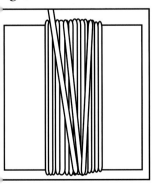 

TASSEL

Cut a piece of cardboard 3" wide by the desired length of the finished tassel. Wind a double strand of yarn around the length of the cardboard approximately 20 times; cut yarn end. Cut an 18" length of yarn and insert it under all of the strands at the top of the cardboard; pull up **tightly** and tie securely. Leave the yarn ends long enough to attach the tassel. Cut the yarn at the opposite end of the cardboard *(Fig. 32a)*; remove the cardboard. Cut a 6" length of yarn and wrap it **tightly** around the tassel twice, ¹/₂" below the top *(Fig. 32b)*; tie securely. Trim the ends.

Fig. 32a   **Fig. 32b**

FRINGE

Cut a piece of cardboard 8" wide and half as long as specified in instructions for finished strands. Wind the yarn **loosely** and **evenly** around the length of the cardboard until the card is filled, then cut across one end; repeat as needed. Align the number of strands specified and fold in half.
With **wrong** side facing and using a crochet hook, draw the folded end up through a row or stitch and pull the loose ends through the folded end *(Fig. 33a)*; draw the knot up **tightly** *(Fig. 33b)*. Repeat, spacing as specified. Lay afghan flat on a hard surface and trim the fringe.

Fig. 33a   **Fig. 33b**

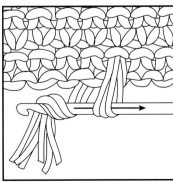 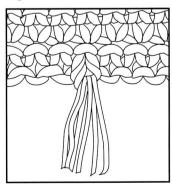

139

STARCHING & BLOCKING

TIPS

1. If using the same fabric stiffener for both white and colored items, starch the white items first in case thread dye should bleed into the solution.
2. A good blocking board can make pinning easier. You can use heavy cardboard, an ironing board, ceiling tile, etc.
3. Use stainless steel pins to prevent rusting. Pins with balls on the end are easier on the fingertips. Fabric stiffener will permanently damage pins used for sewing. These can be set aside for all starching projects.
4. Fabric stiffener can be returned to the bottle after starching if it has not been contaminated with particles and dye. Clip one corner of the bag, then squeeze the bag, forcing the solution to flow into the bottle.
5. An acrylic spray can be used after starching to protect the piece from heat and humidity.

Note: Refer to the following instructions for each specific project.

HAT MAGNETS (Shown on page 44.)

Read all of the following instructions before beginning.

1. Wash each piece using a mild detergent and warm water. Rinse several times in cool, clear water. Roll each piece in a clean terry towel and gently press out the excess moisture. Allow pieces to dry **completely**.
2. Pour fabric stiffener in a resealable plastic bag. Do not dilute stiffener. *Note:* This method is permanent and will not wash out.
3. Immerse dry pieces in fabric stiffener, remove air, and seal the bag. Work stiffener thoroughly into each piece. Let soak for several hours or overnight.
4. Remove Hats from stiffener and squeeze gently to remove as much excess stiffener as possible. Blot with a paper towel several times to remove excess from holes.
5. Cover blocking board with plastic wrap. To shape crown of Hats, roll a piece of plastic wrap in a ball and insert in the Hats. Pin brims of Hats at regular intervals to blocking board, being careful not to split threads when inserting pins between the stitches. Roll one edge of Hat #3 toward top.
6. Allow Hats to dry **completely**.

EASTER BONNET (Shown on page 117.)

Read all of the following instructions before beginning.

1. Follow Steps 1-4 of Hat Magnets.
2. To shape crown of Hat, stuff center of Hat with plastic wrap. Pin brim of Hat at regular intervals on plastic covered blocking board, forming a 18½" diameter circle and being careful not to split the threads when inserting pins between the stitches.
3. Allow Hat to dry **completely**.

HOLY NIGHT ANGEL (Shown on page 129.)

Read all of the following instructions before beginning.

1. Wash each piece using a mild detergent and warm water. Rinse several times in cool, clear water. Roll each piece in a clean terry towel and gently press out the excess moisture. Allow pieces to dry **completely**.
2. Stuff Head with polyester fiberfill.
3. Pour fabric stiffener in a small bowl. Do not dilute stiffener. *Note:* This method is permanent and will not wash out.
4. Immerse Arms, Wings, Halo, and Dress in fabric stiffener, being careful not to immerse Head. Work stiffener thoroughly into each piece. Let soak for several hours.
5. Remove pieces from stiffener and squeeze gently to remove as much excess stiffener as possible. Blot with a paper towel several times to remove excess from holes.
6. Place Dress over plastic covered cone, and pin bottom of Dress to plastic covered blocking board, forming an 8" diameter circle. Stuff Sleeves with plastic wrap, shaping as desired.
7. Insert 2 straws in each Arm, meeting half way at elbow, and also in Ring. Stuff top of Arms with plastic wrap to shape, making sure they will fit in armholes; bend Arms so that they will touch each other when assembled. Remove straws while Arms are slightly damp.
8. With **right** side facing, pin Wings and Halo to plastic covered blocking board, shaping as desired.
9. Allow to dry **completely**.

embroidery stitches

STRAIGHT STITCH

Straight Stitch is just what the name implies, a single, straight stitch. Bring needle up at 1 and go down at 2 *(Fig. 34)*. Continue in same manner.

Fig. 34

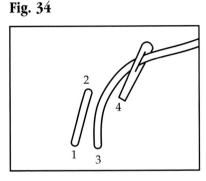

SATIN STITCH

Satin Stitch is a series of straight stitches worked side by side so they touch but do not overlap as shown in **Fig. 35a**, or entering and exiting the same hole as in **Fig. 35b**. Bring needle up at odd numbers and go down at even numbers.

Fig. 35a

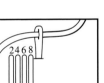

Fig. 35b

FRENCH KNOT

Bring needle up at 1. Wrap yarn desired number of times around needle and go down at 2, holding end of yarn with non-stitching fingers *(Fig. 36)*. Tighten knot; then pull needle through, holding yarn until it must be released.

Fig. 36

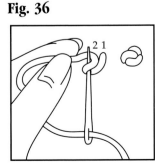

CROSS STITCH

Each square on the Chart represents one sc and each shaded square represents one cross stitch. Thread a yarn needle with a long strand of color indicated. With **right** side facing and bottom edge toward you, bring needle up at 1 leaving a 3" end on back. Work over this end to secure. Insert needle down at 2 (half Cross made), bring needle up at 3 and go down at 4 **(Cross Stitch completed, *Fig. 37*)**. You can work across an area in half crosses and then work back, crossing them as you go. Just be sure that the top half of every cross stitch is worked in the same direction. After each row is worked, weave yarn through stitches on back to point where next cross is worked (long strands of yarn should not show on back). If yarn becomes twisted while stitching, drop needle and allow yarn to hang free untwisting itself. Finish off by weaving under several stitches on back; cut yarn.

Fig. 37

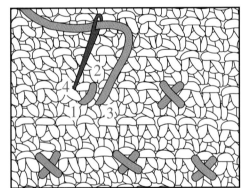

OUTLINE STITCH

Bring needle up from wrong side at 1, leaving an end to be woven in later. Holding thread **above** the needle with thumb, insert needle down at 2 and up again at 3 (halfway between 1 and 2) *(Fig. 38a)*; pull through. Insert needle down at 4 and up again at 2, making sure the thread is **above** the needle *(Fig. 38b)*; pull through.
Continue in same manner.

Fig. 38a

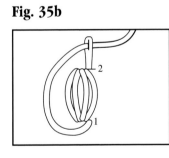

Fig. 38b

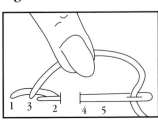

KEEPSAKE BIBS

HOLIDAY HAPPINESS SWEATER

Bunny Ear

Pumpkin Face

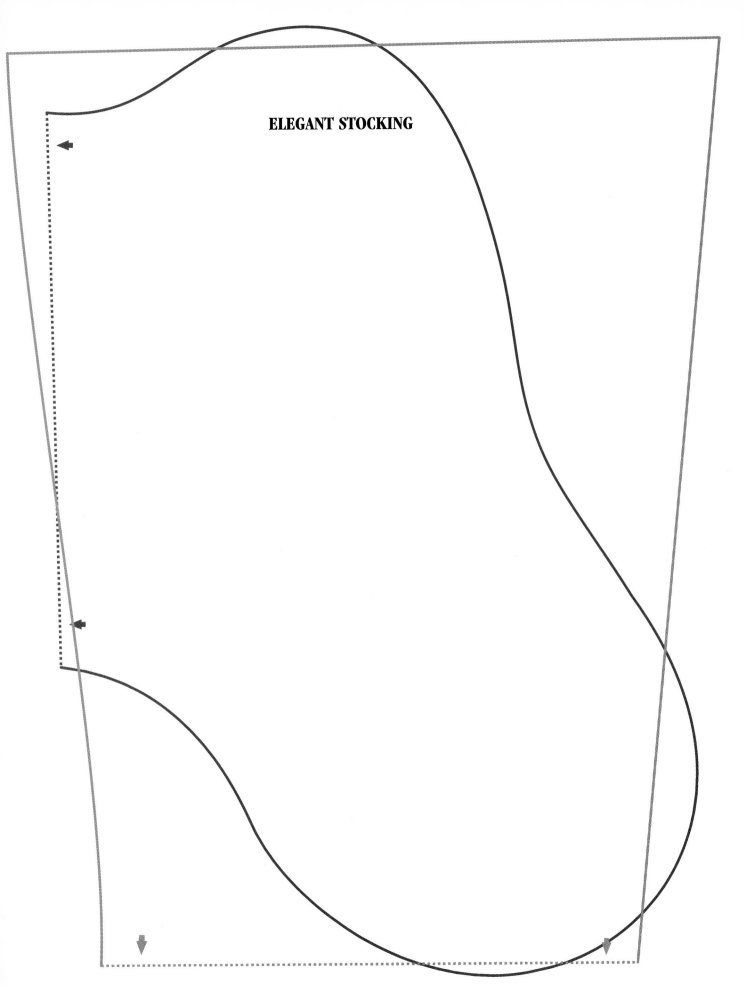

ELEGANT STOCKING

143

credits

We extend a warm *thank you* to the generous people who allowed us to photograph some of our projects at their homes: *Wrapped Up in Afghans* — Steve and Shirley McGran, Bob and Donna Roten, and Dr. Dan and Sandra Cook.

To Magna IV Color Imaging of Little Rock, Arkansas, we say thank you for the superb color reproduction and excellent pre-press preparation. We want to especially thank photographers Larry Pennington, Ken West, Karen Shirey, and Mark Mathews of Peerless Photography, Little Rock, Arkansas, and Jerry R. Davis of Jerry Davis Photography, Little Rock, Arkansas, for their time, patience, and excellent work.

A special word of thanks goes to the talented designers who created the lovely projects in this book:

Pam Anderson: *Watermelon Rag Rug*, page 66
Sherry Berry: *Delightfully Delicate Wrap*, page 88, and *Grandpa's Buddy Afghan*, page 90
Dot Drake: *Summer Flowers Doily*, page 31, and *Fall Pineapples Doily*, page 32
Shobha Govindan: *Classic Coaster Set*, page 58, *"Dressy" Pot Holders (apron)*, page 72, and *Kids' Funtime Caps*, page 98
Sheila Hardy: *Violet Bouquet Afghan*, page 56
Cindy Harris: *Little Pink Piggy*, page 68, and *Turkey Centerpiece*, page 124
Jan Hatfield: *Earthy Mile-A-Minute*, page 10
Alice Heim: *Keepsake Bibs*, page 86
Terry Kimbrough: *Scalloped Curtain Edging*, page 40; *Scalloped Towel Edging*, page 40; *Victorian Washcloth*, page 41; *Flower Dishcloth*, page 45; *Lacy Shells Dishcloth*, page 46; *Cozy Baby Bunting*, page 82; and *Romantic Cover-up*, page 112
Jennine Korejko: *Cozy Reversible*, page 8
Melissa Leapman: *Romantic Lace*, page 22, and *Greek Puzzle Afghan*, page 60
Jean Leffler: *Crayon Afghan*, page 64
Linda Luder: *Holiday Happiness Sweater*, page 100
Fran Marlin: *Luxurious Ripple*, page 20, and *Tic-Tac-Toe Game*, page 74

JoAnn Maxwell: *Easter Bonnet*, page 116
Janet McCoy: *Striking Stained Glass*, page 14
Kay Meadors: *Panda Hooded Towel*, page 70, and *Heirloom Christening Set*, page 78
Helen Milinkovich Milton: *Hat Magnets*, page 44
Carolyn Pfeifer: *Comical Clown Faces*, page 76
Mary Jane Protus: *Colorful Western Vest*, page 108
Teresa Smith: *Grandma's Sweetheart Cover-up*, page 92
Martha Brooks Stein: *Granny Stars*, page 6, and *Good-Morning Daisies*, page 18
Rena V. Stevens: *Lavish Cables*, page 12
C. Strohmeyer: *Winter Lace Doily*, page 28, and *Spring Buds Doily*, page 30
Gail Tanquary: *Elegant Stocking*, page 126
Lee Tribett: *Toddler Bikini and Cover-up*, page 104, and *Pumpkin Patch Pal*, page 120
Beth Ann Webber: *Birthday Fairies*, page 52
Maggie Weldon: *Rich Diamonds*, page 16; *Rose Afghan*, page 36; *Hat Towel Holder*, page 45; and *Petite Basket*, page 51
Debra L. Westberry: *Holy Night Angel*, page 128
Lorraine White: *Lacy Accent Pillow*, page 62

We extend a sincere *thank you* to the people who assisted in making and testing the projects for this book: Janet Akins, Rozlyn Anderson, Anitta Armstrong, Belinda Baxter, Jennie S. Black, Pam Bland, JoAnn Bowling, Mike Cates, Lee Ellis, Freda Gillham, Linda Graves, Linda Green, Raymelle Greening, Jean Hall, Kathleen Hardy, Cheryl Knepper, Liz Lane, Patricia Little, Kay Meadors, Libby Norman, Dale Potter, Linda Shock, Donna Soellner, Karan Stewart, Clare Stringer, Margaret Taverner, Carol Thompson, and Sherry Williams.